CHICAGO ARCHITECTURE AND DESIGN

CHICAGO ARCHITECTURE AND DESIGN

REVISED AND EXPANDED

JAY PRIDMORE | GEORGE A. LARSON

WITH PRINCIPAL PHOTOGRAPHY BY HEDRICH BLESSING

ABRAMS, NEW YORK

EDITOR
Nancy Cohen

EDITORIAL ASSISTANT
Jon Cipriaso

DESIGN
HvAD
Henk van Assen and Amanda Bowers

PRODUCTION MANAGER
Maria Pia Gramaglia

Library of Congress Cataloging-in-Publication Data

Pridmore, Jay.
   Chicago architecture and design / Jay Pridmore, George A. Larson ; with principal photography by Hedrich Blessing.—
   Rev. and expanded ed.
       p.   cm.
   Rev. ed. of: Chicago architecture and design / George A. Larson, Jay Pridmore ; with photography by Hedrich-Blessing. 1993.
   Includes bibliographical references and index.
   ISBN 0–8109–5892–9 (hardcover : alk. paper) 1. Architecture—Illinois—Chicago. 2. Chicago (Ill.)—Buildings, structures, etc.
   I. Larson, George A. Chicago architecture and design. II. Larson, George A. III. Hedrich Blessing (Firm) IV. Title.

NA735.C4L37 2005
720'.9773'11—dc22

                    2005001008

Printed and bound in China
10 9 8 7 6 5 4 3 2

harry n. abrams, inc.
a subsidiary of La Martinière Groupe
115 West 18th Street
New York, NY 10011
www.hnabooks.com

Contents

FOREWORD

HALO BUILDING

5800 WEST TOUHY AVENUE, NILES, ILL.

2001

MURPHY/JAHN

When I arrived in Chicago in 1966 to study at I.I.T. [the Illinois Institute of Technology], I came because I regarded Chicago as the architecture capital of the world. I wasn't the only one. There were people here from all over the world—Germans, Italians, Swedes, Asians, and many other ambitious young people studying and getting jobs in Chicago. One reason, of course, was Chicago's history. We were fascinated by the Chicago Fire, the Columbian fair, the early skyscrapers, and much more. It is not to exaggerate to say that young architects regarded a visit to Chicago as equal in importance to a pilgrimage to Rome or Athens.

Of course, my coming to Chicago was for more than its history. In the 1960s Chicago was the working center of postwar modernism. Most prominently this meant Mies van der Rohe, who was directing the school of architecture at I.I.T. and designing some of the greatest buildings of the century. When I arrived Mies's apartments on Lake Shore Drive had already gone up; the IBM building was being designed. And Mies was not alone. Bertrand Goldberg had recently completed Marina City. S.O.M. had built Inland Steel and was about to build Sears and John Hancock.

What more could a young architect want? Nothing. Young architects were intense, passionate, curious. I remember shortly after I arrived there was a rumor that the plans for Mies's Krupp building [which he designed for the manufacturer's headquarters in Essen, Germany, but was never built] were floating around Chicago. I never saw them, but I remember people saying that they would pay money to get a copy of those mysterious documents.

It's been a while since I have seen that kind of enthusiasm about architecture in most architectural offices, much less the general public. There's also been a lot of poor architecture lately—in Chicago and everywhere else. Construction is shoddy. Form is tired and forgettable. Clients have seemed indifferent to this state of affairs, and another thing is sure: Young architects are not flocking to Chicago to launch their careers.

But things always change, and they are changing for the better. For the first time in a long time I have seen a much more open attitude about architecture, and the results are beginning to show. Perhaps the new buildings at I.I.T. are an example of new things to come. The student center and the dormitories are unlike anything else in Chicago—so much so that Chicago purists objected strongly when these buildings were introduced. They were nontraditional, different, and even seemed to go against the grain. Generally, they have been well received.

But to me good new architecture is not just a matter of doing things differently. You can always do something different from what someone did in the past. Good new architecture is about doing things better. It is absolutely critical to bear in mind that the best new buildings of our period may look different, but they are also being built with much higher standards of construction.

To me, this is one of the real traditions of Chicago: Doing things better.

The future of architecture will bring the architects and the engineers much closer together. This collaboration will do many things. Number one, it will create buildings that are economical and efficient. The collaboration will lead to new form too, as architects discover new ways to use new materials, new systems, and new methods of construction.

This idea is not new. In old Chicago, John Wellborn Root was as talented an engineer as he was an architect. Sullivan could hardly have built such artistic buildings without Adler engineering them in revolutionary ways. More recently the collaboration between the architect Bruce Graham of S.O.M. and his engineer collaborator Fazlur Khan gave rise to John Hancock and Sears Tower.

There are many other elements of Chicago's architectural heritage. We're a city of sleek towers and big shoulders. We're a city that loves elegance but needs to be gritty and real. But for me at this time, the real power of Chicago's past is in the interaction between engineer and architect, the mutual respect between the nuts and bolts of building and the artistic expression of architecture.

Will Chicago once again become the worldwide center of architecture? Perhaps not. Our profession is global now. Architects travel around the world. Their ideas can be applied in Berlin and Bangkok as appropriately as in Chicago. But architecture still has to respond to local conditions, local ideas, and local history. That is why I am very curious about the next decade or so of Chicago architecture. New technologies and new architects will find new ways to interpret our tradition in great new buildings. Some may be soaring skyscrapers, others more modest structures like a single-room occupancy hotel that we are designing for the North Side. I'm convinced that there are bright spots on the architectural horizon, and that Chicago may once again reassert itself as one of the most energetic architectural cities of the world.

—HELMUT JAHN, MURPHY/JAHN ARCHITECTS

PREFACE

PRIVATE RESIDENCE

MICHIGAN AVENUE

1994

**LARSON ASSOCIATES;
STAIRWAY BY JAMES CARPENTER**

Chicago is one of the most exciting cities in the world for architecture and design. Chicago is where the story of twentieth-century architecture unfolded, where the icon of our business world—the skyscraper—first took shape. Chicago is where Frank Lloyd Wright designed furniture, carpets, textiles, china, and glass walls to complete the design of his projects. And it is where my life changed course.

In the summer of 1952, at the age of seventeen, I left my hometown Detroit to visit Chicago, where I discovered a brand-new building that made an indelible impression on me. That revolutionary building was 860 Lake Shore Drive, designed by Mies van der Rohe, and it ignited my lifelong passion for this city and its architecture.

I returned to Chicago after graduating from the University of Michigan, College of Architecture and Design, and joined Skidmore Owings and Merrill. It was the firm's great era, with Bruce Graham, Myron Goldsmith, and Walter Netsch, and it was a heady time, with projects such as Inland Steel, John Hancock, and Baxter Travenol. Some years later I formed my own office and worked on corporate headquarters for Sara Lee, General Motors, Ford Motor, Northern Trust, AON Corporation, and others, as well as many private residences.

One of the greatest pleasures of my career was my role as teacher. I considered it a privilege to educate clients about architecture, design, color, texture, and materials. We spoke of space, proportions, light, and the integration of form and function. Because there is nothing better than an educated client—someone who can fully participate in the design process—I would take clients on tours of the city, the United States, and sometimes the world. We would look carefully at great buildings to understand what made them great. I hoped to convey my passion for architecture, as well as a new way of looking at buildings.

In many ways this book is an extension of that teaching process, directed at a broader audience. It examines Chicago's best works of architecture, the common threads that tie those projects together, and what it is that makes buildings and spaces memorable and lasting. It will help readers everywhere understand the principles that made Chicago the most important architectural city of the twentieth century and continue to influence architecture worldwide in the twenty-first.

Chicago Architecture and Design is filled with stunning photographs from the collection of Hedrich Blessing, the Chicago studio. Jack Hedrich is a longtime friend who allowed us to use these photographs before giving them to the Chicago Historical Society. This book would not have been possible without his generous contribution.

Hedrich Blessing's magnificent photographs combine with vivid text by my collaborator, Jay Pridmore, to illustrate what makes Chicago's best buildings aesthetically and even spiritually moving. Together the words and images bring to life Chicago's wonderful architectural heritage, which is beautifully expressed through its buildings' interiors as well as exteriors.

That heritage lives on today, not only in Chicago but across the globe. As architects increasingly travel and build in locations distant from their origins, they are sharing ideas and expanding upon Chicago's architectural tradition in intriguing new ways. The internationalization of the field has made the world seem smaller since this book first appeared in 1993. *Chicago Architecture and Design* has been thoroughly revised and expanded to examine those and other developments that have taken root over the last dozen years.

Generations of dedicated, creative architects and designers in Chicago devised ingenious yet simple solutions to the problems of space that were an enduring legacy to the city, and subsequently to the world. In fact, some of the finest architecture being built in Chicago today has been designed by extraordinary professionals who are not from here. The great Japanese architect Tadao Ando, who built a remarkable private residence here in 1997, is typical of this worldwide trend.

But it's important to remember that Chicagoans respond to the work of internationally acclaimed architects like Ando because, thanks to their architectural heritage, they recognize and demand the very best. Chicago's great tradition continues to inspire and inform the architecture of the twenty-first century. This book celebrates that tradition and this exceptional city.

—GEORGE A. LARSON

ACKNOWLEDGMENTS

We owe deep gratitude to the firm of Hedrich Blessing, which made its photographic archive available and enthusiastically supported both the first and second editions of this book. Jack Hedrich and Bob Shimer were immensely helpful, and the firm's photographic and laboratory staffs helped make assembling the illustrations a pleasure. Sadly, Michael Houlahan, Hedrich Blessing's president, passed away while this edition was in production. His importance to this book is immeasurable.

Another person indispensable to this book's preparation was Wajih Alkayed, who brought the eye of an architect to his tireless photographic research.

Many people with indispensable knowledge of Chicago architecture granted interviews and provided archival information and advice. One of the most important was Tim Samuelson, cultural historian of the City of Chicago, whose knowledge of Chicago architecture is encyclopedic and whose generosity is unbounded. Two others who repeatedly provided incisive counsel were architect John Vinci of Vinci-Hamp and Ward Miller of the Richard Nickel Committee, whose collections and knowledge are always exciting to tap.

Among the many people interviewed were architects with first-hand knowledge of the forces driving Chicago architecture. They include Thomas Beeby, Laurence Booth, the late Jacques Brownson, George Danforth, the late Joseph Fujikawa, the late Myron Goldsmith, Wilbert Hasbrouck, John Holabird Jr., Thomas Gunny

Harboe, Helmut Jahn, Paul Janicki, Dirk Lohan, the late William Keck, Ron Krueck, Frederick Phillips, George Schipporeit, Gene Summers, and John Thorpe. Others who provided important advice were the late designer Jody Kingery, developer John Buck, and historians Carol Callahan, Susan Dart, Wim de Wit, Paul Myers, and John Zukowsky.

Where photos from Hedrich Blessing's archive were unavailable, a number of photographers generously assisted, including Langdon Clay, Doug Fogelson, Mati Maldre, Greg Murphey, David Seide, and Tony Soluri. People at various archival collections and local architectural firms also kindly helped find new and in some cases rare images. We are grateful to Larry Arbeiter and Bill Harms of the University of Chicago; Zurich Esposito of the Chicago Architecture Foundation; Lori Hammer of Booth/Hansen; Tony Jahn of Marshall Field's; Pam Kane of Skidmore, Owings and Merrill; Tony Kempa, formerly of Lohan Caprile Goettsch, and Susanna Craib-Cox, currently of that firm; Melissa Koff of Wood + Zapata; Shelby Kroeger of Gensler; Gail Catlin of Hammond Beeby Rupert Ainge; artist Martyl Langsdorf and architect Jeff White, who respectively reside in and work at the Schweikher House; Arthur Miller of Lake Forest College (and co-author of *Classic Country Estates of Lake Forest*); Nicole Robertson of Loebl, Schlossman and Hackl; Taber Wayne of Tigerman-McCurry; Shirley Paddock, a Lake Forest historian; Powell/Kleinschmidt; Caryn Torres of Water Tower Place; Mary Woolover of the Burnham and Ryerson Libraries of the Art Institute of Chicago; and Ed Uhlir of Millennium Park. Special thanks to Helmut Jahn and his colleague Keith Palmer of Murphy/Jahn for graciously contributing the foreword.

Thanks also go to a good friend and a great patron of Chicago architecture, John Bryan, former head of Sara Lee Corporation.

Paul Gottlieb, the late president of Abrams Books, who was instrumental to bringing the first edition of this book from idea to reality back in 1993, has our lasting appreciation. We are particularly grateful to the staff of Harry N. Abrams for their long-term faith in this project and for assigning editor Nancy Cohen of New York to it. She set a new standard for patience, attention to detail, and a discerning eye, qualities that every writer covets in an editor. To Eric Himmel, Harriet Whelchel, Leslie Dutcher, and Jon Cipriaso of Abrams, thank you.

CHAPTER 1

THE ROOTS OF MODERN ARCHITECTURE

GLESSNER HOUSE

1800 SOUTH PRAIRIE AVENUE

1887

H. H. RICHARDSON

At Glessner House, Richardson achieved his objective of truth and clarity with a monumental granite design. The front door, like the rest of the milestone building, reflected impregnable strength and love of craftsmanship.

Chicago's reputation as the creative center of American architecture stretches back well over one hundred years. The nation's most fertile architectural minds headed for Chicago in the 1870s, seeking fortune and fame in a city poised to grow as no city had grown before. Since then the city has produced generations of important architects and a host of influential styles. It spawned the first skyscrapers and fostered the evolution of the urban office building; it nurtured Frank Lloyd Wright's earliest dreams and provided a canvas on which Mies van der Rohe defined the modern architecture of his time.

In the twenty-first century Chicago continues to captivate ambitious architects, attracting them to visit, perchance to build. Today architecture's reach is global, and the art is less reflective of individual cities than once it was. But Chicago remains an architectural environment of rare power. Both Chicago's own architects and those with towering reputations established elsewhere find the city's grand spaces and big ideas irresistibly challenging. Chicago's claim to being one of the world's great centers of urban design—bolstered by a long list of architectural milestones—remains uncontested.

Yet Chicago's destiny as a great architectural center would have seemed far-fetched in the early 1800s. New York was one of the world's great ports and Boston

the so-called Hub of the Universe, while Chicago—named after the Indian word for a native onion, *checagou*—was a marshy, unpromising place on the shores of Lake Michigan. It was sparsely settled and relatively distant from the bustling river towns of Cincinnati and Saint Louis, then considered the gateways to the American West. But change came swiftly after 1829, when the Illinois legislature voted to build a canal at the site to connect the Great Lakes to the Mississippi River.

Prospects of the canal triggered Chicago's first real estate boom. Records show that one small lot sold for $100 in 1832 and for $15,000 three years later; builders, hot in pursuit of riches, built neither for the ages nor for aesthetics, simply throwing up dwellings and warehouses as needed. The real estate bubble soon burst, but the waterway became a reality in 1848, the same year the first railroad train steamed west out of Chicago. Those two breakthrough developments nourished an explosion of growth unprecedented in any city anywhere. Meat packers and farm equipment manufacturers made Chicago an industrial center. Warehousers and merchants arrived. So did assorted vagabonds and, in time, architects.

A TRADITION OF INNOVATION

Although early Chicago, in its rush to build, was little

WATER TOWER

MICHIGAN AVENUE AT CHICAGO AVENUE

1869

WILLIAM W. BOYINGTON

One of the oldest structures still
standing in Chicago, the Water
Tower's own water supply probably
saved it from the Great Fire. Its
turrets and rusticated limestone
reflect Boyington's admiration for
medieval builders. Oscar Wilde
called it a "monstrosity with pepper
boxes stuck all over it," but it
became a popular landmark. In this
classic Hedrich Blessing photo from
1930, it provides a rare glimpse of
the city's early architecture.

THE HOMESTEAD

SHERIDAN ROAD AT COLLEGE ROAD,
LAKE FOREST, ILL.

1860

ARCHITECT UNKNOWN

This image of Arcadia was the home
of Devillo Holt, one of the city's
many wealthy merchants. Architects
of the day used pattern books to
build houses for the bourgeoisie
in Greek Revival or Italianate style.
Generally constructed of lumber,
which was plentiful, most such
houses in Chicago were leveled by
the fire; outside the city, several, like
this one, remain.

disposed to architectural niceties, it did embrace inventive building techniques. In terms of innovation the city began to distinguish itself as early as 1833, architectural historians agree. That was the year a local builder named Augustine Deodat Taylor created what is regarded as the first balloon-frame structure, Saint Mary's Church.

Balloon frames were a revelation at a time when standard wood-frame construction relied on posts and beams of heavy timber, laboriously assembled with hand-carved mortise-and-tenon joints. Balloon frames, which used newfangled factory-made materials, such as milled two-by-fours and common nails, were light and quickly made. That type of construction has changed little even to this day: Narrowly spaced studs and beams run the length of the building, held together by nails, and relatively thin joists hold up the floors. "A close basket-like manner of construction" was how balloon frames were described when they were introduced to a congress of professional architects at the American Institute in 1855.

Traditional builders sneered at "balloons," as they called them, for their lightness and presumed fragility, but they caught on quickly in Chicago, where carpenters were chasing the real estate boom. Ironically, balloon-frame construction became widespread elsewhere but was not to last in the city where it had been developed. Shortly after the Great Fire of 1871, the mayor—who had been elected on the Fireproof ticket—outlawed wood construction. The balloon frame vanished from the city of its birth, by banishment or burning—even Augustine

Deodat Taylor's pioneering project had been consumed by the flames. What remained, though, were the conditions that created the innovation in the first place. They included ambition, impatience, a willingness to improvise, and what seemed like a limitless future.

ELEMENTS OF STYLE

Like any frontier town, old Chicago had been designed primarily by builders, not architects. But elements of architectural style began to infiltrate the city as it gained size and wealth. The first known to impart a sense of such aesthetics in Chicago was the remarkable John Van Osdel (1811–1891), regarded as the city's first trained architect. At the time, professional training probably meant little more than a skill at reading plans and understanding specifications. Van Osdel was in fact largely self-taught, but as his career progressed he developed an encyclopedic knowledge of the building styles fashionable in more refined places.

Van Osdel had moved west from New York in 1836 at the behest of William Butler Ogden, Chicago's first mayor. Ogden had earlier moved to Chicago from the East, with the express purpose of getting rich from the resources of the wilderness. Once he did he had no intention of living in a log cabin. So he hired Van Osdel to build him a Greek Revival mansion of wood, "a palatial residence with cupola and classical porticos," as described by the press at the time. It was a successful commission by all accounts and led to more. In the years that followed Van Osdel built prolifically and in nearly every style for which he could locate a pattern book. In 1851 he designed the Second Presbyterian Church at Wabash Avenue and Washington Street in Gothic Revival style. Later he fixed on the French Second Empire style, with its steeply pitched mansard roofs. That caught the eye of the tycoon Potter Palmer, who was in the process of relocating Chicago's fashionable shopping district to his own real estate holdings on State Street. In the 1860s Palmer hired Van Osdel to design a great department store, which he rented to Marshall Field, and the Palmer House Hotel, the closest approximation of a Parisian hostelry on the American frontier.

State Street soon became the city's rialto, a pocket of elegance amidst the slapdash construction of a fast-growing city. The palatial Marshall Field's emporium and the grand Palmer House Hotel, which Van Osdel had designed in elaborate mansard style, attracted an increasingly refined clientele. Despite the muddy roadway that soiled the skirts of the carriage trade, State Street did all it could to mimic the boulevards of Napoleon III.

CHICAGO'S FIERY APOCALYPSE

Although mid-nineteenth-century Chicago had touches of European-style gentility, the prevailing impression was of a chaotic frontier settlement on the make. Chicago could awe with the bustling commerce and ambition that led it brashly to claim to be the epicenter of the growing nation. But, like other early American cities, it had a dark side. "Wolves during the night roamed all over where the city now stands," wrote an early history of the prefire period, perhaps metaphorically describing the thieves and panderers who had the run of the town. So mixed was this image of a powerful yet fundamentally amoral place that when the Great Chicago Fire cut its wide swath through the city, leaving some ninety thousand people homeless, many commentators viewed it as a blessing. In articles and books published after the disaster writers sought to describe a physical force of almost unbelievable power. The perception that stuck was of hellfire and brimstone. Most Chicagoans understood the fire to have had a cleansing purpose; those who remained were meant to rebuild something glorious.

Enthusiasm in the fire's wake was in no way illusory. Within days new buildings were going up. Within a month five thousand new houses had been constructed, and new commercial blocks were soon established on the charred downtown streets. Land values quickly caught up to prefire levels, then surpassed them. Even the rubble that workers hauled away was put to good use as landfill to extend buildable land out into the lake. Three weeks after the fire *Harper's Weekly* wrote that Chicago "will be made a better city than it ever could have become but for this fire." One result would be a "better building system."

FIELD, LEITER & COMPANY	RELIANCE BUILDING
STATE STREET AT WASHINGTON STREET	STATE STREET AT WASHINGTON STREET
1868 (DESTROYED 1871)	1895
JOHN VAN OSDEL	DANIEL H. BURNHAM & COMPANY

Van Osdel mastered the French Second Empire style, which he imagined would remind Midwesterners of Paris. This store, which later became Marshall Field's, was one of the new "palaces" lining State Street, Chicago's shopping district. Its exterior of Connecticut white marble led it to be known as the "Marble Palace" but did not save it from the fire.

The Reliance Building is an iconic link between the traditional masonry of old Chicago and the transparent weightlessness to come. Its terracotta is marvelously detailed; its expansive glass windows presage the technical and aesthetic accomplishments of Mies van der Rohe. Richard Nickel, pioneer preservationist, took this photo in the early 1960s, when the building had been relegated to low-end tenants. It has since enjoyed a splendid restoration.

This slant on the news did not pass unnoticed by Eastern architects, and many bought tickets for Chicago with all due haste. Yet most of the newcomers had neither the disposition nor the skill to provide Chicago with a building system even remotely better than the one that had burned. New buildings, like the old ones, were mostly dark and clumsily ornamented. Streets remained clogged. The most stirring innovation, some people believed, was the addition of salt to mortar, which kept it from freezing and allowed bricklayers to work year-round.

In fact, had Chicago's postfire history gone differently, the apocalypse might have been used to explain not an architectural renaissance but an aesthetic disaster. The need to rebuild as quickly as possible far outpaced the development of a homegrown architectural sensibility. Innovators at the time were understandably more interested in fireproofing than aesthetics; they were also busy developing hydraulic elevators. And most of the dozens of masonry piles that went up within weeks and months of the fire exhibited a clunky ordinariness that made John Van Osdel's prefire palaces look like works of genius, rather than the attractive derivatives they were.

Nevertheless, a few of the architects who headed to Chicago after the conflagration did have a greater vision, and their names—John Wellborn Root, Daniel Burnham, and Louis Henry Sullivan among them—are etched into America's architectural history. Chicago gave those men what architects say they covet most of all: a clean slate. And it provided wealthy, progressive clients—real estate and business magnates who called for bigger, more spacious buildings that were unbeholden to conventional approaches. Chicago, as it turned out, welcomed the boiling creativity of these few architects, and as they realized new designs and new building systems they attracted other architects with new ideas of their own. So began a succession of architectural innovation—and sometimes genius—that continued through much of the twentieth century.

IN SEARCH OF AN AMERICAN STYLE

In the immediate wake of the fire, however, architectural distinction remained elusive. Among the better-known buildings to emerge was the home of retailer Marshall Field on Prairie Avenue. That was then Chicago's Gold Coast, home to the merchant-princes and captains of industry who spent lavishly for comfortable, civilized homes. The Field house was designed in 1876 by Richard Morris Hunt of New York, an architect highly praised and highly paid for his graceful eclecticism. In fact, Hunt treated the commission with more restraint than he did many of his more famous mansions, which often resembled fantastical châteaux with turrets and

towers. "Must you wait until you see a gentleman in a silk hat come out of it before you laugh?" Louis Sullivan once quipped about Hunt's designs.

A discernible self-consciousness underlay architecture of this elaborate sort, as if wealthy Chicagoans felt they should protest the plain industrial character of their city. This self-consciousness was to influence Chicago culture for many years—and a "second city" mentality still runs deep. Nevertheless, a negative reaction to faux French architecture and other poor copies was apparent even then. People who found ornamental European style out of place in Chicago called instead for buildings in keep-

ing with the surroundings, even if they didn't know what those buildings should look like. In 1883 a lengthy and surprisingly apt *Chicago Tribune* article complained that a Swiss-style cottage built recently in the city would be more at home on a mountain top. It had little business in Chicago, which was filled with similarly inappropriate buildings vaguely connected to classical Greek styles and other faraway points of reference, the critic wrote. "So long as this subserviency to the crude wishes of wealthy persons is submitted to we shall never have anything worthy of the name of architecture; we shall simply remain exponents of crudeness, the rampant self-assertion of ambitious nouveaux riches."

In the construction frenzy just after the fire, out-of-place buildings were going up all around. Gone but not forgotten is the old Board of Trade Building, located on Jackson Boulevard and LaSalle Street, where the newer and far more elegant Board of Trade stands today. The old one, designed by William W. Boyington and completed in 1885, was a conglomeration of Renaissance, Gothic, Byzantine, and a number of less discernible styles jumbled together like a medieval horror. People who liked architecture could take satisfaction that, not long after it was built, its footings began to fail, whereupon its tall, unattractive tower was dismantled as a hazard to public safety.

Among those who derided Boyington's Board of Trade was Montgomery Schuyler, the nation's most influential architecture critic at the time. "There are not many other structures in the United States, of equal cost and pretension, which equally with this combine the dignity of a commercial traveler with the bland repose of St. Vitus," he wrote sarcastically (Saint Vitus being the patron saint of dancers, young people, and dogs). Schuyler also wryly complained about anarchists seen demonstrating outside the building, which was Chicago's financial center. "It was very ungrateful of them, for one could go far to find a more perfect expression of anarchy in architecture."

To put his views of Chicago into a larger context, it is helpful to know something about Montgomery Schuyler. Not an architect but a journalist with a literary bent, Schuyler dropped out of college and got his first job on the *New York World*. Like most well-read Americans of his day, he was dedicated to the writings of Emerson, Thoreau, and Whitman. As he wrote about art and culture, he often concerned himself, as they did, with the search for a distinctly American voice.

As Schuyler's interests extended to architecture, he discerned that many monstrosities being constructed in American cities at the time resulted from two overriding faults. One was pretension. The other was Europe. Both were inappropriate in America, he said, at least in large, undiluted doses. Schuyler believed that a truly American architecture would grow only from design that expressed the country's democracy, simplicity, and honest strength.

THE SEVEN LAMPS
Many of the architects working in Chicago in the late 1880s were, like Schuyler, seeking a new style that dis-

tinctly reflected the spirit of the young, promising nation. In that pursuit, they directed their attention not only to the future but also to the past—and not only to America but to Europe as well. Among the most influential texts they studied were the works of the English critic and philosopher John Ruskin.

Ruskin's prose was ornate and dense, and his logic sometimes fell prey to emotion. But Ruskinian principles came to be regarded as baseline absolutes in the discussion of the direction of Chicago architecture—much as Sigmund Freud's theories were in the development of psychoanalysis. *The Seven Lamps of Architecture,* published in 1849, when Ruskin was just thirty years old, was the book that rose to the top of every architect's reading list decades later. Ruskin was not an architect but an Oxford-educated aesthete whose life reached a turning point during a tour of France and Italy. There, upon witnessing buildings that had stood for centuries, he recognized that excellence is timeless. Medieval cathedrals, wrote Ruskin, were masterpieces of craftsmanship, their masonry so precise that "that after six hundred years of sunshine and rain, a lancet could not be put between their joints." They were built for the ages and, to the extent that they endured, represented architecture's highest virtue. Good architecture was good forever, Ruskin concluded, and well-designed structures ever fresh to the eye.

In *The Seven Lamps,* Ruskin analyzed what he believed to be the qualities of great architecture. His "lamps" were Sacrifice, Truth, Power, Beauty, Life, Memory, and Obedience. They were simple and profound, and though the concepts sometimes contradicted one another, they sounded valid beyond question. Of Sacrifice Ruskin stated that great architecture can and should be costly, not for self-aggrandizement but for the exaltation of public life. (Ruskin was referring to cathedrals, but Chicago architects applied his point to commercial buildings.) Of Obedience he wrote that the rules of proportion are inviolate; those that govern structures that have proven to be timeless should apply to the proportions of any building, grand or modest, as well.

Perhaps the most inspiring of the "lamps" was Memory, which reminded architects that they were building not only for their own age but for the ages to come. "Therefore, when we build, let us think that we build for ever. . . . For, indeed, the greatest glory of a building is

not in its stones, nor in its gold. Its glory is in its Age, and in that deep sense of voicefulness, of stern watching, or mysterious sympathy, nay, even of approval or condemnation, which we feel in walls that have long been washed by the passing waves of humanity."

ORGANIC ARCHITECTURE

Perhaps Ruskin's most significant contribution to the development of American architecture was his notion that architecture should be "organic," a quality that referred to the integration of beauty and purpose. The term "organic architecture" has shifted and expanded in definition since Ruskin coined the phrase, but his organic ideal called for every aspect of a building's design to be inextricably related to that building's use. Nature provides an analogy: A tree consists of leaves, branches, bark, and myriad other elements, each essential to the tree's function and each harmoniously related to the whole. Likewise a cathedral expresses in its physical structure the soaring spirituality that is its deepest purpose. Organic architecture came to mean that a building's overall sensation—its Life, as Ruskin put it—was an outgrowth of its form. Form included a structure's plan and elevation as well as less tangible quali-

STUART HALL, UNIVERSITY OF CHICAGO

5835 SOUTH GREENWOOD AVENUE

1904

SHEPLEY, RUTAN AND COOLIDGE

The university's trustees selected an emphatic Gothic style to underscore the new institution's great intellectual mission. In contrast to classical architecture's commercial connotations, the Gothic reflected craftsmanship, reverence, and moral uplift. Gothic-style courtyards provided an enclave amid a booming Chicago.

THE AUDITORIUM (DETAIL)

MICHIGAN AVENUE
AT CONGRESS PARKWAY

1889

ADLER AND SULLIVAN

Organic architecture held that
a building and its details could
simultaneously express mechanical function and natural
form. The Auditorium's original
"electroliers"—lost decades
ago—were re-created (above)
from surviving photos during
Booth/Hansen's elaborate
restoration of what is now
Roosevelt University's Ganz
Hall recital room.

FRANK LLOYD WRIGHT
HOME AND STUDIO

951 CHICAGO AVENUE, OAK PARK, ILL.

1889–1909

FRANK LLOYD WRIGHT

Light was an essential ingredient
of Wright's organic architecture.
In his library (right) it helped
suggest an indoor-outdoor space—
with protection from the elements
but freedom from enclosure.
The room feels like a clearing
in the woods.

ties, such as its relation to its site, the suitability of its
materials, and the needs of the people who would use it.

Chicago architects grabbed upon the organic idea,
applying it to their quest for a distinctly American architecture. Their organic architectural response to the
needs of the people who would build and inhabit downtown Chicago produced something entirely new: skyscrapers rising ten, eleven, and a then dizzying twelve
stories above the street. The skyscraper provided maximum space on minimum real estate, strict economy
in construction, and abundant natural light, basic hall-
marks of the new American architecture.

No idea has so consistently bound Chicago architects
over the years as the organic ideal. To Louis Sullivan,

who wrote tens of thousands of words on the subject,
organic architecture could enhance human life in practical and profound ways. Tall office buildings, for example, could relieve earthbound congestion; they could
also make the spirit soar. Structure, utility, beauty, and
spirituality could become one in a building, he believed,
as they do in a tree.

Frank Lloyd Wright would later enlarge the concept of
organic architecture, forging new relationships between
buildings and the natural conditions around them: He
used horizontal roof lines to celebrate the flat Midwestern prairie and oak trim in regions where oak trees were
plentiful. And more than any architect before or since,
Wright understood architecture not as an object but as
an experience that should correspond to or elicit human

Religious architecture often conveys the organic ideal that a building serve both practical and spiritual purposes. Unity Temple's sanctuary is at once low, cavelike, and filled with light; it is intimate but also seems much larger than it is. Wright's mastery of geometry and his materials, colors, and amazing chandeliers create a space that first fascinates, then inspires awe.

feeling. The organic ideal inspired Sullivan, Wright, and countless architects since to design something entirely new in response to changing human needs. Organic architecture became the touchstone of modern design.

THE EMBRACE OF SIMPLICITY

Some of the earliest manifestations of the architectural theories under discussion in late-nineteenth-century Chicago were the works of Henry Hobson Richardson (1838–1886), one of the most important architects of his generation. The critic Montgomery Schuyler would become Richardson's champion. The two men first met in 1874, when Schuyler landed a part-time job on a short-lived publication called the *New York Sketch-Book of Architecture,* one of the first magazines in the country aimed at architects and not builders (who often believed architects were unnecessary). Richardson was editor at the time, and his idea that a building's form should reflect its structure would have a profound effect on Schuyler.

More than a decade later, in his widely read column in the *Architectural Record,* Schuyler lavished the highest

praise on many Richardson designs, which were distinguished by thick walls, pitched roofs, majestic profiles, and great stone arches inspired by the Romanesque. Schuyler's articles helped transmit the language of "Richardsonian Romanesque," which was adopted by many other architects pressing toward a strong, simple American style. With Richardson's examples in mind, Schuyler believed it was possible to repair "the estrangement between architecture and building—between the poetry and the prose, so to speak, of the art of building, which can never be disjoined without injury to both."

Schuyler traveled to Chicago to write an article that appeared in the *Record* in 1891, in which he claimed that the buildings he found there were a "welcome surprise to the tourist from the East." His interest in visiting the city was piqued, in all likelihood, by the buildings Richardson had designed there just prior to his death in 1886. What pleased Schuyler most about Chicago was that, in the five years since, the great Richardson's lessons seemed to have rubbed off on it. Although he found clinkers like the Board of Trade, Schuyler also witnessed buildings of dignified simplicity

MARSHALL FIELD
WHOLESALE STORE
ADAMS AND FRANKLIN STREETS
1887 (DEMOLISHED 1930)

and power. He declared that Chicago architecture was the architecture of the future. This, he said, was the indigenous art America was waiting for.

The Wholesale Store

In Chicago's central business district, called "the Loop" because of the streetcar line ringing it, Schuyler was excited to find a Richardson building that has since assumed the dimensions of myth. This was Marshall Field's Wholesale Store, completed in 1887, demolished in 1930. It filled an entire city block and exerted an influence that was powerful and immediate. Before construction began, Richardson was interviewed by a *Chicago Tribune* reporter who seems to have paraphrased the architect, writing that "beauty will be one of the objects aimed at in the plans, but it will be the beauty of material and symmetry rather than of mere superficial ornamentation." That idea, so concisely expressed, rang with crystal clarity to the up-to-date architects of the time.

The Wholesale Store commission represented a propitious union of architect and client. Marshall Field, the store's owner, was not only an innovative merchandiser who had amassed one of the largest fortunes in the country, but a patron of the arts; he eventually endowed what later became the Art Institute of Chicago and the Field Museum of Natural History. In these early days of the company, Field's merchandise operations included a retail store of great refinement, as it does today, and a much larger wholesale division. The Wholesale Store was designed to serve professional buyers who journeyed to Chicago from throughout the West to stock their own stores. The extraordinary fact that every merchant west of the Mississippi—and quite a few east of it, too—depended upon Chicago and largely upon Field's as a principal source of goods inspired the architect to design a structure that changed the scale of downtown Chicago in a single stroke. The Wholesale Store would be grand if not imperial, Richardson resolved, and he challenged himself to come up with something of rare power.

Since the Wholesale Store no longer exists, we can judge the building only through photographs—which depict a forceful design of unadorned simplicity, massivity, and rhythmically repeating arches—and contemporary accounts. Reports are that it was simply the most impressive thing ever created in Chicago. Sullivan, often an emotional writer, called it "a monument to

trade, to the organized commercial spirit, to the power and progress of the age." As late as 1921 Austrian-born architect Rudolf Schindler visited Chicago and wrote that Richardson buildings "appear like meteors from other planets" in the middle of otherwise bland cities. This is testimony to the originality and impressiveness of Richardson's building, which was meant most of all to be utilitarian.

The Wholesale Store was original but not without antecedents. Symbolically, there is no question that Richardson meant to express the merchant's power, and he reached into history for a starting point. Both Richardson and Field had visited Florence shortly before the Wholesale Store was designed, and it is no coincidence that the massive dimensions of the Field store resemble those of Palazzo Pitti, palace of the powerful Medici family. The palace has a solidity and a beauty that could easily inspire an architect bent on simple designs—and it also lent Richardson an attractive allusion to Renaissance Italy's great banker-prince, Cosimo de' Medici.

But Richardson was no copyist. While he admired old Tuscan forms, he had other things in mind to give the building life of its own. We know from photos in Richardson's collection that Roman aqueducts enchanted him, and distinct echoes of their ancient forms resonate in the Field building. To reinforce the simplicity of the place, Richardson folds in yet another influence, this one thoroughly un-European. The rear facade reveals rows of large arched windows like those common to the most American of all commercial structures at the time, New England industrial mills. Their practical effect, of course, was to allow natural light to stream in. Artistically, they helped the building demonstrate a broader point: that the essence of varied designs from the past could be blended into something original and cohesive. The Wholesale Store strongly foreshadowed what modern architecture would come to be—practical, original, and respectful of the past, but in no way welded to it.

Glessner House

Another Richardson building, Glessner House on Prairie Avenue, was designed with equal mastery and had equal influence on architects who viewed it. It came late in Richardson's career, completed in 1887, a year after the architect's premature death at the age of forty-seven.

Today, in a part of the city that has become grittily industrial, the stone facade of Glessner House has a forbidding look; even in its day it must have appeared austere. Nevertheless, its originality and resolve have dazzled other architects since the day it went up. Mies van der Rohe visited Glessner House shortly after arriving in Chicago in 1939. Later, when it was threatened with destruction, Philip Johnson initiated an effort to raise funds to buy it. In 1970 a number of working architects undertook its restoration as a labor of love; there's a story that when they needed to see Richardson's plans, a set was found in the office of Mies, who had died the year before.

As is often the case with great architecture, understanding the relationship between client and architect is helpful to understanding the design. The Glessners were New Englanders who had recently moved to Chicago, where John Jacob Glessner was making a fortune in the manufacture of farm machinery. The Glessners were of an intellectual bent and were greatly impressed by the writings of John Ruskin and William Morris, the English poet, artist, and designer who spearheaded the Arts and Crafts movement. In the Ruskinian tradition, Mr. and Mrs. Glessner regarded architecture as an expression of moral condition and, when they hired Richardson, then the nation's leading architect, they expected something quite distinct from the pseudo-French châteaux that lined Prairie Avenue.

The Glessners wanted no less than a work of art. When Richardson inquired about the family's preferred floor plan, Mrs. Glessner protested. "Oh, no, Mr. Richardson, that would be me planning the house. I want you to plan it." During their interview, Richardson noticed a photograph of the stable at Abington Abbey, a medieval English structure, on the wall of their home. Richardson asked if they liked the stable, a plain stone building with a pitched roof. They said they did—it had a rustic simplicity much admired at the time—whereupon Richardson asked for the picture to take back to his studio. "I'll make that the keynote of your house," he told them.

That he did, but again, with nothing derivative or pretentious about the result. The abbey stable gives Glessner House notes of domestic charm, but the facade also recalls the fortresslike formalism of an early palazzo. The fortress idea likely was reinforced by conditions that Richardson found in Chicago as he was designing the house. Civil unrest was in the air, as was highlighted by an entry in the Glessner family diaries. On May 4, 1884, the Glessners were in their Washington Street home reviewing the final plans sent by Richardson's office.

GLESSNER HOUSE

1800 SOUTH PRAIRIE AVENUE

1887

H. H. RICHARDSON

While most wealthy Chicagoans were building elaborate mansions, the Glessners appreciated the virtues of Arts and Crafts design. Their home was simple but impressive in its strength and craftsmanship. The exterior (opposite, above) suggests both permanence and the turning of the building's focus inward. The large south- and west-facing windows on the courtyard (opposite, below) admitted floods of light. The interior decoration exemplifies the homey Arts and Crafts style of William Morris. Exposed oak beams and fine woodwork characterize the interior, including the dining room (right) and entry-hall staircase (overleaf).

THE ROOTS OF MODERN ARCHITECTURE

A comfortable library—not a formal parlor—was the center-piece of the house. Richardson and the Glessners haunted antiques shops for rugs and light fixtures, valuing each piece by the extent to which it reflected the hand of a craftsperson.

They were interrupted by an explosion and gunshots— the famous Haymarket Riot was raging only a few blocks away. Given such strife, the urban rich, even a liberal family, might understandably look favorably upon living in a fortress.

Richardson's reposed exterior is gentler than the average stockade, of course, but it is his interior that points to the emerging direction of modern architecture. Indeed, the very plainness of the outside walls seems to announce that the real interest of this house is inside. That point might have gone unnoticed by the public at the time but would have been striking to the architects who were intently considering architecture's impact on the people who used it.

Richardson provided rich interior detailing, such as the William Morris tiles and medieval-style ironwork that typified organic architecture's celebration of craftsman-ship and true, undisguised materials. But Glessner House's most organic feature was something more sub-tle: a floor plan that was almost revolutionary in its day— and so influential ever since that it might now easily be overlooked. The Glessner plan is open and expansive, with one room flowing through large openings into the next. The effect is almost that of a single, unified space. Although walls and function define specific rooms,

the plan was a radical departure from the convention of firmly delineated chambers.

Richardson broke with another convention by choosing an asymmetrical layout when most mansions of the period embodied classical symmetry. He did so for a very practical reason. Asymmetry enabled him to orient most of the rooms around a light court on the south side of the main wing, filling the uncommonly large spaces with maximum natural light. Space and light, we shall see, became an obsessive concern for Chicagoans, perhaps because the climate so often draws them indoors. That was especially true for the Glessners, who resided in Chicago only in the wintertime, when sunlight is at a strict premium, and summered in New Hampshire.

Numerous other features mark Glessner House as an early modern design, and many of them were tied to the architect's, and the clients', emphasis on practicality, not showiness. One good example, now frequently over-looked, might have raised eyebrows among the Glessners' more conservative friends: The primary room of the house is not a fancy parlor for receiving special guests— as would have been typical at the time—but the library, a room used by the family every day. A place for books, not punch and cookies, as the nexus of the home reflected the hope that intellect and family interaction,

The openness, embrace of hand-crafts, and responsiveness to its occupants that Richardson conveyed at Glessner House represented a great turning point in American architecture.

rather than superficial conventions, would be the cornerstone of modern life. It was a decidedly idealistic statement, but as an architectural decision the mere placement of this room represented a turning point.

Richardson was most active in the Boston area, so it is natural to wonder why two of the most important projects of his career took place in Chicago. One answer is the clients; another is the city itself. Field was by no means a typical client, nor were the Glessners, and the fact that such progressive people thrived in Chicago had everything to do with the city's character. Just as thoughtful architects found Chicago inspiring and promising, so did its businesspeople, its writers, and its countless other citizens who forged new directions, in the process opening minds to new possibilities. Chicago's stimulating environment enabled and encouraged creativity that in architecture brought forth entirely new designs for buildings that pushed against the limits of what had been done before.

CHAPTER 2

THE CHICAGO SCHOOL

THE ROOKERY

109 SOUTH LASALLE STREET

1888

BURNHAM AND ROOT

Chicago School architects, interested in finding beauty in the means of construction, celebrated wrought iron and used glass more prolifically than ever before. The Rookery's oriel staircase was made with the extravagant care worthy of a monumental sculpture.

Before the turn of the nineteenth century, Chicago was so clearly the city of the future that it was attracting not just architects to build it, but writers to chronicle, dissect, and try to understand it. What old Chicago lacked in social order and refinement it made up for in ambition and explosive growth, and where architects found a wildly fertile ground for new construction, writers discovered an irresistible energy that inspired their own artistic breakthroughs. Chicago was the birthplace of a new, sometimes harshly realistic American literary style, including the widely read novels of Theodore Dreiser, Frank Norris, and Upton Sinclair. Aptly, one of the best sellers of the period—*The Cliff-Dwellers,* written in 1893 by Henry Blake Fuller—was set in none other than a Chicago skyscraper.

While architects have sometimes served as protagonists in books and movies, in *The Cliff-Dwellers* the author gives the central role to the Clifton, a fictional Loop office building with safe elevators, central heating, and windows aglitter with the names of prestigious tenants. Fuller's skyscraper was an undisguised microcosm of Chicago's unsubtle social order at the time: A beer hall in the basement served the masses off the street; better restaurants and a barber shop were perched in the tower eighteen stories above.

The Clifton symbolized upward mobility—as well as the ever-present threat of financial and social collapse. Predictably enough all is not well inside. Ambition and fortune collide in close quarters and seemingly at random. Morals are challenged. Reputations are crushed.

In an early scene Ogden, a young transplant from Boston, overhears shouting in an adjacent office; it is the wealthy banker, Brainard, berating his daughter about her recent engagement as if "dealing with the concerns of an ordinary business acquaintance." Sadly, Ogden himself marries a shameless social climber and is forced to embezzle money to support her ways. The plot is full of cruel turns, but the central idea is clear: Materialistic striving narrows lives. The symbol of urban life is the skyscraper, which was invented and enjoyed its earliest development in Chicago.

Few people read Fuller today, but he vividly portrayed the intensity of Chicago life in those highly charged times. He used architecture as a metaphor for power and acknowledged it as an expression of wealth. Indeed, much of the staggering industrial fortunes accumulated in Chicago in the Gilded Age helped finance the city's fast-growing skyline. It was natural that tall buildings would intrigue writers as backdrops to their stories. Some portrayed them as dark and leering, others as bright and fantastic—but always they recognized that buildings had the power to touch people's emotions.

In the real world real architects were interested in tapping emotions, too, as John Wellborn Root did with his first great building, the Rookery. Built in 1888, it is still the noblest edifice on LaSalle Street, though dwarfed by the modern towers rising around it today. Emotion also drove Louis Sullivan's design for the Auditorium Building he developed with his partner Dankmar Adler. The seventeen-story Auditorium was not only Chicago's

HOME INSURANCE BUILDING

135 SOUTH LASALLE STREET

1885 (DEMOLISHED 1931)

WILLIAM LE BARON JENNEY

Iron supports, elevators, and taller urban buildings were all in development when Jenney designed Home Insurance, but it was one of the world's first buildings to include all of those elements. Supported entirely by a steel skeleton and covered by nonbearing walls, it has been called the "first modern skyscraper."

tallest building when it was completed in 1889, but it also contained one of the world's finest opera houses. The Rookery and the Auditorium were epicenters of Chicago when they were built. People who never even walked inside of them were aware of their importance to the city. What was not widely understood at the time was that they were among the era's most influential architectural works and would remain landmarks of what became known as the "Chicago School" of architecture.

The Chicago School, or "Chicago commercial style," as it is also called, revolutionized architecture. Before its advent, many architects had covered buildings with ornament unrelated to inner structure—columns that did not support, openings that did not admit light. By contrast, the Chicago School demonstrated that architecture could and should reveal the engineering underlying modern construction. Celebrating, rather than concealing, structure became an aesthetic imperative. It gave rise to a gracefully proportioned, wholly original style, with buildings that combined "rational" engineering and "emotional" ornament into an organic whole. As the Chicago School evolved, its proponents would write enthusiastically of its simplicity, economy, strength, and even democracy. In time, Chicago office towers came to be regarded as a classic architectural form.

The Chicago School—the name was coined years later—counts Root and Sullivan as its most lyrical and successful members, but the movement began before either of them reached his prime. Its development goes back to the Great Chicago Fire of 1871, to the building frenzy that immediately ensued, and to the few brilliant architects who migrated to the city with unbounded enthusiasm. Although plenty of bad architecture went up in the rush to replace what had been lost, the need to build at an unprecedented pace created conditions under which certain architects flourished. The best of them eagerly embraced new technologies in their efforts to build more efficiently and economically. They happily discarded the old conventions that imitated European architecture—whose heavy ornamentation was an unnecessary luxury under the circumstances—and opened themselves to creating new ways of designing urban buildings.

WILLIAM LE BARON JENNEY

Like many other Chicago architects of the time, William Le Baron Jenney (1832–1907) had arrived from elsewhere. He moved to the city before the fire—and before

most members of the Chicago School—not because it was refined, which it certainly was not, but because it was raw and unformed. He had seen a good bit of the developed world already. Born in Massachusetts, Jenney attended Phillips Academy in Exeter, New Hampshire, then went to engineering school in France. In Europe he was exposed mostly to classical architecture; the formal tradition of the beaux arts was standard fare in schools on both sides of the Atlantic. But he also learned the fundamentals of metal construction, skills he brought back and used during the Civil War as an army officer assigned to the important work of bridge building.

Jenney is remembered as a practical sort, though one who enjoyed the trappings and pleasures of polite society. In Chicago he was known as a bon vivant who would sometimes wander through his office with an armful of dressed duck for the evening's dinner, or pass time spinning tales to entertain his draftsmen. As a designer, however, he chose utility over embellishment, so much so that Louis Sullivan, who worked for Jenney for a short period, wrote that the title "architect" applied to Jenney "only by courtesy of terms."

Considering Sullivan's assessment, Jenney was an unlikely candidate for architectural immortality, but he remains a giant in his field. His reputation rests primarily on his creation of an icon of architecture: The Home Insurance Building, built in 1885 and now demolished, is regarded as the world's first skyscraper. That attribution is debatable but, undeniably, office buildings before Home Insurance almost invariably were constructed with heavy masonry weight-bearing walls and rarely rose more than five or six stories. Jenney instead devised a cast-iron frame that entirely supported his ten-story office building, and covered it with a non-weight-bearing curtain wall of masonry. Home Insurance was completed in a fraction of the time of most other Loop office buildings, and Jenney was credited with the invention of a remarkable and revolutionary approach. Metal frames, curtain walls, and skyscraping heights became common.

Was William Le Baron Jenney the true father of the skyscraper? Perhaps, though there's plenty of credit to go around. Iron frames, for example, were not new, having been used as interior supports in conventional masonry buildings. Safe elevators—another prerequisite for skyscrapers—dated at least to 1857, when they appeared in a New York department store at the corner of Broome

Street and Broadway. And another building framed entirely in metal, evidently in Minneapolis, may actually have preceded Home Insurance. Nevertheless, it was Jenney's building, with its cast-iron supports—which some still regarded as untrustworthy—that was recognized as the milestone, if not for its primacy, then for its influence. Jenney was in Chicago, after all, and it was in Chicago that architecture's great movement skyward occurred.

There is no question, however, that Jenney was an architect ideally suited to his times. His metal-frame technique cut months off construction, and efficiency if nothing else made him a success. His pragmatic approach and his disdain of applied ornament made him a favorite of profit-oriented developers indifferent to architectural immortality. Jenney's innovation served practical ends, and as the metal-frame office building developed it provided another useful advantage: Its iron skeleton permitted larger windows than did masonry construction, the better for bringing natural light and fresh air inside. With that in mind, Jenney went on to develop the so-called Chicago window, a wide fixed pane with narrow movable sashes on both sides. The Chicago window was quickly adopted by architects and developers attracted by its practical simplicity and became a classic form.

Despite Jenney's success and broad influence, some later critics suggested that his innovations sprang not from great inspiration but almost unintentionally, from conditions of time and place. Lewis Mumford wrote that Jenney "seems to have gone about his work absent-mindedly—often instinctively doing the right thing but never conscious enough of it to give a rational account of his purpose." But Mumford was from New York, where condescending attitudes about Chicago prevailed, and may have been too dismissive. Others viewed Jenney as an artist way ahead of his time. The Swiss architectural historian Sigfried Giedion cited the second Leiter Building on State Street, which Jenney designed in 1889 as a simple department store loft, as a ground-breaking modern work. In *Space, Time and Architecture* (1941) Giedion raved about the building's simple proportions and the way its details correspond to the steel frame underneath. He wrote that Jenney achieved what far more self-conscious modernists like Le Corbusier attempted to do years later. "The Leiter building marks

a starting point for this kind of architectural purity and should not be ignored in the history of architecture."

JOHN WELLBORN ROOT

In 1872 the young Georgia-born architect John Wellborn Root (1850–1891) departed New York for Chicago. He arrived with $300 in his pocket and a portfolio of experimental designs. Fortunately he had practical experience as well, as a construction superintendent on the train shed at Grand Central Terminal, and he presented those credentials along with his designs at the office of P. B. Wight. Wight, a distinguished architect and contemporary of Jenney, later explained that he was deeply impressed by Root's drawings and his grasp of "the constructive principles of the best Gothic work of the twelfth and thirteenth centuries." It's likely, however, that he was most interested, at least initially, with the young man's ability to help him get his buildings built.

Root himself was passionate about architecture and a tireless, discerning observer of the art. A wide range of designs was emerging in Chicago in the postfire boom, and the young Root made a pastime of touring the city on foot, often with other architects, and judging new buildings as "architectural" or "not architectural." Those whose structure was apparent in the design tended to meet his approval; those buildings that did not reveal structure—especially those laden with meretricious detail—he deemed "French."

His employer's buildings were of the first category. Among Wight's innovations was the technique of fire-proofing tall buildings by cladding the frames with hollow courses of ceramic tile. So Root's involvement in practical work on practical buildings reinforced the lesson he had first learned when working on Grand Central's great iron and glass canopy: that true beauty in architecture was not superficial, but derived from function. "Styles grow by the careful study of all the conditions which lie about each architectural problem," he later wrote.

Root had an obvious talent for design himself, and within a year Wight was ready to make him a junior partner in his firm. But Root had other ideas and was pulled in a different direction. Daniel Burnham (1846–1912), another draftsman in Wight's office, was eager to establish a firm of his own. He proposed to Root a partnership, in which Burnham would handle the busi-

THE ROOKERY

109 SOUTH LASALLE STREET

1888

BURNHAM AND ROOT

The great arch in the Rookery's powerful exterior masonry leads to an open, light-filled atrium.

ness end and Root would do most of the design. So it was that Burnham and Root left Wight's office in July 1873—just three months prior, as bad luck would have it, to a business-busting financial panic.

The firm suffered from the business drought for at least a year. Burnham and Root secured some residential commissions, but they were something of a consolation prize, not the commercial work they'd hoped for. The business remained disappointing for several more years, until Burnham's talents of persuasion and Root's creative ability to design foundations in Chicago's marshy soil won them the kind of work they sought—tall office buildings in the Loop. Their ten-story Montauk Block, built on Monroe Street in 1882, three years before Home Insurance, boasted brick bearing walls that rose

more than one hundred feet. It was a technical marvel, not only for its height but for its concrete slab foundation, which was devised to distribute the large building's weight in marshy soil. The Montauk also used iron beams to reinforce the structure within. Both devices were relatively new at the time and Root's mastery of them was notable. But what was most remarkable about the Montauk was its lack of decoration. Root clearly agreed with Peter Brooks, the building's developer and investor, who said, "the building throughout is to be for use and not for ornament. Its beauty will be in its all-adaptation to its use." Root followed those instructions with such a deft sense of simplicity and proportion that one architectural historian later gushed, "what Chartres was to the Gothic cathedral the Montauk Block was to the high commercial building."

THE ROOKERY

A transitional building in the history of architecture, the Rookery's exterior walls were of true masonry construction but its interior supports were cast iron. The elaborate decoration was a highly original mix of motifs, including Moorish, Venetian, and Byzantine. It was called a manifestation of "Root's fervid and fanciful pencil."

The Montauk may have been the first building ever referred to as a "skyscraper." (The term was previously used to describe high-masted sailing vessels in New York Harbor.) Notwithstanding its historic stature, the Montauk was later demolished; like many of John Wellborn Root's early Chicago School buildings, its elegant simplicity went unappreciated until too late. One that survives, however, is a widely loved masterpiece that demonstrates with rare poetry how a commercial structure can be enchanting and practical at the same time. This is the Rookery, which still exhibits many of the charms that made it successful when it was completed in 1888. It proves that some aspects of good office building design are advantages forever—ample light for offices, for example, and open areas for congregating and shopping on levels close to the street. Root

devised ways to incorporate such features and in doing so changed the course of American architecture.

Chief among the Rookery's attributes is a large light well in the center, which not only illuminates the interior but also allows for an enclosed atrium. The Rookery's glazed glass interior courtyard—one of America's first retail arcades—proved to be one of the most striking and most influential exemplars of the Chicago School. In the Rookery's atrium, balconies, stairways, and a network of beams and supports evoke weightless, limitless space—calling to mind the Piranesi engravings that Root was known to collect. The Rookery was thoroughly modern in its time, the result of Root's mastery of cast-iron and other building technologies that were then new. But it was timeless as well, designed and realized by

Root's Rookery was a lacy cage of unequaled splendor. Only the fantastical art of the Renaissance artist Piranesi, whose prints Root collected, could match the curious passages and skyways that the architect constructed through this grand atrium space.

an artist who understood that glass and steel were components of the architecture, but that light and space were the true heart of the Rookery's grandeur.

Indeed, John Root was a thoughtful and cultured man, and many believe that he, not Louis Sullivan, would have become the guiding light of Chicago architecture had his career reached maturity. Root also wrote lucid essays in magazines for architects about their responsibility to create an American style. Toward this objective he saw Chicago as a great opportunity. Root was inspired by businessmen and developers whose need for tall, profitable buildings was uncompromisingly clear. Root believed that by meeting skyscrapers' practical require-

ments, he could express their psychology or spirit as well. "Reason should lead the way," Root wrote, "and imagination take wings from a height to which reason has already climbed."

Root must be regarded as the consummate *organic* architect, though the term was not widely used during his life. His choice of a Richardsonian exterior for the Rookery, for example, was not arbitrary. Root intended it to evoke solidity and strength, heightening the contrasting sense of light and openness upon walking inside—which is indeed what the visitor experiences. No artist was more orderly, yet none more elaborately wove various images together. Just how entirely Root's

THE ROOKERY

The Rookery was one of the country's first buildings to make use of a large light court, which filled it with natural light and created a glass-enclosed court-yard—an early shopping center. The light court also illuminated the stairways (opposite), whose windows (seen at extreme left) opened to it.

imagination "took wings" is evident in one of the Rookery's most important motifs, drawn from the building's name, which was inspired by a bit of local humor.

That story relates to Chicago's old City Hall, the previous occupant of the site, which was known for two things: corrupt politicians within and dirty pigeons without. In an inspired moment a passerby called it a "rookery," which stuck. Even when the old building came down the nickname persisted, to the chagrin of the developers, who were intent on a more dignified name for their new building. But it amused Root, who set the name in stone with his grand design and immortalized the joke with laughing crows carved on the granite arch outside. Inside, the ornithological imagery took flight. The atrium resembles an aviary, albeit an elegant one. Root's etched marble panels and ornamental rails (altered in a 1907 renovation by Frank Lloyd Wright) are winding and complex, some say nestlike. The space seems to defy gravity;

it's quite a rookery indeed—and proof that Root's imagination could soar at the slightest provocation.

Monadnock's "Egyptian-like Effects"

The Rookery shows that Chicago School buildings were not always bereft of ornament. A later Root skyscraper, however, demonstrates how much architectural power could be found in restraint. This is the Monadnock Block, whose first half Burnham and Root built in 1891. (The Chicago School firm of Holabird and Roche extended it to the south a few years later, echoing much of Root's design.) The ornament inside and out is spare but wonderfully wrought. On the surface, the Monadnock may be Root's plainest work, but it might also be his most thoughtful.

Here again the clients—and their pragmatism—played an important role in the design. Correspondence between the developers—Peter Brooks, the New England

Root's all-masonry building won immediate praise for its sleek profile, which impressed fellow architects, and its true economy, which delighted real estate investors. The protruding bays were an elegant new touch for tall buildings—and they also added rentable floor space. The addition echoes the original but is distinguished by the overhang at the roof line (in the background at left, opposite). The proportions and restrained detail mark Root as one of the great artists of his time. Even the ornament serves a purpose: In the stairways (above and overleaf) iron provided strength as well as beauty and also allowed light to penetrate.

millionaire who had previously built the Montauk, and his Chicago partner Owen Aldis—indicates that they were obsessed with the building's practicality. The Monadnock should have "no projecting surfaces or indentations," according to a letter from Brooks, who believed that in the smoky Loop "projections mean dirt" as well as "the lodgment of pigeons and sparrows." Instructions from the developers indicated, essentially, a brick box. Predictably, Root satisfied that requirement and gave them substantially more. The Monadnock *is* plain—its elegance comes from sleek projecting bays that run vertically down the sides of otherwise flat brick walls. To us they are a masterpiece of profiling; to Brooks and Aldis they were perfect because they increased rentable floor space.

But Root's good clients were not mere boors or mercenaries, blind to art. Through them we learn something about Root's innermost ideas for the design. Well before the developers saw anything like finished plans, Aldis wrote Brooks that Root's "head is now deep in Egyptian-like effects." There's no indication that Aldis comprehended why Root was studying Egyptian masonry, yet there's a tone of admiration in his letter. Root, he said, was determined to produce a building "harmonious and massive and artistic."

The result was a masonry skyscraper—Aldis and Brooks still distrusted steel—that made an impact when it was built and has impressed architects and critics ever since. At ground level the rusticated base slopes back, almost subliminally reminiscent of an ancient pyramid. From the base the walls rise straight up, largely unornamented. At the top the walls flare out ever so slightly, replacing the expected cornice. Root's design is simple and handsome, but it is so unlike other tall buildings that one naturally wonders what inspired it.

A clue to Root's idea can be found in one of the Monadnock's few decorative images: carvings of papyrus in panels high above the street. Combined with Root's reported study of "Egyptian-like effects," these reliefs, almost invisible from the ground, lead us to the intriguing realization that the building is remarkably similar in profile and proportion to the sleek papyrus-shaped columns found in ruins of ancient Egypt. From there, one can imagine the building's vertical bays as having the long graceful line of stalks of papyrus that Root evidently knew from his studies. It's not that the Monadnock resembles papyrus plants any more than it does an oak tree. It seems rather that Egypt provided the architect with a flurry of ideas to ignite his imagination.

But why Egypt? Here again the answer is conjectural but plausible, given what we know of Root and his circle at

the time. Egypt may have jumped forth in Root's imagination from a purely functional concern. The marshy subsoil of Chicago, it was well known, was much like that of the Upper Nile. In previous buildings, in fact, he had borrowed the pyramid form for footings to help distribute the weight of his heavy skyscrapers. This may have led Root to the papyrus motif. Papyrus, of course, did not grow naturally in Chicago, but papyruslike alliums did. One such allium, the wild onion Indians called "checagou," had given the city its name.

What could be more "organic?" While this interpretation is speculative, the integration of functional elements with symbolic ones came naturally to Root. Images of ancient Egypt, home to history's most basic form of masonry construction, inspired his imagination to do what he believed all architecture should do—"take wings from a height to which reason has already climbed."

LOUIS SULLIVAN

Perhaps the most important, and decidedly the most enigmatic, figure in the history of Chicago architecture is Louis Sullivan (1856–1924). It was he who succinctly articulated the modernist idea that architects ever since have considered, struggled with, and taken to heart: "Form ever follows function." Sullivan's immortal maxim is deceptively simple. It seems to say that architecture should be largely unadorned and utilitarian, but many of Sullivan's designs—and particularly his interiors—are ornate beyond the most extravagant dreams. Sullivan decorated with rich mosaics, carved wood, elaborate plaster moldings, and murals of the most romantic inspiration. And yet Sullivan never neglected the structural concerns of the Chicago School, of which he is regarded as a central figure. He insisted on decoration that revealed rather than concealed structure and explained in his voluminous writings that ornament in architecture was "a luxury, not necessary." Nevertheless, he added, "I believe just as firmly that a decorated structure, harmoniously conceived, well considered, cannot be stripped of its system of ornament without destroying its individuality."

Sullivan remains an intriguingly contradictory character. His status as one of Chicago's two or three most famous architects, and also as the great prophet of modernism, is itself counterintuitive, as few of his buildings either resemble the rest of the Chicago School or look "modern." His enormous influence on the architecture of the twentieth century also seems peculiar, since his practice peaked in the 1890s, when he was still young, and went into almost total eclipse a decade later. Yet countless ideas in the development of modern architecture were his, and he showed the way for later generations. The reason is that in his buildings and his writings Sullivan defined and expressed the tenets of organic architecture with more resolute passion than anyone before or since.

Extending Ruskin's view that a building could reflect the spirit of the people who built it, Sullivan wrote that a building could itself take on the force of life. Space could seem vibrant. Building materials could appear as they were found in nature. Light could imbue a building with life cycles of its own. And in the critical relationship between organic architecture and the people who inhabited it, ornament could strike sublime chords. "We have in us romanticism," he wrote, "and feel a craving to express it. We feel intuitively that our strong, athletic, and simple forms will carry with natural ease the raiment of which we dream, and that our buildings thus clad in the garment of poetic imagery, half-hid as it were in choice products of loom and mine, will appeal with redoubled power, like a sonorous melody overlaid with sonorous voices." Sullivan's florid prose can be difficult to decipher, but his meaning bursts forth with tremendous power in the spaces he designed.

"Large Ideas Tending to Metaphysics"

Sullivan was born and raised in Boston. He was a rebellious student but even as a youth was drawn to the city's rich architectural environment. In 1872 he enrolled at Massachusetts Institute of Technology, which offered the country's first professional school of architecture, and there he took classes from the esteemed professor William R. Ware. Ware's lectures were known mostly for his exhortations that American architecture had deteriorated into a gaggle of European styles. Railing against architects for what he insisted was their rampant bad taste and unscrupulous practices, Ware wrote, "The rules of professional procedure became corrupted and lost." Sullivan agreed heartily with Ware's assessment but dropped out because M.I.T.'s remedy was to inculcate the beaux arts, with its reliance on Greek and Roman forms. More promising, Sullivan thought, would be practical experience. He went to Philadelphia, where he worked for Frank Furness, the well-known designer of uninhibited structures that in some cases looked like Byzantine fantasies.

When built, the Auditorium was the tallest building in Chicago (opposite, below left). It was regarded as the world's finest opera house and also contained offices and a hotel. A banquet hall, later restored and converted into a recital space (opposite, above left), has art-glass transoms, birch capitals, and nature paintings—each a unique work of art. Lauded as a milestone of indigenous American architecture, the Auditorium drew heavily on the best traditions of the past. The facade's enormous corbels (opposite, right) are almost primitive in character. Architects searched world history for architecture that reflected the still young nation.

But the real point of interest for architects at the time was not Philadelphia but Chicago, so Sullivan headed west, joining his parents there. When he arrived in 1873 the seventeen-year-old Sullivan was fascinated, even intoxicated, by the city—as he would be throughout his career—although Chicago was then crude and dirty almost beyond belief for the Easterner. "But in spite of the panic," Sullivan wrote in his autobiography, "there was stir; an energy that made him tingle to be in the game." (Sullivan wrote *The Autobiography of an Idea,* as it was entitled, in the third person.) He applied for a job as a draftsman with William Jenney because he was impressed by the straightforward approach that would lead, a few years thence, to the metal-frame Home Insurance Building.

Working with Jenney, Sullivan took pains to perfect his tracing and drawing skills. After a year or so, he concluded that he ought to continue his formal education and in mid-1874 he enrolled in Europe's leading architectural school, the École des Beaux-Arts of Paris. The choice was surprising, as the École taught neoclassicism, which Sullivan had escaped by leaving M.I.T. But the lessons he took to heart were that the power of design was in the floor plan, and that exterior form should grow from a building's interior scheme. That certainly made sense to a young man dismayed by architecture he viewed as a senseless conglomeration. Nonetheless, Sullivan decided to leave Paris before finishing the course.

Sullivan's biographer Robert Twombley thus explained his subject's formal training, and where it next led him: "Louis' architectural education had turned out to be a backwards tracing of academic ideological development. M.I.T. had been a pale carbon copy of the Ecole, so Louis went to the original. But in Paris, he discovered the Ecole to be a modern outpost of ancient and Renaissance design. So Louis went to Italy. . . . After that, there was no place else to go."

In the Sistine Chapel, Sullivan was thunderstruck by the frescoes and their creator. He found in Michelangelo an inspiring genius for communicating through art what was otherwise inexpressible. Michelangelo was "the first man with a great voice," he wrote. "The first whose speech was elemental." The experience also suggests that Sullivan was open to learning, but preferred doing so on his own rather than in the classroom.

After Italy Sullivan returned to Chicago, where he resolved to produce architecture that would be less historical and more "elemental." He began to work with a variety of architectural firms, mostly as a freelance designer of decoration and ornament. Many of his designs of this early period were successful enough to attract attention—and to secure him a large commission in the late 1870s for the stenciled ornament in the interior of Sinai Temple, a prominent Chicago synagogue. But despite the favorable reviews of this and other work, Sullivan remained baffling to critics familiar mostly with the pattern books. In one article about the young designer a journalist wrote, "Mr. Sullivan is a pleasant gentleman, but somewhat troubled with large ideas tending to metaphysics."

Indeed, the architect seemed to encourage an aura of inscrutability. When asked to explain his style he replied, "That is an exceedingly difficult question to answer. I cannot give it words. I prefer that you speak of it as the successful solution of a problem. The vaguer you are in such matters, the better I shall be pleased."

If writers and the public were unsure how to assess Sullivan's work, other architects definitely appreciated it. In 1883 Dankmar Adler (1844–1900), who had designed Sinai Temple and other projects Sullivan had worked on, invited him to join his well-established firm as partner in charge of design and decoration. The firm of Adler and Sullivan thrived for fourteen years, initially in the design of theaters and the buildings that housed them. Success came in no small part because of Adler's skill as an engineer. But in spaces where ornament counted, Sullivan was much valued for the colorful and curious patterns that characterized his designs. While architectural historians are careful to give Adler due credit for the firm's success, it was Sullivan's contributions that brought the firm's truly revolutionary architecture its greatest public acclaim.

The Idealism of His Times

Sullivan was wildly idealistic, yet his ideas were formed largely by the intellectual climate in which he lived. He was a lifelong reader and enthusiastic follower of Transcendentalist writers such as Emerson, Thoreau, and Whitman. Their philosophy grew from faith in the power of nature—which they viewed as a pulsing, spiritual organism—and in the divinity of mankind. If man was part of nature's vast, mysterious plan, it fol-

Following pages: The Auditorium lobby was designed by Louis Sullivan. Though it was he who decreed, "Form ever follows function," his lobby's beams and arches support nothing and its columns are inessential. No matter: The lobby's main function was to reflect the immensity of form and dazzle the eye. The massiveness of the staircases had a mundane function, to accommodate crowds. But the lush vegetal motif, with branches and leaves growing in and from the stair rails, ceilings, and walls, imbued the building with a natural, almost weightless energy.

lowed that the nation's rich wilderness would give rise to a distinctly American character. Sullivan was just one of many architects determined to capture that character's indomitable force in the art of architecture.

That kind of idealism infused Adler and Sullivan's commission to design the Auditorium Building. The developer, Ferdinand Peck, viewed opera and classical music as a force for social good and believed that building an opera house could help make Chicago a model of moral uplift and democracy. However, Peck was practical enough to realize that a great palace of the performing arts would not pay for itself, and so he envisioned the theater as part of a hotel and office complex. Revenues from paying guests and tenants would go a long way toward supporting an opera house for all Chicagoans.

Peck's idea to break down conventional barriers between rich and poor, commerce and the arts, was unprecedented. It would require equally unconventional engineering. Occupying half a city block, the seventeen-story building would be the largest in the nation at the time. Dankmar Adler deserves immense credit for the Auditorium's unique plan and construction techniques. With unmatched facility, Adler designed a structure with two sets of masonry bearing walls—one around the exterior and the other around the theater space inside—and a structural web requiring so much cast iron that the order staggered the Pittsburgh mill supplying it. Adler's virtuosity in surmounting technical problems was essential to the building. He devised a foundation system that remains a wonder in the soggy soil close to Lake Michigan. He also created a remarkable series

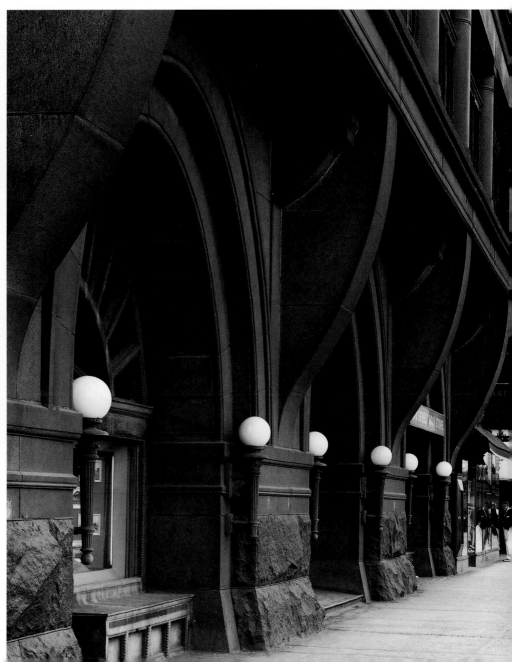

of clear-span spaces, including the theater, that made the interiors soaringly impressive.

To Sullivan fell responsibility for the Auditorium's architectural expression, a task he viewed in philosophical and unabashedly poetic terms. While rational engineering was necessarily the underpinning of what would be the country's largest building, Sullivan's organic ornament, seamlessly integrated with the whole, would make it one of the most ethereal ones as well. The prose and poetry of architecture could become one. And architecture in its highest form would achieve the Transcendental ideal, breaking down the barrier between the material and the spiritual, between reason and emotion.

Sullivan's designs for the Auditorium surprised the world in many ways, and one was an exterior that appeared distinctly plain compared to much of the architect's other work. The reason for this, according to some accounts, was a remark by John Wellborn Root, whose firm had lost the coveted Auditorium commission to Adler and Sullivan. Sullivan "couldn't build an honest wall without covering it with ornament," Root is supposed to have said. The Auditorium's austere exterior walls, clearly influenced by Richardson's Wholesale Store, may have been Sullivan's effort to prove otherwise.

But if the exterior was plain, the interior soared. Today the lobby of the Auditorium Hotel is faded, but it still transmits an emotional impact found in very few interiors. Huge columns appear to support a structure of tremendous mass. (The fact that these columns were not actually bearing the building's weight did not negate the importance of the sensation, in Sullivan's view.) In contrast, leafy designs in plaster panels everywhere grow with apparent weightlessness from the walls. Stories abound about Sullivan's search for draftsmen and tradesmen who could achieve the subtle effects of his decorative concepts. While his young assistant Frank Lloyd Wright was drawing botanical designs, Sullivan hovered over his shoulder. "Make it live, man," Sullivan instructed. "Make it live." He would meet for hours with his Norwegian modeler, Kristian Schneider, to emphasize how ornament should appear to grow right from the plaster, as natural as ripples on a pond.

Attention to detail of this sort is evident throughout the Auditorium, from the lively grain in the Mexican onyx in the hotel lobby to the lyric symbolism in the murals. But

to say that Louis Sullivan designed pleasant spaces is like saying Henry David Thoreau wrote manuals for nature buffs. Both artists strove to touch the spirit. And nowhere is the effect of the Auditorium's ornamental detail more stirring than in the simple and majestic space of the Auditorium Theater. Its structural and decorative elements are intricately and subtly woven together, the very definition of Sullivan's form-follows-function design. The ceiling's span is articulated by a series of arched beams liberally decorated with gold leaf and dotted with a constellation of electric light bulbs; the great vaulted space crescendos from front to back in a dazzling tour de force.

Also amazing about the theater is something that cannot be seen: its acoustics. They are nearly perfect, thanks to a complex relationship between the overall dimensions of space and the arched vaults above. Opera singers who came from Europe were enchanted by the fidelity of the sound, and when Chicago's Civic Opera moved from the Auditorium after forty years, the designers of the new opera house used the Auditorium Theater as an acoustic model. Adler as engineer deserves most of the credit for the way sound moves through the four-thousand-seat space, but the Auditorium's blend of visible and invisible elements is the ultimate in organic architecture. Sullivan often referred to musical art as architecture's nearest relative. Here they become one.

"The Tall Office Building Artistically Considered"
After the Auditorium, Adler and Sullivan's work focused—as did all Chicago—on office skyscrapers. For a while the firm was favored by developers who wanted castles in the sky. And as he and Adler rose to the top of their profession, Sullivan's pronouncements were published and pored over by architects everywhere. In one of his more lucid essays, "The Tall Office Building Artistically Considered," published in *Lippincott's Magazine* in 1896, he set out to describe the form. "It is lofty," he wrote, "the force and power of altitude must be in it, the glory and pride of exaltation must be in it." He listed the three elements of a skyscraper in almost classical terms. It has a base, which attracts the eye; it has a shaft, or the office tiers, uniform in all ways; and it is topped by a capital or attic "to show," he wrote, "that the series of office tiers has definitely come to an end." He went on to compare the skyscraper to a branching oak or a drifting cloud, expressing for the first time what came

61

Wright called Charnley the first "modern" house in history. Some have noted that its exterior resembles a simplified version of a small French palace that was widely published at the time. But something indisputably original was going on here—not least because the building's real interest lay inside.

on his many words. At the head of this class was Frank Lloyd Wright.

A collaboration between Sullivan and Wright yielded one of the most wonderful interiors in all Chicago. This is Charnley House, built in 1892. Some controversy surrounds the building. One issue is the claim that it is architecture's first modern house, as Wright insisted that it was. Others have disagreed, saying it is a throwback—and apparently a direct borrowing from a small eighteenth-century French palace illustrated in textbooks at the time. Another issue is its authorship. Who was the real designer, Sullivan or Wright?

Without settling the first question, what is clear is that some features of Charnley House are unmistakably modern. Its three-story skylight and spare ornamentation

distinguished it from other houses in Chicago at the time. Its unrelenting focus on the interior is notably modern as well. As for the Sullivan-Wright matter, today's consensus is that Sullivan was responsible for the layout, and Wright for the interior and detailing. Long, narrow Roman bricks and plain moldings give Charnley an overall horizontality, which we can attribute to Wright. The fine wooden screen along the stairway is also pure Wright, while the symmetrical plan and heavy exterior walls suggest Sullivan's hand. The use of so much wood in a house built for a lumber family reflects a commitment to organic architecture and could have originated with either man.

From an academic distance, specific authorship of specific features attracts attention. But more important than detailed attribution is that Charnley House repre-

to be organic architecture's dictum: "Form ever follows function."

Sullivan was a leader, albeit an eccentric one. While other Chicago School architects followed an essentially Sullivanesque scheme in straightforward lofts and office blocks, Sullivan himself took off on fanciful flights, lavishing his buildings in ornament. But his ornamentation never disguised the structure of his skyscrapers; rather, the leafy spandrels and the cornices that seem light enough to float highlighted the powerful thrust of the steel frames within. Those inherent, seeming contradictions imbued Sullivan's buildings with immense vigor and lasting beauty. Although Sullivan's written explanations of his purpose were largely inscrutable, when people *saw* his buildings they understood.

As his career developed Sullivan continued to elaborate on the idea of organic architecture. Witness the Carson Pirie Scott department store in Chicago, completed in 1904. It is a tall building for its time, expressing vertical thrust as skyscrapers do, but organically connected as well to the horizontality of the street. The balance of those two simultaneous movements is perhaps the build-ing's most startling effect, one that has been imitated but never equaled by architects ever since.

Carson Pirie Scott is more than an attractive loft building. It is a textbook case of form intertwined with function. At the outset of the commission, Sullivan paid particular attention to the site, where the department store was already a going concern. He watched its daily activity. What he discerned was a kind of theater, with windows as stage set for an audience of well-dressed women. With function in mind, Sullivan devised Carson's most distinctive form, the cast-iron ornament that wraps around the base of the building. It frames large street-level windows that transform simple window shopping along a stretch of State Street into a theatrical event. And like a veil, it provides delicate counterpoint to the otherwise masculine profile of Chicago architecture.

Charnley House

Sullivan was the most influential architect of his time, and yet his work was inimitable, so particular were his solutions to the problem at hand. Philosophically, how-ever, Sullivan's concept of organic architecture made a profound impression on the next generation of Chicago architects. Many regarded him as their master and hung

CARSON PIRIE SCOTT & COMPANY

A powerful Chicago School loft rises above street-level windows veiled in delicate cast-iron frames. The department store building is remarkable for a clarity of form that leads the eye across its horizontal line as well as up its then remarkable height. This photo shows the building after its cornice was removed in an attempt at modernization.

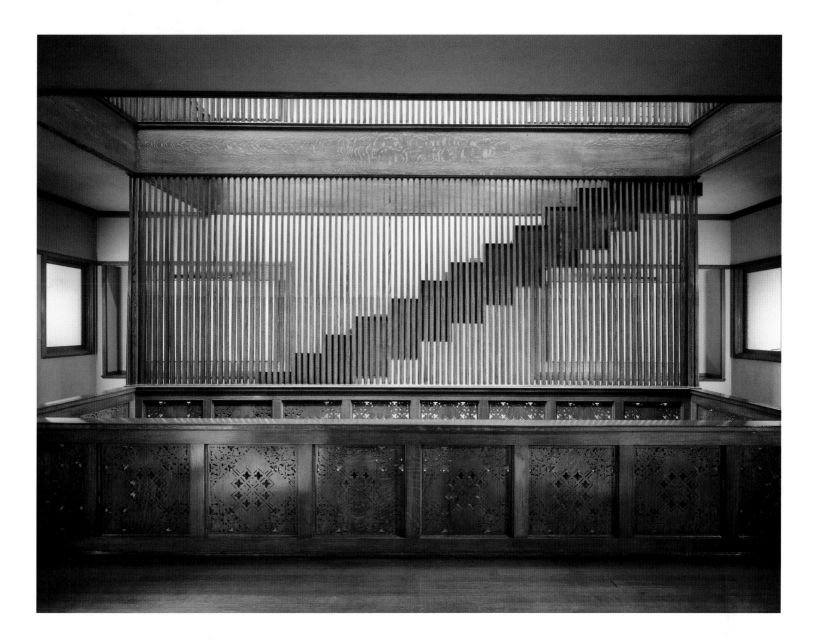

sents a design with a foot in two generations. In it we
see with rare clarity how architectural ideas can be
transmitted. Inside the house itself, the work of one
designer is inextricable from that of the other. (While
Wright insisted that Charnley House was his own design,
one wonders if the enigmatic Sullivan might have
enjoyed the difficulty that later generations would have
in separating their work.) Charnley House shows that,
even in its most artistic moments, architecture is not
created in a vacuum. Rather, it is the result of the
efforts of everyone involved—clients, tradespeople, and
certainly collaborating designers. Architectural genius
lies in putting together all component parts. Trying to
break them up after they have been assembled in a completed design seems quite beside the point.

CLASSICISTS STRIKE BACK

The World's Columbian Exposition, which would open in
1893, presented an exceptional opportunity to showcase
Chicago and its architecture. The fair aspired to be the
greatest exhibition of the arts, sciences, and technology
in history. Burnham and Root had been made consulting
architects for the event, a high honor. The firm would be
responsible for establishing the fair's architectural tone
and choosing the architects for its grand pavilions.

However, in a terrible setback for the Chicago School,
John Wellborn Root died of pneumonia in 1891, at age
forty-one, while he and Burnham were planning for the
event. Indications are that Root had intended to guide
the world's fair to an architecture akin to the styles then

DANIEL H. BURNHAM AND JOHN WELLBORN ROOT

The partners (pictured in their Rookery studio) combined classic proportion with the all-new skyscraper form. Chicago architecture might have taken a different course had Root lived. Burnham, more businessman and less artist than Root, turned the firm toward the classical.

The architects (successors to H. H. Richardson's firm) were instructed to build Chicago's new library in the "classical order of architecture," in keeping with the Columbian Exposition's style. Although the design disavows the simplicity and practicality of the Chicago School, its massive vaults and ample natural light create an impressive interior, a Chicago tradition.

evolving in Chicago, even though well-established Eastern architects, largely unreconstructed neoclassicists, would be involved in the project. But Root's hope that the fair could help bring about an original American style died with him. Instead, the leading New York firms—William Morris Hunt and McKim, Mead and White headed the list—and their refined European neoclassicism came to dominate the Columbian Exposition.

Architecturally speaking, the world's fair was a beaux arts extravaganza that largely ignored the organic ideals of the Chicago School. Its main promenade, the Cour d'Honneur, was organized around a great axial basin, rigidly classical in style. The buildings were intended as temporary and made of a kind of plaster, whitewashed to emulate pristine marble. Conceived as a kind of fantasy, the fairgrounds were called "White City," and its brilliance was heightened by a flood of electric light. Electric lighting was not yet in widespread use, and its deployment on such a vast scale dazzled visitors. "Perhaps dyin' is goin' to be somethin' like crossin' the dividin' line that separates the Midway from White City," said a character in a popular novel entitled *Sweet Clover*, which came out shortly after the fair.

In her biography of Root, Harriet Monroe (the founder of *Poetry* magazine and Root's sister-in-law) acknowledged that the Columbian Exposition was a wonder and a suc-

CHICAGO CULTURAL CENTER

Within the center (above), Preston Bradley Hall (opposite) is one of Chicago's best-loved spaces for lectures, music, and other civic events. Most of its mosaics were designed by Robert Spencer, who later distinguished himself as a Prairie School architect. Louis Comfort Tiffany's firm is credited with designing the hall's massive skylight. The coffered ceiling was modeled after classical forms, but the metal chandeliers reflect Arts and Crafts style.

cess in many ways. Nevertheless, she wrote, "John Root's conception of the Fair differed much from the White City of memory." Under his guidance the result might have been "a queen arrayed in robes not saintly, as for a bridal, but gorgeous, for a festival." Monroe leaves us wondering what a Root-designed fair might have been like. Some faint evidence exists, such as an article for *Inland Architect* magazine, which reported that Root preferred a Romanesque scheme, with touches of colonial and other styles that he believed might contribute to a distinctively American architecture. Moreover, Root would likely have had little patience for plaster made to look like marble. His early sketches called for festive colors. "You've got an exuberant bar-baric effect there—a kind of American Kremlin," said an English artist who saw Root's drawings. They had "lots

of color and noise and life." One wonders if Root sus-pected that classicist forces were angling to dominate this grand project. He might have had an inkling from his partner, Burnham, who unequivocally supported the beaux arts schemes. In the midst of planning, Burnham declared the Romanesque, by which he also meant the Chicago School, quite dead.

Reports of its demise were exaggerated, of course, as the lessons of the Chicago commercial style lived on after the Columbian Exposition, though under different cir-cumstances. The great event had brought Chicago world-wide renown, and the city had pretentiously taken to calling its fair and itself "Paris on the Prairie" (alterna-tively, "Athens on the Lake"). Resistance to its new clas-sical taste was futile. But some spoke up—including

THE CHICAGO SCHOOL

Louis Sullivan, whose Transportation Building at the fair was placed a good distance from the main concourse. He called the fair "naked exhibitionism of charlatanry . . . enjoined with expert salesmanship of the materials of decay." He said it set architecture back fifty years.

It probably wasn't that bad. Certainly, the world's fair represented some backtracking insofar as organic architecture was concerned. But the beaux arts style was an equally legitimate response to conditions. It "provided an ideal setting for the transition from the tycoon of entrepreneurial capitalism to the 'organization man' of emergent finance capitalism," wrote architectural historian William Jordy. The up-and-coming plutocrats were not attracted to Chicago School buildings by architects who valued democracy, but rather to colonnaded halls with white marble underfoot.

What's more, the Columbian Exposition can also be seen in the fullness of time as an enrichment of Chicago

architecture, not a loss. The great event provided the nation's largest canvas ever for city planning from the ground up. With landscapes designed by Frederick Law Olmsted and buildings sited in naturalistic settings, the fair was precursor to the 1909 Plan of Chicago and the City Beautiful movement that influenced many urban centers in the early twentieth century.

It must also be admitted that the fair produced buildings of undeniable excellence. While many were destroyed shortly thereafter, the one that survives remains an icon of Chicago's South Side. Today's Museum of Science and Industry was originally the Palace of Fine Arts, constructed of plaster like the rest of the fair's structures. It was the only fair building to escape razing and in the 1920s and 1930s was rebuilt in limestone. Rededicated, and now one of the city's most popular museums, it stands as a classical masterpiece. It is important for its stateliness and proportions, and also for bringing to Chicago another short-lived master, Charles Atwood.

MARSHALL FIELD'S STATE
STREET STORE

A towering atrium sheds light on
upper-story offices (opposite) and
the selling floors below (right).

Charles Atwood

Charles Atwood (1848–1895) had a troubled career
in Chicago, but better than any architect of his generation he illustrates an impulse to blend the old and
the new, with results that were in some cases deeply
original. Atwood joined Daniel Burnham's firm after John
Wellborn Root's death, although he almost missed the
opportunity. The story is that Burnham had traveled to
New York to interview Atwood, who for reasons unknown
missed the meeting. Burnham put him out of his mind—
until Atwood followed him to Chicago, showed up at his
door, and virtually pled for the position.

Results were very good indeed. The first work Atwood
turned out for Burnham was the Palace of Fine Arts at
the world's fair, which proved the architect to be a
classicist but no mere copyist. Atwood understood the
beaux arts vocabulary well enough to assemble elements
from Greece and Rome (Ionic columns and caryatids
from the Acropolis, the Pantheon's dome and porticoes)
and then, with great design skill, to unify them into what
was widely considered to be the best building at the
fair. Some architects accused Atwood of plagiarism in
the design, perhaps jealously. But Atwood dismissed
his critics: "The difference between me and some other
architects is that I know what to take and what to leave,

and know how to combine things that come from different sources, while they do not." Charles McKim, of
McKim, Mead and White, corroborated Atwood's self-
assessment. McKim, too, had been eager to find errors
in Atwood's classical proportions, but found none.
"Confound him," McKim told Burnham. "He is right
every time."

With Atwood as chief designer, Daniel H. Burnham &
Company flourished. The firm is often considered a bastion of classicism that had waved goodbye to the Chicago
School, but in fact the firm's designs typically blended
aspects of the rationalist Chicago School with elements
of the historicist beaux arts that had preceded it.

For example, the firm's design for a section of the
Marshall Field's store, the Annex (at Washington and
Wabash Streets), has an austerely decorative classical
exterior. Yet its general plan and light-filled interior
rival the most carefully wrought Chicago School lofts.
The firm also built the Railway Exchange (later the Santa
Fe Building), festooning it with enough classical detail
to satisfy any Francophile. But its massive proportions—
its graceful "big shoulders"—are pure Chicago, and its
spectacular atrium would have been impossible without
Root's example in the Rookery.

RAILWAY EXCHANGE BUILDING

224 SOUTH MICHIGAN AVENUE

1904

DANIEL H. BURNHAM & COMPANY

The Railway Exchange (opposite) was influenced by the "white city" classicism of the 1893 world's fair but harked back to the massive proportions of the older Chicago School. The building owes much of its success to its openness and natural light, which streams in from exterior windows and the broad light court (left).

RELIANCE BUILDING

STATE STREET AT WASHINGTON STREET

1895

DANIEL H. BURNHAM & COMPANY

Following pages: Depending upon the angle and the time of day, the Reliance Building can appear as ornate as a Gothic cathedral or as glassy as a Mies van der Rohe skyscraper. Handcrafts were apparent in details throughout, from the elevator grilles down to the doorknobs. By the 1960s, when photographer Richard Nickel took the black-and-white pictures here, Reliance had fallen into decay, but historians and preservationists recognized its lasting value.

Finally, Burnham's firm was responsible for what is arguably the most advanced Chicago School office building of them all, the Reliance Building, completed in 1895. It features more glass and less solid wall than any previous building—a practical solution to developer (and electric elevator mogul) William Ellery Hale's demand for abundant light in a building too small for a light court. Reliance keeps one foot in history with antique touches and Gothic ornament that proved Atwood's mastery of medieval as well as classical forms. But the glassy building straddles the future as well: Many today label it a harbinger of the International style that would flourish under Mies van der Rohe a half century later.

Discerning the actual authorship of the Reliance Building is complicated, which underscores the diversity of the styles and ideas it contains. Documents show that Burnham's partner John Wellborn Root was working on the project when he died, but he didn't get very far. It was Atwood who opened the Reliance to the light with great expanses of glass and who designed its ornamental bands of terra-cotta with a complexity worthy of medieval artisans.

Brilliantly restored in a project completed in 1999, the Reliance collects accolades that its practical developer and busy architects could never have predicted. But beyond its historical importance and lasting value, this wonderful building makes an important point: "Schools" and "styles" and "movements" provide analytical tools for understanding the history of architecture, but rarely explain the creation of a truly original building.

CHAPTER 3

FRANK LLOYD WRIGHT AND THE PRAIRIE SCHOOL

FRANK LLOYD WRIGHT HOME AND STUDIO

951 CHICAGO AVENUE, OAK PARK, ILL.

1889–1909

FRANK LLOYD WRIGHT

Wright's house, begun early in his career, shows the influence of the Shingle style, a rustic, simplified take on fussy Victorian homes, but his geometric treatment was distinctively bold. His Home and Studio is a virtual catalogue of seminal ideas about light, materials, space, and the spirituality of architecture.

Not everything Frank Lloyd Wright (1867–1959) wrote about in his autobiography actually happened just as described; his relationship with the truth was fragile, to say the least. But the way he recounts his early days working in the office of Louis Sullivan has the ring of authenticity and reflects the high regard in which he held the man he remembered as his *Lieber Meister* (dear master). When they first met in 1887 Sullivan's career was shooting skyward, and Wright was a confident twenty year old. Sullivan was looking for a draftsman to make finish drawings for the Auditorium Building, and Wright wandered in with samples of his work. Wright's drawings evidently did not include the kind of decorative design Sullivan was looking for, because he told the young man to return with other drawings that had more ornamental detail.

If this resembled a rebuff, Wright did not take it that way. "He looked at me kindly and *saw* me. I was sure of that much," Wright wrote years later. Wright stayed up late several nights to complete the exercise and returned to Sullivan with new drawings and hopes of getting the job.

Sullivan looked at his work and said, "So you are trying to turn Gothic ornaments into my style just to please me, are you?"

"You see how easy it is to do," replied Wright, who no sooner had said it than knew he shouldn't have. "I had displeased him," wrote Wright. "Unconsciously I had reduced his ornament to mere 'sentimentality.'"

Despite that rocky start Sullivan hired Wright, and a relationship of genuine mutual respect developed. But the personal melodrama continued, eminently understandable given two intense architects with egos as large as their talents. As soon as Wright took his place in Adler and Sullivan's practice, he found himself continually humiliated by the moody Sullivan, who treated draftsmen as he did most other people, including clients—as lesser mortals. Sullivan's bad humor was not the only hazard in the office. Wright was surrounded by haughty and less talented co-workers, who on one occasion lured him into a ridiculous and bloody boxing match in the drafting room.

FRANK LLOYD WRIGHT HOME AND STUDIO

The stairway illustrates the pronounced geometry Wright brought to architecture. The space is indisputably modern, despite classical adornments such as the plaster frieze.

The situation improved, and the lessons Wright learned in his five years with Sullivan ran deep. But scenes at the outset of their relationship revealed an important dimension of both men: their emotion. Vividly and palpably, emotion comes through in the buildings of Sullivan and Wright—and it is the quality that distinguishes all Chicago architecture at its best. Wright could be ill-tempered, and throughout his life inner drives led him to wildly erratic behavior, excused only by the brilliant expression of his work and his ability to inspire generations of architects who followed him.

THE WRIGHT HOME AND STUDIO

On a wide street in suburban Oak Park, Illinois, the dark Shingle-style house attracts little attention at first glance amidst its larger neighbors. A second glance reveals some intriguing distinctions—including an oversized gable and, often, groups of people milling around outside. This is the Frank Lloyd Wright Home and Studio, where Wright lived and worked for twenty years. Since its 1974 conversion into a museum and study center, the Home and Studio has become a popular attraction; it provides an unparalleled introduction to this most complex of architects.

Wright began building the house in 1889 and the attached studio in 1898. He moved out in 1909, concluding what we now regard as his early career. The house testifies to how fruitful that period was. A guided tour of the Home and Studio shows with great specificity how Wright moved from a kind of Shingle style—the modernized Victorian form that H. H. Richardson, among others, had used in wood-frame designs—to the long, low-slung Prairie style that remains his most distinctive mark on modern architecture. But the tour does more than illustrate Wright's formal development from one school to another. It demonstrates the architect's belief that buildings should be "intimately interrelated with environment and with the habits of life of the people," revealing details not only of the home he built for himself but of the life he lived there.

One such detail is that in 1909 he abandoned his wife and six children here, running off to Europe with a client's wife. Guides at the museum, who refer reverently to "Mr. Wright," do not dwell on this episode. But it is impossible not to wonder about a decision that appears self-centered and reckless in the extreme—and clashes so tantalizingly with the mastery and control evident in his architecture. And it was not an isolated instance. Other dramas and difficult episodes occurred at the Home and Studio, including Wright's traumatic break with Sullivan in 1893. The story is that Sullivan had provided a loan for the land and construction. All went well for a year or two—until Sullivan discovered that Wright was designing houses on a freelance basis after hours. That was forbidden by the terms of his contract, and Sullivan fired him. Wright found more clients of his own, but the touches of Sullivanesque ornament in the house recall Wright's painful estrangement from his *Lieber Meister.* The two did not reconcile until shortly before Sullivan's death, almost twenty years later.

A restoration completed in 1988 re-created with great care the appearance of the Home and Studio at the moment Wright left it. Such specificity required intensive research based on photos and interviews with the surviving Wright children. The year 1909 was a controversial endpoint for the yearslong restoration, as it meant destroying many changes that Wright himself made for his family in later years. Yet the Frank Lloyd Wright Home and Studio Foundation chose that year, justifiably, as the zenith of Wright's Prairie style. By then Wright had already committed twenty years to the house, which now vividly showcases how his design evolved over time into the style most closely associated with him.

Viewed from the street, the Home and Studio appears just this side of traditional. The triangular peak in front

may be more modern than other houses'—plainer and more geometric—but not too unlike other Shingle-style structures that went up in Oak Park and elsewhere in the Chicago area at that time. Inside, too, many features appear almost conventional. A plaster frieze of classical heroes, for example, wraps around the staircase. Apparently Wright's mother liked classical sculpture, and he used it when he could, especially early in his career. But only at first glance does the frieze appear unremarkable; another look shows it is slightly oversize, wider than might be expected for the staircase. That detail of measurement helps enlarge the front hall's scale, demonstrating Wright's subtle command of proportion and space.

Among Frank Lloyd Wright's revolutionary contributions to architecture, the most important and most widely adopted was his dedication to opening up interior space and making it flow from room to room. The subject appeared in his writings again and again. "As a young architect," he wrote, "I began to feel annoyed, held back, imposed upon by this sense of enclosure which you went into and there you were—boxed, crated." A quest to eliminate that claustrophobia by rethinking interiors resonates throughout his work. "The conception of the room *within*," he wrote. "The architecture of the within—that is precisely what we are driving at, all along. And this new quality of thought in architecture, the third dimension, let us say, enters into every move that is made to make it—enters into the use of every material; enters the working of every method we shall use or can use."

An early example of Wright's concept of inner space is the Home and Studio's inglenook, the seating area around the living room fireplace. Finished in light-colored wood, the alcove has a traditional feel we don't associate with modern architecture. An earnest epigram carved over the fireplace, "Truth is Life," seems peculiarly dated. But even though the inglenook evokes old Scandinavia, it more significantly foreshadows Wright's command of interpenetrating space, according to John Thorpe, an Oak Park architect and a founder of the Home and Studio Foundation. The idea was that two distinct spaces could be made to seem like one, or one space like two. Here, a roaring fire can warm the entire living room, making the inglenook part of the larger space, while the small benches built in on either side of

Following pages: Wright always said that dinner provided "a great artistic opportunity." Details such as the floor tile, carved grille, and leaded glass make his dining room a model of the American Arts and Crafts movement. The master bedroom demonstrates Wright's celebration of Americanism with murals of idealized natives on the midwestern plains.

YE'VE LEFT A GLIMMER STILL TO CHEER
THE MAN—THE ARTIFEX
THAT HOLDS IN SPITE O' KNOCKS AND SCALE
O' FRICTION WASTE AN' SLIP,
AN' BY THAT LIGHT—NOW MARK MY WORD—
WE'LL BUILD THE PERFECT SHIP.

In extremely limited space, Wright created a remarkable, comfortable workroom (opposite). Here his team of architects turned out designs that blended natural light, uncommon space, and a "conception of the room within." Wright designed the reception hall of his studio (right) as a calming indoor-outdoor space, meant to soothe the most excitable client.

the hearth carve out an intimate setting separate from the living room.

Such details are subtle and today may hardly attract notice, as interpenetrating spaces and open floor plans became common in residences of the 1900s. But this home, where the entry hall leads to the living room, which leads to the study, which leads to the dining room, does engender a unique impression of openness and ample space that belies the small size of the individual rooms. "It is like the walls are Japanese screens that have been slid back on tracks," noted Thorpe. The analogy to a traditional Japanese house might be useful—although any oriental influence is subtle, and citing direct antecedents for Wright is risky. Sometimes Wright would exaggerate his debt to things Japanese, even appearing in oriental garb so outlandishly inappropriate that he embarrassed his friends; other times he resentfully would deny any such influence.

Perhaps more than any other Wright-designed house, the Home and Studio became a laboratory for his ideas about architecture, specifically for elements he described as "organic." Like Sullivan before him, Wright sought the organic in his materials, in his colors and forms, and most emphatically in his rejection of what he saw as hidebound styles. In organic architecture, "a bank will not look like a Greek temple," he said at a lecture in England in 1939. "A university will not look like a cathedral, nor a fire engine house resemble a French chateau." Defining what each of those structures might look like instead would be hard, in the absence of an established American tradition—and so much the better for the iconoclast. Wright repudiated "preconceived form fixing upon us either past, present or future," exalting instead "the simple laws of common sense—of super sense, if you prefer."

The experience of being in a space designed by Wright conveys the organic more clearly than his words do. One of his most concise explications, and one of the most

FRANK LLOYD WRIGHT HOME AND STUDIO

The playroom is a masterpiece of proportion, designed for children and made to appear larger than it is. The large windows dramatize what lies beyond the room's walls.

marvelous spaces in all of his work, is the children's playroom upstairs in the Home and Studio. The space is a great barrel vault, where Wright again manipulated scale. The room appears larger and higher than it actually is because many features—window seats, bookcases—are scaled to a child's size, as well as to a child's imagination. Intricately designed leaded-glass windows, installed low to provide a child's-eye view, expose and frame the treetops outside, creating a sense of being in the sky. Wright also used scale and perspective to make the balcony at the end of the room seem higher and deeper than it could practically be. Tall and forbidding, dissolving into darkness, the balcony added an element of mystery to the room, the architect's son David Wright remembered.

Elsewhere in the building, Wright honed his effort to "destroy the box" and dissolve the divisions between the built environment and the natural one—among his most significant contributions. His studio's entrance hall feels small but not confined, with light streaming in through green and gold stained glass reminiscent of sun glinting through the leaves of a lush forest. Small windows at eye-level, leafy ornament on the walls, and rich natural finishes in the woodwork reinforce the effect of a composed natural environment, which Wright intended to calm clients and other visitors to the office. "The outside may come inside, and the inside may and does go outside," he wrote. Elsewhere he expanded upon the idea: "Landscape and building become one, more harmonious. So the life of the individual was broadened and enriched by the new concept of architecture, by light and freedom of space."

Elmslie, a student of Sullivan
and a contemporary of Wright,
designed this clock for Sullivan's
Henry B. Babson House in
Riverside, Illinois. Made of fine
mahogany and brass inlay, the
clock has the smooth surfaces
and straight lines that are
associated with the Prairie style
but also prefigure the streamlining
that would become fashionable
in the 1920s.

THE PRAIRIE SCHOOL

Although Frank Lloyd Wright is the best known and most
influential proponent of the Prairie style, the movement
did not spring from him alone. He was but one of a
group of young, passionate, likeminded architects who
lived in or near Chicago and came together at the turn
of the nineteenth century. They shared ideas and a common goal: to develop a distinctive American architectural style. They also had common heroes, among them
Louis Sullivan and Sullivan's own beloved Walt Whitman.
Whitman believed that a primal creative force resided
in America, possibly centered in the Western prairie.
Sullivan exhorted younger architects to be "not a merchant, broker, manufacturer, businessman, or anything
of that sort, but *a poet who uses not words but building
materials as a medium of expression.*"

Most Prairie School architects built primarily houses.
They were interested in simple, horizontal lines and if
pressed admitted that the prairie itself had inspired their
long, low architecture. All sought to design interiors
of flowing space flooded with natural light; many aimed
to create organically integrated environments, designing
furnishings—decorative accessories, furniture and cabi-
netry, rugs and other textiles, art glass windows and
lighting—that reinforced the architecture's lines. Beyond
that, each member of the Prairie School defined the
style in his own way—so much so that the most precise
label for each architect's style is his own name, whether
Frank Lloyd Wright, George Washington Maher, William
Purcell, George Grant Elmslie, or Walter Burley Griffin.

The genesis of the Prairie School (the term was not in
common usage until 1964, when most of its original
members were dead) traces back to 1893, when many
of those young architects began moving into studios in
Steinway Hall, a new Loop office building on Van Buren
Street. Steinway tenants came and went, often sharing
space, sometimes sharing commissions, and frequently
reminding each other that they were unbound by tired
architectural forms or doctrine. Wright was among this
group, whom he later nostalgically called "the Eighteen,"
though the number was hardly constant. Other members
included Richard Schmidt, Myron Hunt, Dwight Perkins,
and Howard Van Doren Shaw, all of them at that point
more ambitious than successful, which left them with
plenty of spare time to mount exhibitions of their work.
Under the auspices of the Chicago Architectural Club
they also held lectures on a broad range of subjects. A

PLEASANT HOME

HOME AVENUE AND PLEASANT
STREET, OAK PARK, ILL.

1898

GEORGE W. MAHER

Pleasant Home (left and opposite)
is one of Maher's best-known
examples of his "motif-rhythm"
theory, his idea for an indigenous
American style. His ornamental
designs for Pleasant Home involve
thistles and honeysuckle, native
to the Midwest, and a lion meant
to symbolize owner-client John
Farson, a powerful Chicago banker.

frequent speaker and a friend of the Eighteen was
Joseph Twymann, an Englishman who managed a furniture showroom in Chicago. While Twymann's Gothic-
style furniture might not have appealed to these modern
young men, his message did: He exalted the artist
as craftsman, a concept that came directly from the
English Arts and Crafts movement and its prophet,
William Morris. The movement's adherents not only
placed the highest value on craftsmanship, but regarded
it as the antidote to spirit-deadening industrialization.
Twymann emphasized that an architect was first and
foremost an artisan and that he should be faithful to the
materials at hand. Plaster should not be made to look
like marble, nor glass to look like rare jewels. Twymann
declared, and the Prairie School architects came to
believe, that the moral soundness of society depended
upon the honesty and integrity of the built environment.

Many of the Eighteen also became founding members of
the Chicago Arts and Crafts Society, organized in 1897
and the second such club in the United States, the first
being in Boston. It convened at Hull-House, the social
settlement house founded by social worker Jane Addams.

The club's members included social workers as well as
artists, reflecting Addams's conviction that handcrafts
restored the self-worth that the machine age had torn
away. The social reformers—some of whom believed that
home design could directly influence morality—welcomed architects, too. The challenge of translating such
idealism into new schemes and concepts in architecture,
particularly residential architecture, made the so-called
Progressive Era a stimulating time for the incipient
Prairie School.

A sign of the intellectual ferment was Frank Lloyd
Wright's address to the Chicago Arts and Crafts Society
in March 1901. His speech, entitled "The Art and Craft
of the Machine," marked a turning point in the discussion of handcraftsmanship's virtues; it changed the
terms of the Arts and Crafts argument only slightly, but
in time altered the character of residential architecture
significantly. In the speech Wright praised William
Morris for preaching simplicity in crafts and construction.
Morris's principles were indispensable to architects,
Wright said, and he had shown the way in the fight
against "the innate vulgarity of theocratic impulse in

art as opposed to democratic." Yet Morris was wrong to summarily dismiss machines, Wright insisted. Machines represented "the modern Sphinx—whose riddle the artist must solve." To illustrate he used one of the most common materials used to build American homes— wood. "The machine teaches us that certain simple forms and handling are suitable to bring out the beauty of wood," he said. Wright thus began to promulgate his own love of plain wood, decorated primarily by its natural grain—best revealed by mechanical tools that cut and smooth—rather than by fussy carvings.

All the Prairie School architects championed such truthful use of materials. "Art and Crafts stands for the idiomatic use of materials—leaded glass in a leaded glass way, wooden structures in the way called for by wood," Milwaukee architect Elmer Grey declared in the *Architectural Record* in 1907. But the architects interpreted their common conviction with individual approaches. Some found inspiration in the medieval past. Others kept their eye on the beginnings of European modernism, particularly the Secession (the Austrian expression of the sinuous French Art Nouveau), which sought beauty in linear grace. (A number of the Eighteen, including Wright, visited the 1904 Saint Louis World's Fair to see the German pavilion and architect Joseph Olbrich's Secession interior.)

And as architecture took its early, tentative steps toward modernism, its practitioners followed Wright's lead, seeking to reconcile their art's deeply human practice with powerful new machines. Grey, who later became a partner of Myron Hunt, was concerned that modern construction's large size and the complexity of mechanical systems such as elevators and electric lights could militate against craftsmanship, but he shared Wright's recognition that machines could benefit architecture. Grey proposed to resolve the contradiction with greater communication between architects and tradespeople. He called for the establishment of permanent halls where the trades could assemble, where leaded-glass makers, metalworkers, tile painters, and brick manufacturers could show and discuss their wares with the architects who used them. Grey's idea was not realized at the time, but no one disagreed that craftsmanship should be evident throughout the modern house, no matter how advanced its mechanical systems.

GEORGE WASHINGTON MAHER

Most Prairie architects were levelheaded thinkers who viewed down-to-earth practicality as the underpinning of good architecture. Yet a few extended their thoughts into fuzzier realms. A case in point was George Washington Maher (1864–1926), one of Chicago's most successful residential architects at the turn of the century. Maher

MADLENER HOUSE

STATE STREET AND BURTON PLACE

1902

RICHARD E. SCHMIDT

Madlener had the presence
of a Renaissance palazzo, but
its simple lines and precise
proportions also reflect the
commercial buildings of the
Chicago School, which held
important lessons for Prairie
architects like Schmidt and his
associate Hugh Garden.

assumed the role of architectural prophet in this period,
writing voluminously that modern design would evolve
only when architects set old forms aside and developed
deeply personal styles. He urged architects to penetrate
their clients' minds, since architecture springs from
deep inside the psyche. The superrational ancient Greek
expressed a sense of order in classical architecture,
he wrote in *Architectural Record*. The Goth, by contrast,
was "cradled in mysticism [and] gave expression to his
aspiration in the perpendicular line." Maher also argued
that modern homes, to achieve a more personal expression, should be "influenced by local color and atmo-
sphere in surrounding flora and nature. With their vital
inspiration at hand, the design naturally crystallizes
and motifs appear which being consistently utilized will
make each object, construction, furnishing or decoration
related."

Maher's "motif-rhythm theory," as he called it in an
attempt to codify his ideas, updated the timeless notion
that patterns and rhythm underlie good architecture.

Maher drew his ornamental motifs from nearby nature;
they included the thistle, a plant native to the prairie,
and the honeysuckle, another native, which he said represented friendship. He believed the repetition of such
motifs throughout a house design would coalesce into
an architecture that "completely harmonizes all portions
of the work until in the end it becomes a unit in composition"—in other words, a work of original art.

Maher presented his motif-rhythm theory as design
doctrine, though in retrospect it was really an idea about
decoration. In one of his more successful houses,
Pleasant Home (so named because of its location at the
intersection of Pleasant Avenue and Home Street in Oak
Park), Maher found inspiration in the leonine personality
of his client, investment banker John Farson. Maher
repeated several motifs, most prominently the lion's
head, throughout the large Prairie-style house. The lion
appeared in countless ways—as exterior ornament, on
mantels, in carved furniture—wherever conventional,
perhaps classicized, ornament might otherwise have

appeared. Pleasant Home was intended to be an expression of Farson's individuality, though critics wondered if the result was not more expressive of Maher's own needs and temperament.

In 1904, five years after Pleasant Home's completion, a writer in *Architectural Record* praised Maher's philosophy while conceding that he "is struggling not very successfully at formal expression." History tends to agree. Little is written today about Maher without acknowledgment of his shortcomings as a designer or mention of some of his least successful efforts. Speculation is that his grand notions led to his frustrations as a designer, which may in turn have led to his suicide in 1926. Nevertheless, Maher's determination to find inventive solutions, his good fortune in securing large commissions, and his ability to publish his work made him influential as an early Prairie architect.

MADLENER HOUSE

Despite the high-flown rhetoric surrounding the Prairie School, early Prairie houses were often most successful when their objectives were understated. A distinctive example is Madlener House, which is on the North Side and is now home of the Graham Foundation for the Advanced Studies in the Fine Arts. Designed by Richard Schmidt (1865–1958) and his associate Hugh Garden (1873–1961) for a wealthy brewing family, the house is built of brick, with large imposing windows looking out

to the street; its exterior proportions resemble those of an Italian Renaissance palazzo. Yet Madlener House was strikingly modern when it was built in 1902, owing to a variety of influences. Clearly its architects were mindful of the Chicago School and the potential for elegance in stark simplicity. They also appear to have been influenced by the simple geometry and classical sense of proportion of Secessionist architecture, photos of which the German-born Schmidt undoubtedly came across in German magazines.

Inside Madlener House, Schmidt and Garden went to the edge of being modern, but no further. Large, interpenetrating spaces show the Wrightian influence. The rich finishes—broad panels of highly polished French walnut, moldings with intricate geometric detail—are likewise up-to-date. What is lacking, however, is an organic relationship among all the parts. One critic who found the exterior "stately without being grandiose" objected when he got inside. Among his complaints was that the windows, which seemed well proportioned from the street, did not bring maximum light inside. The interior plan also exhibits a symmetry, perhaps at the expense of natural light, that most Prairie architects were careful to avoid.

The building makes clear that Schmidt and Garden were in command of elements of the modern without being truly modern themselves. They were eclectic designers,

a label implying they were not driven by conviction to advance the cause of a particular style. A later remark by Hugh Garden bears this out. He said that experience had taught him to match each type of structure with its ideal style: Tudor for country estates, Renaissance for city homes, Chicago School for commercial structures. That must have sounded like blasphemy to any true proponent of the Prairie style, whose touchstone was originality. Perhaps Garden was simply more candid than other architects. Or he and Schmidt had a rare gift for making formulas appear original. At any rate, Madlener House remains a handsome building in a fine neighborhood. Whether or not it perfectly incarnated the architectural dictates of its day, it has aged well.

ROBIE HOUSE: THE CLASSIC PRAIRIE STYLE

What we think of today as the quintessential Prairie style is Frank Lloyd Wright's. He was the author of the horizontal lines, the wide eaves, and the flowing interiors that have been adapted in a thousand ways in the modern American house. Others followed and many imitated Wright, but his Prairie houses stand alone as classics, partly because their designs are so quiet and reposed, partly because they have become icons as unmistakable as a Greek temple or Florentine palazzo.

Wright's Prairie period came to an end in 1909, when he ran off to Europe with his mistress. He later returned to the United States to work in a number of different styles only vaguely related to the Prairie. These included his Maya-influenced California houses, built mostly in the 1930s, and the almost primeval Taliesin West, Wright's home and studio in Scottsdale, Arizona, which he began in 1937. In the post–World War II era Wright designed his Usonian houses with simple Prairie features and an eye toward mass production. But of all the buildings Wright created over the long sweep of his career, his early Prairie houses most completely represent the architect's mind at work. And none of those buildings does this quite so well as Robie House, built in Chicago's Hyde Park in 1909.

MADLENER HOUSE

Love of rich material—a Prairie School keynote—is evident in the French walnut used throughout (below). The interior's largely rectilinear forms contrast with a touch of sinuous Art Nouveau above the mantel (below right).

ROBIE HOUSE

WOODLAWN AVENUE AND 58TH STREET
1909

FRANK LLOYD WRIGHT

Robie House is Wright's classic
Prairie-style home. Wide eaves,
long brick walls, leaded glass, and
a constant play of shadow and light
are among its influential features.
Wright's design meant to satisfy the
owner's demand for a clear view of
the outdoors that did not compro-
mise the privacy and warmth inside.

At Robie House, as in most masterpieces of organic
architecture, success owed greatly to the active involvement of the client. Frederick Robie was no tycoon, but
a mechanically minded bicycle-factory owner. Bicycles
were an advanced and modern technology at the time,
and Robie was himself an innovative thinker. When he
was planning his house, he explained to a builder that
he didn't want a cluttered Victorian home; he found
such places old-fashioned and effeminate. He wanted
something up-to-date and designed as efficiently as,
well, a finely tuned bicycle. The builder sighed and told
him that he probably wanted to build "one of those
damn . . . Wright houses."

With Wright Robie got what he wanted. Instead of knick-
knacks and clutter, his home was filled with unique
touches and the latest conveniences, many of them
designed specially for this home. Features uncommon

at the time included a garage connected to the house,
efficient electric lighting (with custom-designed fixtures
integrated with the architecture), burglar and fire alarms,
and even a built-in vacuum system with pipes threaded
throughout the house. Such devices may surprise people
who have heard stories of Wright's alleged indifference
to mechanical function and his buildings' leaky roofs.
(He once told a client who complained of a dinner ruined
by a leaky roof to relax and move the table.) But Wright
designed Robie House with a precision that suited
Robie's modern lifestsyle—and his plans for it were so
painstakingly accurate that Robie's contractor told the
owner that he "might as well have been making a piece
of machinery."

More important than things mechanical in Robie House
were things ineffable: light and space. Here again the
collaboration between client and architect came into

101

ROBIE HOUSE

The complex geometry of the exterior provided seamlessly open and light-filled spaces inside. Wright exercised maximum control over his interiors, far beyond the architectural design: At Robie and many of his other Prairie houses, he designed each piece of furniture as well as other decorative elements, found furniture and art-glass makers to produce them to his specifications, then placed each item for maximum effect.

FRANK LLOYD WRIGHT AND THE PRAIRIE SCHOOL

COONLEY HOUSE

RIVERSIDE, ILL.

1908

FRANK LLOYD WRIGHT

Coonley was one of the few homes
Wright built at this stage of his
career that were unrestricted by
budgetary constraints. It has been
called a "palazzo among Prairie
houses," but its impressiveness
lies in its expansive horizontality—
not in an imposing height—and
its flowing spaces.

play. "Light has always been somewhat of a specialty of
my disposition," Robie explained to Wright. His other
requirements included a broad view of the outdoors, but
utter privacy from passersby. That seemingly impossible
contradiction meshed perfectly with Wright's objective,
in Robie House and throughout his career, of finding
new ways to connect interior and exterior space.

Needless to say, the result was unconventional. The
exterior is long and low, with oversized eaves cantilevered an alarming distance from the rest of the house.
The eaves were made possible by steel beams developed
for shipbuilding, a practical if unusual technology, and
apt for a house neighbors called "the battleship." Other
practical conditions—including a distaste for damp
basements and Robie's request for open, yet private
views—inspired the architect to raise the main floor over
an above-grade ground floor. The height, the eaves, a
deep balcony, and profuse art glass combined to create
a house that is as harmonious as it was unprecedented.

The interior of Robie House even more subtly achieved
the objectives of architect and client. Wright tran-
scended the limitations of conventional interiors by
eliminating the walls that would have divided the main
floor into a series of individual rooms. The large, open
interior space, which allows free movement throughout,
is defined by a long stretch of south-facing windows
that fill the house with light. Other features—the hearth,

for example, and rugs—delineate specific areas for dining, for receiving guests, and for sitting.

Words can scarcely convey Robie House's simultaneous
evocation of spaciousness and intimacy, but Sigfried
Giedion in *Space, Time and Architecture* does as well
as anyone. In Frank Lloyd Wright's "constant endeavor
to find interrelationships between various separate elements," Giedion wrote, Robie House was a triumph that
"brought life, movement and freedom to the whole rigid
and benumbed body of modern architecture."

COONLEY HOUSE: A "COUNTENANCE OF PRINCIPLE"

Wright believed that the Prairie house, designed for
practicality and built of common and locally available
materials, should be economical. However, his innovative projects frequently ran over budget—infuriating
many clients. One of his Prairie houses that was unrestricted by cost was Coonley House, built in 1908
in suburban Riverside, Illinois, for Avery and Queene
Coonley. The Coonleys were as progressive as they were
wealthy, types we now consider activists. They were
involved in the Chicago settlement house movement.
They were also committed Christian Scientists, which
was a new and liberal-minded approach to religion at
the time. They hired Wright with full knowledge that he
was the most advanced architect available.

COMSTOCK HOUSE II

1613 ASHLAND AVENUE,
EVANSTON, ILL.

1912

WALTER BURLEY GRIFFIN

The paired Comstock Houses (only Comstock II is shown, below left) exhibit the architect's interest in the ties between indoor and outdoor space, as did the work of his mentor, Frank Lloyd Wright. At Comstock Griffin also applied his ideas about interpenetrating space to the yard and garden the neighboring houses share.

Before the couple began contemplating a Frank Lloyd Wright design, Mr. Coonley had said he wanted "something colonial." It would go well in Riverside, a town of curving wooded streets laid out in 1868–70 by the firm of Frederick Law Olmsted and Calvert Vaux. But the Coonleys realized something was lacking in the colonial style, and Mrs. Coonley suggested that they hire Wright. It was a good match. In their meetings Mrs. Coonley expressed her belief that the house should be a "countenance of principle," a phrase inspired by her study of Christian Science. "Principle" is one of the seven synonyms for God used by Mary Baker Eddy, the church's founder. It implies the oneness of all being and the aspiration that life be conducted in a setting of harmony and grace, free of error.

Such thinking fit snugly into Wright's ideas about architecture. The outcome was a masterpiece, dazzlingly harmonious and vividly metaphoric. The interior plan of Coonley House is largely open, with spaces articulated from above by an unpredictable geometry of wood beams, skylights, and intricately carved grilles in the ceiling. Other features—the garden, for example, and the playhouse glinting with some of Wright's most original art glass—confirm that a classic Prairie house's richness is in its details.

But Coonley House also has an unmistakable grandeur of dimension—not the lofty heights associated with a palace or cathedral, but a striking horizontality, extravagant in its expansiveness and the free movement it invites. Wright expressed the philosophy behind such a design in a particularly flowery passage in his autobiography: "A free country and democratic in the sense that our fore-fathers intended ours to be free, means *individual* freedom for each man on his own ground. . . . Why not, now that the means comes to hand, let his line of action be *horizontally* extended: and give him the flat plane expanded parallel to the earth, gripping all social structure to the ground!" The architect's own explanation might amount to gibberish had he not left behind the wonderful spaces that prove his point far better than his words ever could.

WALTER BURLEY GRIFFIN

The Prairie School had many architects whose brilliant accomplishments were ultimately eclipsed by Frank Lloyd Wright's towering artistic shadow. For others, a broad interest in applied arts and design beyond architecture made them hard to categorize, further blurring recognition of their contributions. Walter Burley Griffin (1876–1937), too often forgotten in the annals of Chicago architecture, suffers on both counts. He was a Renaissance man whose career on three continents embraced architecture, urban planning, landscaping,

and even inventing building materials. While his interest in related arts ought not weaken his standing as
an architect, the fact that he worked for many years in
Wright's studio long relegated him to corollary status.
Yet Griffin made a deep mark on Chicago with dozens
of early modern suburban houses, and his career was
among the Prairie School's most important.

As a teenager, Griffin watched the construction of the
1893 World's Columbian Exposition; the audacity of
the Cour d'Honneur and the vast, winding greenbelts
surrounding it dazzled him. Blending architecture and
landscape became Griffin's particular interest, and in
architecture school at the University of Illinois he took
a number of horticulture courses as electives. He was
later exposed to the ideas of Jens Jensen, the landscape
architect whose own Prairie style celebrated native
landscapes and called for the indigenous flora of the
Midwest. Jensen was designing public parks and private
landscapes—he worked with Wright on Coonley House—
with an approach to nature that had obvious appeal for
architects with an "organic" turn of mind.

As a result of those influences, when Griffin began his
own practice in 1907 he conceived exterior space much
as other Prairie School architects designed interiors.
Among his early, small-scale works were the Comstock
Houses, a pair of homes that he planned in Evanston,
Illinois. The detached single-family structures share
a garden and a garage structure between them, allowing
Griffin to design outdoor space that interpenetrates
much as the flowing interiors of typical Prairie homes
do. Griffin went on to incorporate his idea of shared
space in planning whole suburban neighborhoods. While
he often did battle with rigid notions of private property,
his efforts won critical acclaim. "Always there is that
consideration in his town planning problems of the convenience and happiness of all its citizens," *Western
Architect* magazine wrote in an article about Griffin.
Living in one of his houses "becomes not a thing of joy
to him alone but an integral part of a symmetrical plan
which adds to the beauty and value of his neighbors'
belongings."

One can wonder what might have been Griffin's fate—
and Chicago's—had he remained in the Midwest. But in

CHURCH OF ALL SOULS

1407 CHICAGO AVENUE, EVANSTON, ILL.

1903 (DEMOLISHED 1960)

MARION MAHONY GRIFFIN

Marion Mahony was one of Wright's most talented employees; she married another Wright protégé, Walter Burley Griffin. Her clients for the Church of All Souls were Unitarians who wanted something fashionably Gothic. The resulting design gracefully mediates between the perpendicular and the horizontal. The random-cut limestone exterior, along with ivy, made the church appear to be part of the natural landscape, a high virtue in the Prairie canon.

1912 he entered and won an international competition to plan and design Australia's new capital city, Canberra. Griffin's scheme included a scenic river, swelling lakes, and vistas of nearby mountains. It combined formal boulevards and naturalistic features, recalling the 1893 fair as well as the Prairie School's predilection for native landscape. Griffin moved to Australia to oversee Canberra's development, and his Chicago career came to a close.

Griffin and his wife, Marion Mahony, a former Wright protégée, spent the next twenty-one years working in Australia, where he devised a new building system. His concrete "knitblocks" could be assembled into a variety of practical forms and were well suited to unwooded countries like Australia, where a shortage of construction lumber was a constant problem. Interestingly, Frank Lloyd Wright's 1930s California houses used a textured masonry building system that certainly borrowed from Griffin's innovation.

THE CLOSE OF THE PRAIRIE SCHOOL

Among the other members of the Prairie School, none personified its idealism more than George Grant Elmslie (1871–1952). A draftsman and designer in the office of Louis Sullivan from 1889 to 1909, Elmslie became a skilled specialist in Sullivanesque ornament. He was

not only talented with the pencil, but also unstintingly loyal; he was the last employee to remain with Sullivan as his practice dwindled away. Even after Sullivan's death, Elmslie continued to exalt the humanism and poetry of the master's work.

In 1910 Elmslie opened his own office with another progressive Chicago architect, William Purcell (1880–1965), and for about ten years they enjoyed a busy practice. They designed commercial structures, the most enchanting of which was the Edison Shop on Wabash Avenue, completed in 1912 and later demolished. It was a four-story storefront with balconies and an almost residential air. If city streets everywhere were lined with buildings as open and friendly as photos suggest this one was, urban life would be a more gentle proposition indeed.

Purcell went into semiretirement in 1920 because of ill health, and Elmslie, like many architects, later ended his career embittered. World War I had drained idealism from society, and fewer clients were interested in his frankly progressive houses. Ultimately, Elmslie was reduced to designing banks and commercial buildings on behalf of other, often lesser, architects who got the credit for them.

But he and Purcell were not entirely forgotten. By the 1930s European modernism was on the rise in America, and some scholars wrote that Purcell and Elmslie represented a historical link between the Prairie School and the International style of Mies van der Rohe. They credited Purcell and Elmslie with having simplified the Wrightian style and further reduced it to its elemental geometry. The connection displeased Elmslie, however, who protested sharply that the Europeans designed according to "formula" and not "inspiration." In fact, the theory that the Prairie School led logically to the International style is arguable, even probable.

Recent decades have also brought renewed recognition to Elmslie, Purcell, and other lesser known Prairie architects, in part due to the attention Wright continues to draw to the Prairie School. Perhaps most surprising is the abundant, if belated, praise for a form that Elmslie and Purcell pioneered. Among their other strengths they became master practitioners of the "bungalow," a small,

brick urban home with a single story at street level and a half-story in a gable or dormer above. In true Prairie tradition, bungalows (named for hutlike dwellings British subjects used in India) combined an appreciation of handcrafts (seen in the woodwork and tiling) with affordable economy. Purcell and Elmslie helped make the bungalow style ubiquitous in their own day. The bungalow so successfully met the needs of families of the period that some eighty thousand of them were built in Chicago neighborhoods between 1910 and 1940.

More recently the bungalow has been canonized as a classic, at least in Chicago. Architectural historians are studying them and presenting lectures on the subject. Enthusiasts are buying them up, and prices for the most refined examples are skyrocketing. And whole neighborhoods that had been dismissed as prosaically middle class are being restored with the care once reserved for more upscale examples of Chicago's indigenous Prairie School.

FRANK LLOYD WRIGHT AND THE PRAIRIE SCHOOL

CHAPTER 4

FROM ARTS AND CRAFTS TO ART DECO

CHICAGO BOARD OF TRADE

141 WEST JACKSON BOULEVARD

1930

HOLABIRD AND ROOT

Powerful vertical lines character-ized big-city architecture in the 1920s and 1930s. The Board of Trade typifies what American architects had been seeking for decades: an emphatically American style that was original, powerful, and appropriate for commerce.

The architects who dedicated themselves to modern and "democratic" ideas in design were not always favored by a class of client that was growing in Chicago in the early years of the twentieth century. Wealthy business tycoons and their heirs, with large fortunes and sometimes pretensions to match, were often blind to the aesthetics and deaf to the philosophical issues with which organic architecture concerned itself. They were unfazed by the buildings Sullivan railed against as mere copies from other times and places. They were scarcely aware that the Prairie style, conceived in the Midwest, was being praised around the world for artistic importance. Instead, those with the greatest means usually ordered the most traditional homes, most often modeled after European estates from centuries past.

A number of historically oriented architects, including Howard Van Doren Shaw and David Adler, emerged to serve that clientele. The gulf separating them from Frank Lloyd Wright and his Prairie School colleagues might appear vast and unbridgeable: Wright and his circle sought a quintessentially American style; Shaw and Adler were highly influenced by old European antecedents.

But even the architects whose work seemed to look backward were inevitably of their own time. The best of the historicists often incorporated aspects of the new

with the old, subtly updating antique styles and demon-strating that some elements of design are timeless. Shaw and Wright were in fact friends early in their careers and occasionally shared office space in Steinway Hall, where the Prairie School was born. Shaw later pursued success in a direction of his own. He became an eclectic with a talent for traditional mansions, but never lost his adherence to organic ideals.

Shaw's break from the Prairie School—and the thriving practice that resulted—drew the scorn of committed modernists like Wright. In a 1918 speech entitled "Chicago Culture" Wright dismissed Shaw's classical and neo-Gothic buildings as stage sets. Describing one Shaw house he quipped, "I utterly failed to imagine entering it other than in a costume. . . . I can see it as great fun (very expensive fun), but how can it be seen as culture when the essence of all true culture is a *development* of self-expression?" Wright's own organic architecture reflected social purpose and progress, he declared, and had little use for historical referents.

Wright was famously prickly, and his speech also hints of his frustration and his envy of Shaw's grand success. Some years earlier Wright lost an important commission to one of Shaw's fellow historicists. He had designed a home for Harold and Edith McCormick, both heirs to

industrialist fortunes, on property overlooking Lake Michigan in the affluent and spacious suburb of Lake Forest, Illinois. It would have been one of his most dramatic residences ever but was never built. New York architect Charles A. Platt got the commission to design an Italianate villa instead.

But if Wright was indignant that Chicago would not bend to his architectural philosophy, he was in the wrong town. Although Chicagoland was the birthplace of several architectural styles, the true spirit of its architecture was found not in an individual school or movement but in diversity. By the early part of the twentieth century, classicism, Gothicism, historicism, and modernism all flourished, often in the same design, even as they appeared to be at philosophical odds. While any history of Chicago architecture is punctuated by the individuals who became household names, the main text concerns a community of architects who were willing to experiment, combine the old with the new, and so thoroughly mix ideas that the evolution of style was anything but orderly.

HOWARD VAN DOREN SHAW

Wright's acerbic view of Shaw's work was understandable—their approaches were so divergent—but history regards Howard Van Doren Shaw (1869–1926) more

kindly. To be sure, Shaw's houses were traditional in appearance, as his clients preferred, but they were also driven by values that were then modern, if not avant-garde. While his designs evoked the medieval past—Shaw certainly read and applied Ruskin's principles to his work—they also reflected the more contemporary Arts and Crafts movement. Like the Prairie School architects, Shaw loved natural wood finishes, humble brick, and art glass that filled rooms with light. And his interest in open interiors and flowing space includes Shaw in the story of twentieth-century modernism.

A fellow Steinway Hall architect described Shaw as "the most rebellious of the conservatives, and the most conservative of the rebels." The idea of rebellion conveys neither Howard Shaw's gentle nature nor his obvious ability to charm wealthy clients. Yet from the beginning of his career he joined other Chicagoans in pushing residential design toward modern ideas. Like the members of the Prairie School, he believed that a house must respond to the particular conditions of its site, its occupants, and its times. Design was creative, not formulaic, and the outcome each time was unique. "Personality is the thing," wrote one of Shaw's many admirers in *Western Architect* magazine on the occasion of the architect's death. While some might detect in Shaw's work

R. R. DONNELLEY &
COMPANY BUILDING

22ND STREET AND SOUTH CALUMET
AVENUE

1912–29

**HOWARD VAN DOREN SHAW AND
CHARLES Z. KLAUDER**

Donnelley printed and shipped
some of the nation's leading
magazines during most of the
twentieth century. Shaw connected the modern firm to the
industry's artisanal roots by
ornamenting the exterior with
colorful terra-cotta printers'
marks. He used Gothic touches
throughout, and the building
retained its medieval character
through continual modifications.
In the late 1920s Klauder, an
East Coast Gothicist, completed
the company's Memorial Library
(opposite right).

only copied historical styles, many colleagues saw features that were "idealistic" and architecturally advanced.

Still, Shaw did not join the quest for a new, wholly
American style. While his Prairie counterparts were bent
on harnessing the machine, Wright's "modern sphinx,"
Shaw focused on connecting the present to the idealized
past. His designs often began with steeply pitched roofs,
and he even added shutters and flower boxes to his windows. That his emphasis on handcrafted detail, natural
light, and flowing interior space aligned him with the
moderns would have surprised the conservative families
who hired him to create settings they imagined fit for
European gentry.

Shaw himself came from a privileged background—his
father was a wealthy dry goods merchant, and both
parents came from well-educated families on the East
Coast. After private high school on Chicago's South Side,
Shaw attended Yale, graduating in 1890, then enrolled
at Massachusetts Institute of Technology for architectural training. He worked, the summer before starting
at M.I.T., at the office of William Le Baron Jenney, but
Jenney's utilitarian commercial style seems to have
had little impact on him. Subsequent travels in England,
France, and Italy strengthened Shaw's resolve to be an
architect and revealed to him the creative possibilities
inherent in traditional styles. "I wish I might remember
everything and have the right idea ready for use, that's
the only way a man may become a great architect," he
wrote to his wife during a trip abroad.

When, in 1894, Shaw opened his practice in the attic
of his parents' Chicago home, his family connections
brought him an instant supply of well-to-do clients.
Many of them asked for houses in the Georgian style,
which then dominated residential architecture, and that
is what Shaw provided. In his first three years of practice,
he designed six houses in Hyde Park, near the University
of Chicago. Although the designs were essentially classical, Shaw put his stamp on each by simplifying it and
stripping it of as much extraneous ornamentation as he
dared. He quickly developed a reputation as an architect
with an approach distinctly his own.

"He designs individual houses for particular clients, and
borrows from anyone or any number of sources as much
or as little as he pleases," wrote the *Architectural
Record* in 1913. "But wide as is the range of his sources

it has significant limits. He rarely gets too far away from
the English renaissance . . . and he will have no dealing
with frog-eating Frenchmen. Few contemporary
American architects are so entirely free from French
influence as he is."

Shaw's freedom of design—especially from French-style
formality and mansard roofs—earned him a lifetime
of praise and prosperity. His flexibility was admired by
the critics and—more important—by clients who were
convinced they would get a suitable "Italian villa,"
or a small "Gothic castle," or whatever they wanted by
hiring Shaw. He knew well how to charm fellow members
of the upper class, sending bouquets to clients on move-
in day and paying courtesy calls once they had settled
in. Where his counterpart Wright was irascible, Shaw
was polished; while Wright pushed the limits of architecture, Shaw took originality only so far as circumstances
allowed. As a result he was uncommonly successful;
he was never without important commissions and he was
enormously prolific, designing more than two hundred
buildings over the thirty-two-year span of his career.

Ragdale's "Cultivated Shabbiness"

The purest articulation of Shaw's architecture is his own
Lake Forest home, Ragdale. Its gables, plain plaster
walls, mullioned windows, and lushly planted landscape
make the place look like a hobbit's lair. It was the kind
of escapist fantasy that must have made staunch modernists look askance, but it was well suited to its owner's
individuality—a quality important to the architecture
of any age. Ragdale became a kind of laboratory, where
Shaw tested ideas for design and craftsmanship. He
named it as a family joke, as he'd seen a house called
"Ragdale" in England and liked its sound "of cultivated
shabbiness," the sense that the place was forever unfin-
ished. Besides being designer, Shaw worked there as
carpenter, bricklayer, gardener, and painter along with
hired hands. He was never so happy as he was when
dressed in old knickers and working on the house.

Old World craftsmanship gives Ragdale a look of studied
informality. The entrance hall has woodwork of un-
painted oak, and between the hall and the dining room
are six large panels of leaded glass. Window seats,
Stickley chairs, and Mission oak with pewter inlay are
typical of the unpretentious interior decor. A carefully
planned rusticity prevails outside as well. Narrow paths
wind through the fifty-acre property, with rustic trail

RAGDALE

1230 NORTH GREENBAY ROAD, LAKE
FOREST, ILL.

1898

HOWARD VAN DOREN SHAW

Ragdale was Shaw's home and
a laboratory for his ideas. His
passion was for the English Arts
and Crafts movement, which
was related to but more traditional
than the Prairie School. He filled
his home with stacks of books,
colorful rugs, and his own
handmade furniture, which was
often whimsical in form and
detailed with pewter inlay. Yet
dignity and repose characterized
all his work, which was frequently
for clients whose taste was more
pretentious than his own.

signs at every intersection. The garden has a dovecote
and a sundial inscribed with verse.

Another outdoor feature of the Shaw home is the
Ragdale Ring, a small theater where plays by Shaw's
wife, Frances, were staged. Some who were in the audience later recalled that poets such as Vachel Lindsay,
Carl Sandburg, and William Butler Yeats attended pro-
ductions at the Ring, but their visits are undocumented.
Still, the absolute truth of such events is not essential
to Ragdale's spirit. Its architecture is poetry itself,
devised to transport the imagination to simpler times.

DAVID ADLER AND HIS "GREAT HOUSES"

By the end of Shaw's career, his gentle forays into the
past were coming to seem old-fashioned. Tastes were
moving away from the humble Arts and Crafts in the
1920s, a more aggressive decade marked by social
change, economic expansion, and the rise of mass con-
sumerism. Yet modernism was not always the response
to modern times. In the wake of upheavals like World
War I and the Bolshevik Revolution, many American
capitalists sought the comfort and stability of conservative, aristocratic homes.

The architect who best embodied the era, for Chicago's
upper classes at any rate, was one of Shaw's former
draftsmen, David Adler (1882–1949). Adler built extravagant residences for the scions of great wealth, much

of it accumulated by the robber barons of the Gilded
Age. If Shaw's modest-looking designs expressed a
certain moralism, Adler's often suggested limitless
resources. Shaw's ideals of organic architecture led to
houses that were imaginative but still deeply responsive
to their conditions, while Adler's homes provided an
escape from the here and now.

Adler drew from farflung sources but almost always built
in styles that his clients could easily name: "Louis the
Sixteenth," "Italianate," and "South African Colonial"
became his repertoire. His approach to architecture was
historicist, eclectic, and unmistakably nonmodern; he
made no attempt to innovate or to contribute to the
development of a new regional or distinctively American
style. "Adler as a Chicago-based architect remains
totally at odds with the canonical Chicago tradition of
innovative commercial buildings of Louis Sullivan and
the domestic Prairie School of Frank Lloyd Wright and
his followers," wrote critic Richard Guy Wilson in the
catalogue for an expansive Adler retrospective at the Art
Institute of Chicago in 2002.

In his own time Adler's success seemed to be proof that
the conservatives had prevailed over the progressives.
The effort to "create an American style has proved a fail-
ure," wrote Thomas Tallmadge in a 1922 *Architectural
Record* article about Adler. Tallmadge, an architect and
onetime member of the Prairie School, termed Adler's

KERSEY COATES REED HOUSE

1315 NORTH LAKE ROAD, LAKE
FOREST, ILL.

1932

DAVID ADLER

Adler's genius was for updating
traditional designs to suit contemporary tastes. Working with
his sister, interior designer Frances
Elkins, he blended many modern
elements into the Reed House's
seemingly eighteenth-century
design. He reduced Georgian style
to its restrained essence, adding
large, bright spaces and sizzling
touches, such as glass spindles in
the bannister and black marble
columns.

eclectic approach "cosmopolitanism" and declared it the current life force of American architecture.

Adler's special mastery was in using old models to build new houses. Indeed, very few architects could use the vocabulary of historic styles so freshly to assemble designs of such harmony. He had "excellent taste," one colleague observed, and the grandeur of his buildings and the rich finishes of his interiors suited his upper-crust clients well. But he was also credited by progressive contemporaries for "modern flair," which points to the fact that Adler adroitly incorporated organic precepts, adding natural light, airiness, and a modern simplicity to grand, historicist styles.

Although Adler came to embody architectural conservatism, his career path was somewhat unconventional. He was born to a prosperous Jewish family in Milwaukee, though he later attended an Episcopalian church, which aligned him religiously with the majority of his clients. He went to Lawrenceville School and then to Princeton, where he was an unremarkable student. After his graduation in 1904 he embarked for Europe and enrolled in the architecture program at the Munich Polytechnikum, where he finished three semesters but for reasons unknown failed to complete his fourth, which would have earned him a diploma. Later he enrolled in the École des Beaux-Arts in Paris, where he completed classwork but declined to submit a thesis. No one knows what pre-

Adler chose a Louis XVI style for the Ryersons, whose fortune derived from the steel industry. The architect brought a modernity to the traditional design with large, open spaces filled with natural light. The oval-shaped dining room is an example of a perfectly proportioned Adler interior; it feels much larger than it really is.

vented Adler from doing what was necessary to receive credentials. Even after he began his successful practice in Chicago he remained unlicensed, and in one apparently perfunctory attempt to pass the state exam, he answered a test question about roof structure by writing, "I have men in my office who take care of that sort of thing." He failed dismally, though later in his career he passed the test and obtained a license.

What Adler did have, in lieu of official credentials, was an uncanny appreciation of and eye for design. When he traveled in Europe he collected hundreds of postcards of buildings he admired; on the backs he often drew moldings, windows, doors, and other details. He kept the cards and probably referred to the pictures throughout his career. Yet he always replicated architectural details in his own way—no one ever accused him of plagiarism—and he annotated his drawings with their

sources. Notes on the drawings for the Edison Dick house in Lake Forest, for example, show that the mantel came from page 49 of *The Architect or Practical House Carpenter,* written by Asher Benjamin in 1830. "Adler's extreme care in selecting details from architectural documents bordered on the creative," one of his draftsmen remembered. Sometimes Adler purchased entire rooms from houses that were being razed or disassembled and worked them into his own designs. With a keen sense of proportion he was able to adapt details, or even combine aspects of disparate models, while ensuring the fundamental relationships of scale were harmonious and sound.

Timeless proportion and not imitative detail is behind the success of one of his better-known houses in Chicago, the Ryerson Residence, built in 1921 on Astor Street. Although the style could be labeled Louis XVI, Adler

WILLIAM McCORMICK BLAIR HOUSE

LAKE BLUFF, ILL.

1926

DAVID ADLER

To take maximum advantage of breezes off Lake Michigan, Adler followed the model of an eighteenth-century "New Netherlands" house, a cottagelike structure whose sections were rarely more than one room deep. Houses in the original vernacular style often ramble, but Blair House flows seamlessly, thanks to the sense of proportion Adler applied to the paneling, moldings, and smallest details.

handled it with a restraint that resulted in a light, stream-lined look inside and out. At their best Adler interiors had "Mozartian spontaneity, grace and elegance in line and decoration," wrote the *Chicago Tribune* at the time. "They are always fresh but never eccentric or startling."

And even as he designed in a vernacular from the past, Adler drew on the contemporary tenets of organic archi-tecture, as seen at the William McCormick Blair House, built in 1926 in Lake Bluff, Illinois. The Blairs wanted an informal home that took advantage of the light and breezes coming off Lake Michigan. Adler accommodated them with a rambling style he called "New Netherlands." The house resembled an eighteenth-century colonial cottage that had expanded over time with a series of one-room additions. The building's single-room depth allowed each room to have windows on two or three sides, providing ample air and light, and the house flows easily from one room to the next.

Despite their enormous success, Adler's styles were unquestionably anachronistic—as he himself knew before his career ended. Upon his election in 1945 to the National Institute of Arts and Letters, Adler noted sadly, "My work is all in the period of the 'great house,' which today, alas, is over."

ART DECO AND HIGH SOCIETY'S JAZZ AGE INTERIORS

As the 1920s progressed, some of the same conditions that spawned Adler's historicism simultaneously were ushering in its opposite: a new and bolder modernism. The Roaring Twenties were a time of expanding wealth, renewed optimism, and frequent travel, one result of which was exposure to European modern design. Some modern styles were too stark for American tastes at the time, but one that instantly appealed to architects and their clients was Art Deco. Art Deco took its name from the Exposition Internationale des Arts Décoratifs et Industriels Modernes, which was held in Paris in 1925 and helped popularize the style. Characterized by a sleek profile, geometric forms, and glossy, often polychrome finishes, the sophisticated Art Deco simultaneously evoked the aerodynamic machine age and the angularity of ancient Egypt.

The decorative possibilities of Art Deco and other mod-ern styles swiftly drew the attention of those who catered to Chicago's smart set. Among them was Robert Switzer,

formerly of the interiors department at the architecture firm Holabird and Roche, who in 1927 opened a shop called Secession, Ltd., on Dearborn Street. The store specialized in modern decorative arts, including the styles from Germany and Austria that provided the shop its name. Switzer and his partner, Harold O. Warner, conceived the business after a trip to Europe, where they bought so much furniture, Switzer later said, they had no choice but to open a store. They quickly found clients flush with money and anxious to replace their tired clas-sical or antique interiors with something colorful, fresh, and new.

Fashionable stores like Switzer's became gathering places for high society during the Jazz Age, and savvy retailers spent freely to keep their interiors up-to-date. Among the architects they called upon for this kind of work was Philip Maher (1894–1981), who renovated Stanley Korshak's Blackstone Shop on Michigan Avenue, which sold ladies' couture. Even better than Maher, Korshak knew what he wanted; he began the project by taking his architect to New York City to see Bergdorf Goodman, one of the nation's glitziest stores. They also had a look at the *Isle de France,* a famous Art Deco ocean liner. The Blackstone Shop that resulted in 1929 was restrained but sleek, as modern as it was exclusive. It was light in color and feel; the furniture, vaguely reminiscent of eighteenth-century French pieces, had smooth lines and glossy surfaces.

Even the usually staid Marshall Field's department store adopted the latest look—evidence of its growing main-stream popularity. By the early 1920s its State Street display windows deployed Art Deco and often abstract imagery to bring attention to the store's up-to-date merchandise. The store's longtime design director, Arthur Fraser, was convinced that modernism made con-sumers think, and that thinking consumers would buy. Fraser's sleek forms, bold colors, and even wigless man-nequins left conservative store executives shaking their heads, but management couldn't argue with the sales that resulted. Fraser had free rein designing the State Street store interior, and his work at Marshall Field's did much to infuse Chicago's popular taste with dashes of modernism.

Luxury apartment dwellers were succumbing to the same trend, and to the same architect who was responsible for the Blackstone Shop. Maher (the son of Prairie architect

George Washington Maher) designed two luxury co-op buildings on Chicago's Gold Coast, completed in 1928. Named simply for their addresses, 1301 and 1260 Astor Street, the streamlined high-rises were marketed as the apotheosis of urban living. The interior layouts featured large rooms and flowing spaces, slick Jazz Age boudoirs straight from a Hollywood movie, but residents were slow to embrace modern decor completely. Some ordered touches of the Art Deco they admired in cruise ships, but most were still tied to the classical; the interior designs Maher's firm executed were filled with traditional moldings and mantelpieces. Eventually the buildings' residents adopted the refined modernism the architect had intended—but by the time some fully took to Art Deco, the style was already retro.

MODERNISM, SKYSCRAPERS, AND THE TRIBUNE COMPETITION

American designers initially applied Art Deco to interiors, but by the end of the decade the streamlined look had transformed entire buildings and reshaped public tastes. Modernism was not universally accepted, however. In 1927, for example, Chicago's Association of Arts and Industries sponsored a debate at the Palmer House on the topic, "Resolved, That the hope of art expression lies in the modern movement." Speaking against modernism

was Miss Marion Gheen, an interior decorator with a wealthy clientele and a taste for traditional furnishings. "Every true artist, in working out the impulse to create that which mysteriously rises within him, is bound to revert to the use of classic forms," she said.

Arguing for the modern side was Alphonso Ianelli, a noted sculptor and teacher at the Art Institute of Chicago. Classical art was exhausted, Ianelli declared. "It is as silly for us to build our Field Museum, stadium, and aquarium in classic Greek architectural style as it would be for us to issue our daily newspapers in the language of classic Greece." His view was not new; it went back to the days of Louis Sullivan. But now, Ianelli insisted, modern design was taking hold, not only in department stores but in office interiors, movie theaters, and the sleek autos people were driving.

Skyscrapers turned out to be a natural subject for Art Deco–style streamlining, too. By the late 1920s a building boom had markedly changed Chicago's skyline, and the so-called Art Deco skyscraper had become the dominant style. It was an antidote to earlier, sometimes ponderous attempts at high-rise architecture. There were classical skyscrapers dripping with ornament, like the 1926 Jeweler's Building on Wacker Drive, which was

1260 AND 1301 NORTH ASTOR STREET

1928

PHILLIP MAHER

Maher distinguished himself as a leading architect during Chicago's Art Deco period. His exclusive apartment buildings featured strong, modernist lines inside and out. The entrance (opposite, right) and lobby (right) at 1301 North Astor have classical proportions, but with materials like stainless steel and bold geometries they suggest something new in architecture: the machine age.

topped by something akin to a small Roman temple. There were the so-called Gothic skyscrapers, exemplified by the Wrigley Building, built in 1921 on North Michigan Avenue; its tower was modeled after the Spanish Gothic tower of the Giralda, in Seville. While these were interesting historical essays, and the Wrigley remains a popular favorite, none had the soaring grace that could best express the protean engineering skill and surging financial confidence the American skyscraper represented.

The architectural turning point—one of the most significant of the century—came in 1922. That year Colonel Robert R. McCormick, publisher of the *Chicago Tribune,* the city's largest daily paper, issued a call for designs for his company's new headquarters. He challenged architects to create "the most beautiful and distinctive office building in the world." The eye-catching inducement was $100,000 in prize money—$50,000 of that, as well as the commission, to go to the first-place design. The Tribune Tower competition attracted 263 entries from around the world. Although it did not instantaneously transform American architecture, the high-profile competition riveted the entire profession's attention, and its finalists' entries came to be recognized as touchstones for modern skyscraper design.

McCormick was looking for a design that reflected both his media empire's grandiose self-image and its commitment to state-of-the-art technology. (The *Tribune* called itself "The World's Greatest Newspaper," less for editorial distinction than its commercial and technical prowess.) The new Tribune Tower would house the world's most modern printing presses, an array of advanced broadcasting equipment, as well as late-model elevators and other conveniences. But, as it turned out, the building itself would not represent the most forward-thinking design.

The winner was the Gothic-inspired entry submitted by the New York firm of Hood and Howells. Raymond Hood (1881–1934)—who had worked for the Gothicist Ralph Adams Cram but would later design the ultramodern Daily News Building in Manhattan—was primarily responsible for the design. His thirty-six-story building, capped by a distinctively ornate tower, became a Chicago landmark. But the design that truly shook the architecture world was the second-place entry, by Eliel Saarinen of Finland. Saarinen's streamlined skyscraper epitomized what modern architects were thinking about at the time and came to have more influence than any unbuilt building in history. It helped launch Saarinen's American career as a major modern architect, and it

FROM ARTS AND CRAFTS TO ART DECO

TRIBUNE TOWER
COMPETITION ENTRIES

1922 (UNBUILT)

TOP LEFT: **ADOLF LOOS**

TOP RIGHT: **HOLABIRD AND ROCHE**

BELOW LEFT: **WALTER GROPIUS
AND ADOLF MEYER**

BELOW RIGHT: **ELIEL SAARINEN**

Loos was an avant-garde architect
from Vienna, where strict classical
forms were emphatically out of
fashion, so many viewed his entry
as a satire on America. Holabird
and Roche's design typified the
skyscraper of the period: powerful,
sober, surmounted by towers, to
be admired from afar. Gropius, who
founded the Bauhaus and admired
the Chicago School, suggested
pure structure and thoroughly
modern materials, in this case
concrete. Saarinen's entry, though
never built, was highly influential.
Its almost Gothic detailing
suggested the timelessness of
powerful architecture, and its
emphatic vertical thrust made it
a monument to America's skyscraping aspirations.

CHICAGO TRIBUNE TOWER

432 NORTH MICHIGAN AVENUE

1925

HOOD AND HOWELLS

Opposite: The winning entry in
the Tribune Tower competition
was controversial. Alfred Granger,
a member of the jury and an
architect, likened it to a human
body, with "flesh and muscles"
covering a fine skeleton. Louis
Sullivan decried it as architecture
"evolved of dying ideas." In fact,
Tribune Tower was a modern
commercial skyscraper disguised
in church raiment.

helped point urban architecture in a new direction, toward sleek, powerful skyscrapers whose design made few references to history.

The controversy that immediately greeted the decision to award the commission to Hood and Howells evolved into a lasting dispute over the relative merits of Hood's and Saarinen's designs. Yet the two buildings are more alike than dissimilar, and both played a role in inspiring the generation of Art Deco skyscrapers that followed. While Saarinen's design is the more widely recognized model, Hood's also features elements of a modern skyscraper that belie its reputation as retrograde or historically irrelevant.

The steel-framed Tribune Tower that was built combined the new with the old more than is commonly realized. The ornate Gothic styling at the top, modeled after the tower of Rouen Cathedral, satisfied Colonel McCormick's deeply conservative impulses. (Some employees called him the "greatest mind of the thirteenth century.") At the same time the tower admirably accommodated the newspaper's modern operations—as it does to this day. In fact, it was the design's modernity that a member of the competition jury, architect Alfred Granger, most praised in announcing the winning entry. "The steel is covered as in the skeleton of the human body, but, while the covering, like the flesh and muscles, satisfies the eye, the frame always makes its presence felt through the covering," he wrote.

Yet the building had vehement detractors, and their criticisms still resonate. If the "flesh and muscles" simile was meant to evoke organic architecture, it failed to convince Louis Sullivan, the movement's prophet. In his 1923 essay on the Tribune competition he compared the flying buttresses around the building's upper stories to "the monster on top with its great longlegs reaching far below to the ground." Sullivan conceded that, without its intricate decoration, the Tribune Tower could be a "rather amiable and delicate affair with a certain grace of fancy," but mostly accused it of being among "those works evolved of dying ideas." Sullivan cut short his blistering critique—"it is cruel to go on, for analysis is now becoming vivisection"—to praise Saarinen's second-place entry as fervently as he had deplored the winner.

Saarinen "grasped the intricate problem of the lofty steel-framed structure, the significance of its origins,

and held the solution unwaveringly in mind, in such wise as no American architect has as yet shown the required depth of thought and steadfastness of purpose to achieve," Sullivan wrote. Saarinen's truly inventive design used abstract Gothic forms to achieve a soaring verticality and, to Sullivan's delight, it was free of extraneous decoration, save for the subtle finials at the top. It combined the romance of a timeless past with the thrusting power of modern urban culture. Simple and powerful piers that soared skyward as if to defy gravity highlighted the underlying structure. It was, in short, Sullivanesque, a term that describes many modern skyscrapers of the 1920s.

In the fullness of time, Sullivan's dismissal of Tribune Tower must be judged an oversimplification. Granted, its upper-story Gothic confection did not influence skyscraper designs in the years that followed. But Tribune Tower's modernity is unfairly overshadowed by its historicism (which itself produced a building that has aged very well indeed). Despite dissenters, the Tribune Tower competition's influence in modern architecture owes nearly as much to the building Colonel McCormick built as to the building that never was.

GRAHAM, ANDERSON, PROBST AND WHITE

By the late 1920s modernism had become so widely accepted that even Chicago's last bastion of traditional architecture—Graham, Anderson, Probst and White—finally and decisively turned to it. G.A.P.W. was the direct successor to Daniel Burnham's practice and the city's most successful architectural firm. It was never radical and rarely on the leading edge of design. G.A.P.W.'s acquiescence to Art Deco influences was a sure sign that modern architecture was not just fashionable but made good business sense for architects and their clients alike.

G.A.P.W.'s chief, Ernest Graham (1868–1936), had worked for Daniel Burnham during the construction of the 1893 Columbian Exposition; he is remembered as the man issuing orders to everyone in sight while riding a white horse. Graham became Burnham's heir apparent not for his design talents but for his business acumen and skill with clients. He also used his connections to invest in commercial buildings that the Burnham firm designed, amassing a fortune in the process. He became part of Chicago's power elite, and after the Burnham firm was renamed as his in 1917, it frequently secured the most desirable commissions in town.

During the firm's first years its designs could not have been more conservative. The classicism of its 1924 Straus Building on South Michigan Avenue—a skyscraper later sold to C.N.A. Insurance Companies—led modernist architect Andrew Rebori to write, "Those entrusted with the design and execution of this huge structure were never once swayed by the emotion of the creative mind. They followed along the smooth path of accepted precedent. . . . The result is massive impressiveness." But the firm was not strictly bound to the past; rather, it reflected the established precepts of its day, and as modern ideas became acceptable, Graham, Anderson, Probst and White responded.

Its first experimentation with the modern was in its building interiors. The exterior of an early 1920s G.A.P.W. design might resemble a structure from ancient Greece or Rome, but the inside would be spacious and filled with natural light. Its 1922 Continental Bank (now Bank of America) Building on LaSalle Street, for example, was clad in customarily classical lines, but inside

sported something new: color. Murals high above the floor of the main banking room were executed by Jules Guerin, whose atmospheric watercolors illustrated Burnham's 1909 Plan of Chicago. (Guerin had been director of color for the 1915 Panama-Pacific International Exposition, which a critic described as "a classical city ablaze with the colors of the Mediterranean"—and a stunning contrast to Chicago's White City of 1893.) Guerin's murals do not verge on anything like the social realism that would decorate many buildings a few years hence—quietly composed, they depict commerce—but the color they bestowed was early evidence that the firm that hired him was entering the modern era.

With the Merchandise Mart, completed in 1930, G.A.P.W. committed to modernism inside and out. Marshall Field and Company, the Mart's builder, had conceived the enterprise to consolidate the wholesale businesses of manufacturers from across the country, allowing retailers to stock their stores with goods found under one roof. This bold, unprecedented plan led to construction of the world's largest building at the time. For reasons as commercial as they were

MERCHANDISE MART

ON THE CHICAGO RIVER BETWEEN WELLS AND ORLEANS STREETS

1930

GRAHAM, ANDERSON, PROBST AND WHITE

The Mart (right and following pages) was the world's largest building when built; its twenty-five stories extend the length of two city blocks along the north bank of the river. The building, with its plain geometric form and rich finishes, marked the initiation of its previously classicist architects to the era of streamlined modernism.

HERMAN MILLER SHOWROOM

MERCHANDISE MART

2000

INTERIOR BY KRUECK AND SEXTON

The Mart continues to function as an important merchandising destination. The interior design for the showroom of Herman Miller, a furniture maker long identified with American modernism, is thoroughly contemporary, with overlapping glass panels and baffled light. Yet it features the same timeless principles—streamlined planes, broad curves, and long corridors—that characterized the Mart's design when it was built.

artistic, the Mart demanded a design that would call attention to itself. To that end G.A.P.W. borrowed from a variety of sources, including Chicago's nineteenth-century warehouses and its twentieth-century skyscrapers. Blocklike and big-shouldered, the Merchandise Mart has the simplified, utilitarian lines and essential modernity of the Chicago School. But it also features the streamlined profile and graceful proportions of the best Art Deco. The warm spotlights that bathe it at night make clear that the Mart is an elegant, harmonious hybrid. It sits broadly along the north bank of the Chicago River, where the city's pioneers settled. Remembering organic architecture's decree that buildings be ideally suited to their site, one can hardly imagine the Merchandise Mart anyplace else.

By the early 1930s Graham, Anderson, Probst and White had definitively broken with its traditional past. Its Field Building on LaSalle Street (on the site of Jenney's Home Insurance Building) provided proof that it, and the architectural world, had moved irrevocably forward. For the Field Building (now LaSalle Bank) the firm designed a stripped-down, streamlined skyscraper with a rocket-like vertical thrust, suited to the jazzy modern world. The design was decidedly practical, as brochures printed for its 1934 opening made clear, touting the no-nonsense amenities that mattered most to the market: high-speed elevators, for example, and alternating current for better radio reception. Its large and dramatic lobby had walkways suspended overhead—reminiscent of the Rookery across the street—but the streamlined effect was more that of a sleek locomotive than of an Impressionist aerie. Then, as now, it feels like a building for people on the move.

"ARISTOCRATIC" MODERNISM: HOLABIRD AND ROOT

The most emphatic modern architecture of downtown Chicago in this era was designed by a firm whose pedigree reached back to the beginning of the Chicago School. In 1928 Holabird and Roche became Holabird and Root, in acknowledgment of John Wellborn Root Jr. (son of the Rookery's architect), who had been with the firm for fourteen years. The change in the firm's name accompanied changes in its approach; it adopted a collaborative method, incorporating the work of the best professionals it could find in design, interiors, sculpture, mural painting, and landscaping. The method allowed new ideas rapidly to crystallize and flourish.

Holabird and Root is best known today for the Chicago Board of Trade, completed in 1930 and a tour de force influenced, no doubt, by Saarinen's Tribune Tower entry. "Every inch a proud and soaring thing," reported *Architecture Magazine* in February 1932, echoing Sullivan's earlier exhortation for urban skyscrapers. The

CHICAGO BOARD OF TRADE

141 WEST JACKSON BOULEVARD

1930

HOLABIRD AND ROOT

Holabird and Root's Board of Trade (also seen on page 110) epitomized the Art Deco era. Its lobby is a model of Deco-style streamlining, with translucent glass, nickel reflectors, colorful marble pavements, and ziggurat shapes that were partly inspired by a modern fascination with ancient Egypt, which was kindled by the recent discovery of King Tut's tomb.

FIELD BUILDING

135 SOUTH LASALLE STREET

1934

**GRAHAM, ANDERSON, PROBST
AND WHITE**

The Field Building's plain modern
facade has a strong vertical thrust,
reinforced by elongated and
abstract fluted columns at the
entry and inside. Notwithstanding
the depression, this was a design
for the Jazz Age.

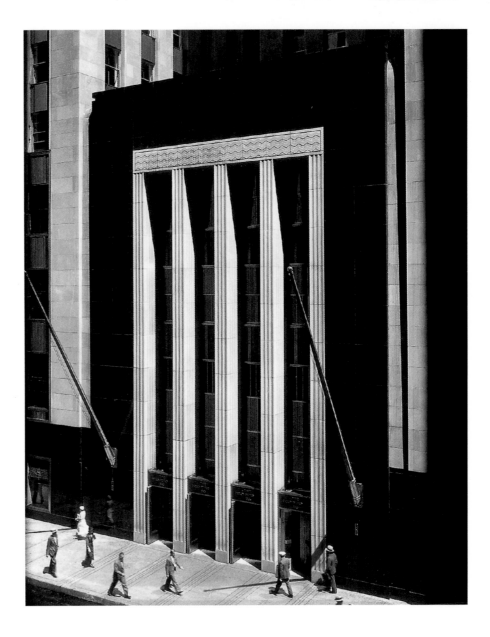

forty-four-story Board of Trade embraced the modern in many ways. Its relentless verticality was broken only by dramatic setbacks, much like recent skyscrapers in Manhattan, where zoning laws prohibited sheer vertical walls and architects made a virtue of zigzagging their way up. Floodlights at night emphasized its bold, modern form. On top, the sculpture of Ceres, goddess of grain, is unabashedly Art Deco. Inside, the lobby's polychrome effects—seen in the floor, walls, and elevators—were designed as chevrons and ziggurats, partly inspired by Egyptian forms made popular by the sensational discovery of Tutankhamen's tomb a few years before. Lamps were hidden behind translucent glass, and nickel reflectors helped diffuse indirect light, a relatively new tech-

nique. Gold leaf and faience added brightness, even flash, to a design that owed little to precedent.

Another Holabird and Root building, 333 North Michigan Avenue, is a milestone of 1920s American architecture, widely influential for its bold profile and also for the financial success it has enjoyed since going up in 1928. Architectural historian Carl Condit called it "aristocratic." So prestigious was 333 that Holabird and Root themselves took offices there, along with several other large architectural firms. Outside, its powerful yet gentle lines owe obvious debts to Saarinen's Tribune entry, as well as to Sullivan's classical tall-building canon, which called for a base, a shaft, and a tower or capital. Its long and narrow floor plate, which assures ample light for all

FROM ARTS AND CRAFTS TO ART DECO

Much like Saarinen's unbuilt design for the Tribune Tower, this building soars upward, as sleek and as modern as a skyscraper of the late 1920s could be. It also recalls the old Monadnock Block with a floor plate that is long and narrow, the better to fill the interior with plenty of natural light.

tenants, takes its lesson from the Monadnock Block, and well it might. John Root Sr. designed the Monadnock, and its later addition was by Holabird and Roche.

The exterior of 333 was stately, but one of Holabird and Root's interiors, also designed in 1928, epitomizes the giddy modernism of the Prohibition era. It was the Tavern Club, an Art Deco drinking establishment for any member who has "ever done any thing, or thought any thing and is of a clubbable nature," according to the club's bylaws. John Root, a member, said its purpose was "to create an environment in which it might be possible to escape from the pressures of the moment by having one's thought directed in the direction of the future rather than the past." The Tavern Club's interior design had nothing to do with old oak paneling and moose heads. Instead it featured murals by John Norton entitled *Pagan Paradise,* a composition of tropical plants and nudes. Furnishings and accents were in pale green, flamingo pink, and jet black. Not everyone approved, of course. On the occasion of its twentieth anniversary in 1948, a member recalled that some early visitors— writers who were "rugged followers of the Carl Sandburg tradition"—frowned upon the decor. "The place looks like a milliner's shop," said one grizzled scribe, who was probably more accustomed to barrooms with sawdust on the floor than to tony drinking clubs.

The Great Depression that followed on the heels of these new buildings drained many people of optimism, but it did not eliminate style. As if creative retailing could be an antidote to bad economic times, Holabird and Root in 1930 built Michigan Square (also called Diana Court),

an enclosed arcade and shopping mall on North Michigan Avenue. The indoor shopping center (which brings the Rookery to mind and foreshadows Water Tower Place by forty-six years) was decorated throughout with polished metalwork and marble. The famous Swedish sculptor Carl Milles was commissioned to create a sculpture of Diana for the atrium, and tenants were encouraged to design their own storefronts, which produced a dazzlingly creative array. "Art Moderne dominates the center portion of the building in a motif that sets Michigan Square apart as truly unusual," a building trade magazine reported shortly after the opening. "Holabird and Root, architects of the building, are to be congratulated for having made so fine a contribution to the fusion of art and business."

This outstanding building flourished through the depression and for decades thereafter, but unfortunately did not survive the reconstruction of North Michigan Avenue. Today a Marriott hotel occupies the site. *Chicago Daily News* art critic Dennis Adrian reported on the building's sad demise in 1973. "The vandalizing of N. Michigan Ave., or what is left of it, proceeds apace. . . . The most recent loss is the beautiful Michigan Square Building, now being wrecked behind a web of scaffolding." Adrian described the "flying staircases that gave a startling effect of suspension . . . and created wonderfully theatrical effect." Although its importance was largely unappreciated at the time of its destruction, it is a credit to the architects that Michigan Square remains one of Chicago's most fondly remembered buildings. As Adrian wrote mournfully, "It would have been a wonderful place to dance."

FROM ARTS AND CRAFTS TO ART DECO

MICHIGAN SQUARE BUILDING (DIANA COURT)

540 NORTH MICHIGAN AVENUE

1930 (DEMOLISHED 1973)

HOLABIRD AND ROOT

Michigan Square was an early enclosed shopping center, harking back to the Rookery and presaging Water Tower Place. It was Chicago's Art Deco jewel, praised for its successful synthesis of art and commerce. Many of its merchants—including the Socatch bake shop (above right)—designed their own storefronts accordingly. With chevrons and glossy surfaces as keynotes, its lively, original design remains unsurpassed. The building was demolished before Chicago realized what it was losing.

CHAPTER 5

THE MEANING OF MIES AND THE RISE OF MODERNISM

DIRKSEN FEDERAL BUILDING

219 SOUTH DEARBORN STREET

1964

LUDWIG MIES VAN DER ROHE

The less-is-more approach—
shorthand for Mies's reduction
of glass and steel towers to their
essence—produces a seemingly
weightless transparency that
sometimes yields ghostly images
of the surrounding city.

"Less is more." The phrase is inseparable from the architect who uttered it, Ludwig Mies van der Rohe (1886–1969). The phrase is also misleading. The glass and steel architecture of Mies van der Rohe may be "minimalist," but as a distillation of ideas ranging from the writings of philosopher Saint Thomas Aquinas to the cubist paintings of Pablo Picasso, there is nothing sparse about it. His architecture's deceptive simplicity can mask its profound lessons, which often are lost— and not only on the general public. Architect Robert Venturi, in his 1966 *Complexity and Contradiction in Modern Architecture,* trivialized Mies's phrase with an alternate slogan: "Less is a bore." That potshot led to an unfortunate misunderstanding of one of the century's great architects, though Venturi was referring more to callow imitations than to the work of Mies himself. In fact, spending time in a Mies van der Rohe space is a rich architectural experience. Learning about what motivated him touches on essential tenets of architecture.

Mies became the towering figure of modern architecture shortly after emigrating to Chicago from his native

Germany in 1938. There he had been associated with the Bauhaus—a school of design founded in 1919 by architect Walter Gropius—and was its director from 1930 to 1933. The Bauhaus espoused a functional, rational architecture that made innovative use of new building techniques and materials, especially machine-made materials like metal and glass; Bauhaus design was characterized by stark geometric forms and an absence of applied ornament. Its position on the leading edge of German architecture brought it in conflict with the Nazis' conservative tastes, which ultimately drove Mies and several other Bauhaus-affiliated architects to flee Germany for America, bringing with them the seeds of what developed into and was later termed the "International style."

Mies's rectilinear architectural vocabulary, as well as signature design features like exposed supports and glass-curtain walls, met with great success in America. But despite his work's wide impact, its substance was often underestimated. Venturi was not the first architect to misunderstand Mies's seeming simplicity. Even Frank

THE ARTS CLUB

109 EAST ONTARIO STREET

1951

LUDWIG MIES VAN DER ROHE

The Arts Club commissioned Mies to design a gallery, dining room, and lecture hall within an existing building, using furniture the club already owned. He created a masterpiece of flowing space. The focal point of the gallery (below left) was Constantin Brancusi's *Bird* (now on exhibit at the Art Institute of Chicago). Mies's solution for a difficult, narrow space at the entrance was a stairway (below right) of renowned elegance and simplicity.

Lloyd Wright, a friend and then rival, was unable to give Mies the credit he deserved.

Mies's relationship with Wright, which began in the late 1930s, had grown out of mutual respect. Mies certainly knew about Wright's Prairie houses by 1911, when Wright's work was published in a prestigious portfolio by Wasmuth Press of Berlin, and there is no doubt that Mies's conception of space and his reverence for materials derived partly from Wright's organic approach to architecture. Wright probably learned about Mies when he traveled in Europe at about the same time; he also saw Mies's work in 1932, when the Museum of Modern Art (MoMA) in New York mounted its milestone exhibition on the International style.

The two finally met in 1937, when Mies was in Chicago making plans to move there and to join the faculty of the Illinois Institute of Technology (I.I.T.). Their meeting came about when an architect they knew in common phoned to say that Mies van der Rohe would like to meet Wright, who was then seventy years old, almost twenty years Mies's senior. "I should think he would," was Wright's less-than-modest reply. This was better than other European architects got from the American master, who was horrifyingly rude when Walter Gropius, for one example, attempted to pay his respects. But Wright genuinely admired Mies and invited him to his home at Taliesin, in Wisconsin, where a visit intended to last a few hours extended to days. With a Wright apprentice chauffeuring, the two architects motored to Racine to see construction in progress on Wright's Johnson Wax Building, then to Chicago and its suburbs to see Robie House, Coonley House, and Unity Temple. Mies was clearly impressed. He later wrote a short essay for a catalogue that was never published but had been intended to accompany a 1940 exhibition of Wright's work at MoMA: "Here, finally, was a master-builder drawing upon the veritable fountainhead of architecture; who with true originality lifted his creations into the light," Mies wrote of Wright.

Architectural egos being what they are, sparks can fly unexpectedly. And fly they did. In 1946 MoMA mounted a retrospective of Mies's work, and Wright swept into the opening of the exhibition with more than average pomp, according to Joe Fujikawa, a student of Mies's and later partner of his successor firm in Chicago. "Wright was pointing at Mies's work and saying things like, 'I did this in 1925,'" said Fujikawa, who was present. "He was giving everyone the impression that he was behind everything Mies had ever done."

Wright must have felt a pang of remorse, for afterward he wrote a letter to Mies explaining his point of view—stopping short of apologizing for his behavior—and inviting Mies back to Taliesin. Mies answered politely that he would of course be glad to make another visit and talk amiably about architecture. But Mies, who became known for the aphorism "Build, don't talk," never went and never saw Wright again. Wright grabbed the last word, naturally, later equating Mies's "internationalism" with communism. Both movements, he suggested, must destroy in order to create—"do this very leveling in the name of civilization," as Wright put it. Mies remained typically unruffled, but never communicated with Wright again.

Despite the personal rift, the artistic connection between Mies and Wright runs deep, most generally in their organic attention to materials and to light and more specifically in the way both planned space. Mies's debt to Wright can be overstated—as Wright himself did— but many of Mies's designs, particularly from his 1913–36 German period, evoke sensations akin to Wright's in dissolving boundaries between rooms and between the interior and exterior. Glass partitions, exterior courtyards, and brick courses extending into the countryside demonstrate a distinct link between Mies and the earlier Prairie style.

MIES, THE ABSTRACT THEORIST

Beyond Wright, an impressively wide range of sources informed Mies's ideas about architecture. Among his influences was the de Stijl group, composed mostly of Dutch painters whose rationalist art concentrated on the rectilinear organization of lines and primary colors. De Stijl (the Style) was an art movement deeply connected to its times—World War I and its aftermath. After that devastation, the rosy world of Impressionism seemed irrelevant, and all representational art was losing its appeal. The theories growing around de Stijl generally intended to cleanse art of all historical reference and subjective emotion. The work consisted of lines, color, and empty space—a reductionism that Mies and his architectural compatriots applied to floor plans as well.

Another influence on Mies was early Catholic philosophy, such as the writings of Saint Thomas Aquinas, though the architect was far from religious in any conventional sense. Aquinas wrote in the thirteenth century that the spiritual world could be discerned by the observation of things that were visible. Through serious contemplation, human beings could perceive in any object—a rock or a blade of grass—its essence as derived from God. For an architect of Mies's sensibility, the idea that a thing as seemingly inanimate as a steel post or sheet of glass might also have spiritual impact was attractive. Thus Mies struggled mightily to assemble his buildings' materials in a way that would express their essence.

Mies was an extremely abstract thinker. That was due in some measure to the fact that he came of age as an architect directly after World War I, when the German economy was in near ruin and there was little actual building to do. It was also a reflection of the philosophical impulses driving European architects at the time. The upheavals that wracked the continent in the early decades of the century gave rise to a utopian intellectualism, a conviction that art could change the world and that design could promote social order. Mies's contemporary, Le Corbusier (1887–1965), the Swiss-born, French-based modernist architect and urban planner, was a major proponent of such beliefs, which he communicated not only through his buildings but also in doctrinaire manifestos.

In that environment Mies became a theorist and an organizer; he was involved with a number of progressive art groups in Berlin, where he had settled. He worked on avant-garde exhibitions and contributed his own experimental building designs, showing his views of architecture's future. One such project, exhibited in 1922, was his Glass Skyscraper, designed for a site on Berlin's Friedrichstrasse. Here he unveiled the alarmingly radical concept of a steel skeleton exposed behind transparent walls of glass. The idea likely had many sources, and Mies might have cited Aquinas as well as Picasso, whose cubist works projected several perspectives at once. But in hindsight the similarities between

this project and the largely unembellished steel frames of the Chicago School are inescapable.

Mies and other young architects endlessly discussed the small points of their work. While Mies later claimed that he did not particularly enjoy debate, it remained the best way for any architect to draw notice during Germany's slump. Mies also formed relationships with the Russian Constructivists then working in Berlin, who saw as their task "not to decorate life but to organize it." And he published articles in magazines explaining what became known as the "New Architecture," still mostly theory and drawing. "We reject all aesthetic speculation, all doctrine, all formalism," he wrote in a style as spare as his architecture. "We refuse to recognize problems of form, only problems of building."

With just a few actual buildings to his credit, Mies van der Rohe's reputation grew, and when Germany's economy recovered in the late 1920s, he was close to the top of a list of eligible architects. Conservatives attacked the New Architecture, to be sure, but the effect of such criticism was increased exposure, and commissions came his way.

Mies: Theory and Reality

Mies never wavered from his theoretical convictions nor shook his not-of-this-world quality, and his works were not always deemed practical by those who used them. His design for the German Pavilion at the 1929 world's fair in Barcelona, Spain, serves as a case in point. One of Mies's most influential designs, the so-called Barcelona Pavilion was an elaborate exhibit for the German building-supplies industry. The commission was one of Mies's first opportunities to realize his concept of modern architecture at full scale and in three dimensions. Under a flat roof the pavilion was filled with freestanding walls, flowing space, and rich materials: giant slabs of polished onyx, thick wool rugs, and travertine floors that extended to the edge of a limpid pool in the rear.

The pavilion's most important aspect was something Mies had previously only imagined in his drawings of projects that were never built—great walls of glass all around. The use of glass was key to the New Architecture for reasons both theoretical and practical. Glass enabled architects to reveal interior and exterior space simultaneously, merging points of view that had been separate, thereby achieving in architecture what

THE MEANING OF MIES AND THE RISE OF MODERNISM

cubists were achieving in painting. Because of Mies's consummate skill for blending those abstract ideas with real building materials, the pavilion (which was dismantled after the fair) is remembered as a milestone in the development of modern architecture. But in spite of its undisputed genius, Mies's work raises a lingering question: Does a great monument of modern architecture also constitute a suitable, comfortable place in which to live? Mies never responded directly but repeatedly suggested that his notions of architectural integrity trumped anyone else's ideas about mere comfort.

A story about Mies's now classic Barcelona chair illustrates the point. Mies designed it specifically for King Alfonso XIII; it was to be the monarch's ceremonial chair during an official visit to the pavilion. On the day the Spanish king was expected, Mies was making a last check of his building when, as he remembered, "To my surprise I found a wanderer sitting in the chair. I ordered him out with the following words: 'For you I made a bench outside by the pool.'" Form—even ceremonial form—rather than human comfort seems to have been the architect's priority—a charge likewise leveled at the Barcelona chair itself, whose ergonomics some consider less than perfect.

The same question of practicality hovered over another of Mies's famed designs, the Tugendhat House, completed in Brno, Czechoslovakia, in 1930. The design is vintage Mies. Its main space, fifty feet by eighty feet, is enclosed by sheets of glass—including a retractable window wall—and partitioned by freestanding onyx walls and an ebony screen. Mies also designed several pieces of furniture for Tugendhat House, a joint effort with his partner during this period, Lilly Reich. Reich deserves much of the credit for the rich fabrics and elegant touches that finished Mies's otherwise stark interiors. The partners left little room in Tugendhat House for non-Miesian elements. They either designed or specified all the furnishings, the piano, and even a sculpture of a female torso.

Critics wondered if the place was too severe to be livable, and a few negative articles about Tugendhat House appeared after it was built. Fritz Tugendhat, the owner, took it upon himself to write a defense of his architect, which was published in the magazine *Die Form:* "It is true that one cannot hang any pictures in the main space, in the same way that one cannot introduce a piece of furniture that would destroy the stylish uniformity of the original furnishings—but is our 'personal life

860–880 NORTH LAKE SHORE DRIVE

1952

LUDWIG MIES VAN DER ROHE

Mies's twin twenty-six-story apartment buildings on Lake Shore Drive (left and opposite) were the first of Chicago's very few steel-frame residential towers. Raising them on their beams above the ground allowed for lobby views that penetrate the glass walls and stretch over the lake into infinite space.

repressed' for that reason? The incomparable patterning of the marble and the natural graining of the wood do not take the place of art, but rather they participate in the art, in the space, which is here art." Notwithstanding Tugendhat's impassioned justification of the project, it is worth noting that the Tugendhats were quick to re-arrange things and bring in pieces of their own after Mies had photographs taken of the new house.

CHICAGO'S HOMEGROWN MODERNISM

Mies would become the giant of Chicago architecture after adopting the city as his home in 1938, and his glass skyscrapers would reinvent the local skyline from the 1940s through the 1960s. But it would be a mistake to think that he imported modernism to Chicago or that he was single-handedly responsible for the next step in the city's architectural evolution. Modernist strains were emerging in Chicago well before Mies's arrival.

Yet for many decades architectural historians tended to regard Chicago exclusively in terms of the Chicago School and Mies. Sigfried Giedion asserted in 1963 that nothing of equal architectural importance to the Chicago School happened in the city until Mies arrived. (He regarded Wright as an eccentric exception.) That view persisted as late as 1976, the year Chicago's Museum of Contemporary Art mounted a major exhibit of Chicago architecture that had been organized in Germany. The exhibit took the position, as stated in the catalogue, that "there were few meaningful architectural events in Chicago in the long years between the depressing development which was introduced by the World's Fair of 1893 and the beginning of the work of Mies van der Rohe at I.I.T. in 1938."

Rancorously challenging that judgment, a group of young architects called the "Chicago Seven" helped org-anize a counterexhibit, "Chicago Architects," with a catalogue written by the Chicago-born architects Stanley Tigerman and Stuart Cohen. The exhibit celebrated nearly one hundred works that did not fit neatly into the Museum of Contemporary Art's exclusionary canon. The counterexhibit proved that the city's architecture— beyond the buildings by the best-known names—had vitality and influence. It demonstrated that visionaries like Keck and Keck, Paul Schweikher, and Andrew Rebori were practicing an American modernism in the prewar years, well before the European modernists found their way here.

Like their European counterparts, American architects were exploring new ideas, but their intentions were generally more pragmatic than idealistic. Modernists on both sides of the Atlantic were experimenting with glass and steel, for example, but while minimalism made European architects think of art theory and abstract paintings, it appealed to Chicago architects because it enabled them to build more quickly and easily. A grow-ing aspect of American modernism, especially in the wake of the depression, was the importance placed on economical building techniques and the use of modest materials.

KECK AND KECK: BUILDING FROM THE INSIDE OUT

All-American pragmatism expressed itself in an inventive-ness that was every bit as visionary as the European modernists' idealism, however, as exemplified by the work of George Fred Keck (1895–1980) and William Keck (1908–1995). As "machines for living" (a phrase Le Corbusier coined to describe the houses he was building in the 1930s), Keck and Keck homes achieved in the early 1930s a level of innovation that has rarely been matched since. The Keck brothers kept track of European design trends, to be sure, but never lost sight of Chicago's values. Those included the central impor-tance of economy, as well as open and flexible interiors, filled with natural light. The Kecks even fought to develop solar energy, making remarkable strides in the technology before an abundance of cheap energy after World War II regrettably sidelined their efforts.

Fred Keck, who some call the firm's creative genius, began his architectural career in Chicago in 1921 and opened his own practice in 1927. His first commissions were simple, mostly conventional suburban homes for clients brought in by friendly real estate developers. Business was good until the depression came along, which was, in retrospect, a kind of blessing. He had long wanted to build in the modern style, but found that introducing change was difficult in good times, when most clients were happy with the status quo. In those days, "We had problems getting financing for anything that was modern and up-to-date," said William Keck, who joined his older brother's firm in 1931.

The depression—and the building industry's need to adapt to the new conditions that ensued—helped the Kecks build their first truly modern and perhaps most

HERBERT BRUNNING
RESIDENCE

The Kecks were preoccupied with
space planning to avoid clutter
and provide openness in relatively
small quarters, such as this living
room. Simple forms and textures
(here including shag carpet) led
to interesting compositions in the
Brunning house and many other
residences designed by George
Fred Keck and his younger brother,
William.

famous structure, the House of Tomorrow, at Chicago's
Century of Progress exposition in 1933. Fred Keck
conceived it as a modern showcase that would demonstrate how the latest building supplies could be used
harmoniously and economically, and he asked the
makers of glass, steel, rubberized flooring, and dozens
of other products to provide materials. His compact
House of Tomorrow—which included a hanger for a
small biplane—was a hit. Tens of thousands of fairgoers
visited the house, and since admission was ten cents,
the investors (including Keck) even made a little money.

To fairgoers, the House of Tomorrow might have looked
otherworldly, or at least European, but the Kecks claimed that it was as American as a Model T. They modeled
its plan after a four-story brick mansion called the
Octagon House, which was built in 1853 in Watertown,
Wisconsin, where the Kecks spent their youth. Octagonal
houses were an early innovation in American architecture, economical to build and designed to maximize
living space and natural light. The Watertown Octagon
had a central core that brought running water from a cis-
tern on the roof and carried heat from a furnace below.
The brochure handed out at the House of Tomorrow
pictured the old Watertown house, along with the Kecks'
commentary: "If the inventive spirit and direct expres-

sion as exemplified in this house, built in the middle
of the last century, had been carried on we should have
escaped the inanities of the post–Civil War period and
the first thirty years of this present century." The Kecks
went on to explain, "The chief concern of the architect
was not to give a specific form to his building, but rather
to find a solution to the many and varied new requirements of a residence in a simple and direct manner.
The causes were considered first, the effects later. He
started from the inside and worked out." The Kecks
knew their house would appear strange at first, but that
people would become accustomed to it and even find
it "right and proper and beautiful."

The House of Tomorrow, like the Octagon, was designed
with a central core for heating and air conditioning
(which "will be considered as necessary as central heating and bathrooms are today," the brochure stated
presciently). The plan is a dodecagon, a twelve-sided
polygon. Not an arbitrary or decorative choice, the architects determined it to be the most efficient shape for
the standard-size glass panels to be used. The interior
design was uncluttered, to convey a sense of space and
freedom. Furniture and interior details were of the simplest form but called attention to themselves with the
interesting use of materials. Flooring, for example, was

HOUSE OF TOMORROW

CENTURY OF PROGRESS (LATER MOVED TO BEVERLY SHORES, IND.)

1933

GEORGE FRED KECK

The House of Tomorrow was an exhibit for the building supply industry at the Century of Progress. Its shape (a twelve-sided polygon supported by a central steel column) was dictated by the standard size of glass panels, which were easy to procure and install. "The plan of the house is as unusual as it is logical," Keck wrote. Basic forms, simple materials, and natural light combined to provide a measure of comfort not then associated with modern design. The hangar suggested the airplane as tomorrow's mode of personal transportation.

THE MEANING OF MIES AND THE RISE OF MODERNISM

NASH MOTORS EXHIBIT

CENTURY OF PROGRESS

1933 (DEMOLISHED 1934)

WHITING CORPORATION

The 1933 fair viewed mass production as the nation's deliverance from the depression and modern design as the way to showcase it. This eighty-foot glass tower displayed Nash's latest automobiles in a constantly moving vertical rotation.

CHRYSLER MOTORS PAVILION

CENTURY OF PROGRESS

1933 (DEMOLISHED 1934)

HOLABIRD AND ROOT

Light and water were integral elements of an architecture meant to inspire hope of a better future, with prosperity—and automobiles like Chrysler's—on the horizon.

of end-grain wood blocks in some cases, bright-colored rubber tile in others. The most influential features of the House of Tomorrow were its chrome-tube furniture and metallic venetian blinds; convenience would soon become an aesthetic.

As the Century of Progress exposition continued into 1934, the Kecks assembled many of the same suppliers for a second project, the Crystal House. More starkly modern than the House of Tomorrow, the Crystal House was supported by exterior trusses and enclosed with glass panels, making the interior entirely open and flexible. The Kecks' talented draftsman Lee Atwood designed

the furniture, much of it modeled after pieces he found in pictures of Mies's European houses. Unfortunately, fairgoers were less enthusiastic about this building than the previous one and did not flock to see the Crystal House; Fred Keck lost his personal investment in it. "I had to decide between being rich or going for reputation," he explained candidly years later. "I was young and built the building and lost my shirt."

While working on their fair projects, the Kecks happened to make many practical discoveries, including recognizing the possibilities of solar heat. The House of Tomorrow went up in the dead of winter, but once it was

149

THE MEANING OF MIES AND THE RISE OF MODERNISM

For his second futuristic house at the world's fair (left), Keck opened up the interior space entirely by placing all the steel-truss support on the exterior.

The client told the Kecks she wanted "the house of the day after tomorrow." Space, light, and convenience were her principal requirements for the weekend retreat (opposite).

enclosed in its glass panels, the tradesmen working inside had to remove their coats. The Kecks quickly realized that they could capture and use the sun's radiated heat and began to incorporate in their designs the then far-fetched notion of energy conservation. For future houses they tracked solar paths and designed eaves of the proper width to admit rays in winter and keep them out in summer—an idea way ahead of its time.

The clients who took a liking to the Kecks' modern houses were by no means average homeowners, but the well-to-do; their neighbors were likely to be living in upscale, traditional houses by David Adler and Howard Van Doren Shaw. Some of those wealthy clients, like Mr. and Mrs. Benjamin J. Cahn, were more unabashedly radical than the Kecks themselves. The Cahns were Chicagoans seeking to build a weekend house in Lake Forest. When Mrs. Cahn met the Kecks she told them that she knew about the House of Tomorrow, but was looking for something different. What she wanted, she said, was "the house of the day after tomorrow."

Mrs. Cahn had some other stipulations. One was that her house require an absolute minimum of upkeep, since she was disabled by a hip injury. In lieu of curtains, which she believed needed maintenance, the Kecks designed exterior venetian blinds, an idea they were

eager to try. Instead of rugs, they provided a kind of rubber tile. Mrs. Cahn also insisted on being able to sit down anywhere in the house to read—but she vetoed having any lamps on tables or on the floor. The Kecks' solution was a system of pinpoint lights in the ceiling, controlled by discretely placed switches.

An attractive luxury of the Cahn House, which cost about $125,000 in 1938, was its floor plan: It formed a graceful arc from one end to the other. This was less than strictly utilitarian, but served two aesthetic functions. The front side curves to embrace the approaching visitor, providing a warm welcome. The convex curve in the back provided a measure of privacy to the bedrooms, each of which opened through floor-to-ceiling walls of glass to views of a prairie landscape designed by Jens Jensen for an earlier house that was torn down to make way for this one.

THE INTERIORS OF MARIANNE WILLISCH

With an abundance of new ideas and techniques at their disposal, architects like the Kecks were finding ways to improve the lives of the people who inhabited their homes—a progressive goal that had only grown in importance since Ruskin and Sullivan first wrote of architecture's potential humanistic impact. The proposition, promulgated by the Kecks, that the best houses were

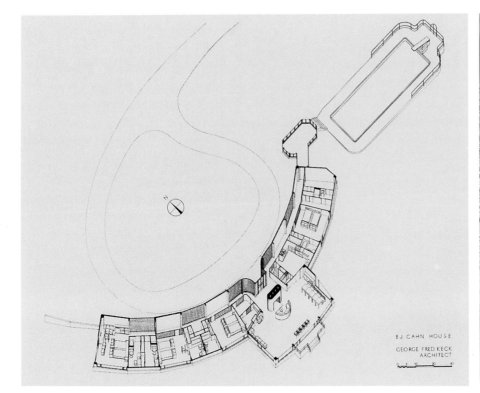

designed from the inside out also helped to raise the profile of interior designers in the 1930s.

The Austrian-born interior designer Marianne Willisch (d. 1984) was a valued collaborator of the Kecks and herself a leading proponent of modernism. In Vienna Willisch had been a member of the Werkbund, a semi-official design guild with links to the Secession and the Bauhaus. She moved to Chicago in 1930 and soon opened a design store, Chicago Workshops, in Michigan Square. She sold a variety of European furnishings—Le Corbusier chairs, for example—and also commissioned furniture and decorative pieces to be made locally. The shop was not a stirring success and it closed after only a few years, but it established Willisch's reputation, and she enjoyed a busy design practice thereafter.

Just as modern structures sought simplicity, so did Willisch's interiors. As she explained in an interview shortly before her death, interiors "should be so organized as to be useful and practical. To do that you have to think not of decorating, but of space planning." She acknowledged that, as a modernist, she had to fight off the "vicious campaign against the Bauhaus, with people saying that the barrenness and coldness of the architecture has spoiled our warm, elegant, and highly

decorated interiors." Yet she could boast that many clients left her modern interiors unchanged for decades, evidence of her designs' comfort and timelessness. "Taste is only a temporary thing," she said. "Style is organic and it lasts. It lasts not only to the end of your days but well beyond your lifetime."

Willisch, whose personality was as strong and striking as her Viennese accent, got to know her clients well, saying she enjoyed the "psychological" aspects of the job. "I will not coerce you," she would profess to clients, but her unyielding insistence on space organization and openness usually prevailed. Typical of her airy designs were storage walls to hide the televisions and stereos she deemed eyesores. She tended to make a virtue of mass production, with chrome furniture, shag area rugs, and glass tabletops among the up-to-date features. Antiques were acceptable in moderation, but not "so-called antiques" from junk stores. Fabrics were another important focus, and their textures and colors were often enriched by the play of light.

Indeed light was the quality William Keck most remembered about Willisch's interiors: "A lot of light . . . light colors. Splashes of colors on the furnishing. . . . Never anything violent at all. . . . Simplicity was her underlying

THE MEANING OF MIES AND THE RISE OF MODERNISM

word and underlined doubly." Keck recalled only a few times, over the course of many collaborations, when she was confounded. One was in the Edward McCormick Blair House, built in 1955 in Lake Bluff, Illinois. Over Willisch's vigorous objections, the client insisted on using a startling rug obtained on African safari. Willisch had to work her otherwise modern design around an animal skin lying in the middle of the floor.

PAUL SCHWEIKHER AND ECLECTIC MODERNISM

Most of the Chicago architects who were exploring the new ideas that helped modernism gain a foothold in the 1930s did not become household names like Frank Lloyd Wright and Mies van der Rohe, but their contributions were significant nonetheless. Among them were Paul Schweikher and Andrew Rebori, both of whom began as architects in the traditional vein, then moved gradually toward modernism.

Schweikher (1903–1997), who was born in Denver, followed his future wife, who had enrolled in the School of the Art Institute, to Chicago. After taking a few drafting courses himself, he realized that drawing was a good way to make a living; after discovering he had a knack for architecture, he got a job in the office of David Adler. Although Adler was anything but a modernist, Schweikher learned invaluable lessons—especially the immutable rules of proportion—from the master. Working on Adler's historical great houses, he later said, he realized that the smallest detail could influence a room's or a building's entire effect, which was as true for modern design as for traditional.

Schweikher then decided to complete his bachelor's degree and in 1927 entered Yale, whose School of Architecture was still tied to the beaux arts. Modernism was creeping in, however, and students' conversations frequently centered on the modern. Schweikher remembered a friend pointing to a picture of an interior designed in the modernist Wiener Werkstatte mode and asking if he thought it was "the architecture of the future." Schweikher replied, "Well, I think so." It certainly was, though Yale students wouldn't have known it from their classwork at the time.

Schweikher returned to Chicago in 1930, after spending a year studying and traveling in Europe. He worked for several local architects, including Philip Maher, whose

design impulses were modern, but whose wealthy clients indulged up-to-date design only to a point. Maher's 1928 apartment high-rises at 1301 and 1260 Astor Street had demonstrated that Art Deco–style streamlining was voguish for those who could afford such luxury. But modernism was also moving toward an emphasis on economy—and Maher's designs often went the other way. In Schweikher's view, Maher's socialite tendencies got in the way of good architecture. He remembered one of their arguments having been over whether a set of details was "Colonial" or "Georgian"—a matter of little inconsequence to advanced architects at the time.

Even when working for others early in his career, Schweikher designed his own work, such as a North Side house with an observatory on top, which the Museum of Modern Art included in a 1933 exhibit on Midwest architects. That year he left Maher and set out on his own, designing suburban residences for the most part, many of them in wood, brick, and other organic materials associated with the Prairie School. His approach also related to more contemporary European modernism, such as that of the Bauhaus and Mies. "The only thing I emphasized was the use of materials," he said. "Instead of painting brick after it was in place, letting the color of the brick stand. Instead of staining wood with dark stains, protecting it with preservatives. It was a kind of simplicity that we hoped to introduce, and directness."

With his plain, unadorned designs Schweikher created useful and comfortable rooms. In 1946 he built one of his most exquisite houses, on a large tract of land in Schaumburg, Illinois, for himself. The house clearly reflects Schweikher's openness to new influences, especially those he absorbed during a trip to Japan in 1937. The Japanese elements of the Schaumburg house—its marked asymmetry, for example, and the flowing space divided by screenlike walls—are a reminder that certain ideas related to modernism did not originate with Wright or Mies, but had ancient and farflung roots.

ANDREW REBORI AND THE FRANK FISHER APARTMENTS

Another important architect active in Chicago through the first half of the twentieth century was Andrew Rebori (1886–1966), whose practice was notable for advanced concepts of modern design and also for their presumed opposite, socially prominent clients. Rebori himself

spanned the cultural spectrum. Born to Italian immigrant parents on the Lower East Side of New York, he moved to Chicago and married a relative of Colonel Robert R. McCormick, publisher of the *Chicago Tribune*. He happily established himself as a local bon vivant, a reputation that helped him attract a well-heeled clientele.

Rebori spanned eras as well, beginning his practice in Chicago about 1911 and keeping his hand in almost until his death fifty-five years later. Stylistically, he covered the gamut. He built the tony Racquet Club in 1923 in something akin to the Georgian style. The following year he built the Riding Club on McClurg Court (today it houses CBS studios); it had traditional detailing but also a tall-trussed roof that revealed a modern interest in making structure a decorative feature. And he easily adopted elements of Art Deco design.

Rebori further exposed his eclecticism—and much more—at his Streets of Paris attraction at the 1933

World's Fair, a kitschy rendition of European nightlife. The featured performer was the sultry fan dancer Sally Rand, whom Rebori claimed to have discovered. The architect was said to have made $700,000 in ticket receipts for Miss Rand's blockbuster performance, in which she revealed and concealed her own personal architecture with a pair of seven-foot ostrich-feather fans.

Rebori's more important and most intriguing contribution to Chicago architecture became a modernist landmark: the Frank Fisher Apartments, built in 1938 on North State Parkway in the well-heeled Near North Side. The painted brick and glass block building epitomized the era's "depression modern" style. Streamlined and sparsely adorned, the Fisher Apartments exhibit Rebori's modern notion that a building's beauty lay not in ornamentation but innovation.

The project began when Frank Fisher, an executive for Marshall Field's, presented Rebori with a long, narrow lot

THE MEANING OF MIES AND THE RISE OF MODERNISM

The client requested an apartment building design that provided the maximum rentable space on a narrow urban lot. Rebori used curves, glass block, and a variety of unconventional techniques to create thirteen uncommon, unornamented duplex units that are far more spacious than the exterior would suggest.

and asked him to design a walk-up building with the maximum number of units possible. It was no easy task. Rebori had to come up with a plan that would allow for apartments spacious enough to suit the upscale neighborhood while also buffering the living space from the noisy street. His solution boldly combined ideas, from a light court reminiscent of older Chicago School buildings, to the undisguised use of building materials. Curving glass-brick walls were stylish and modern; they also maximized usable space and necessitated air conditioning, a new feature in residential architecture. Rebori had created his equivalent of Le Corbusier's "machines for living," absent the doctrine.

Into the four-story design Rebori fitted thirteen small duplexes, with interior balconies that create a series of interpenetrating spaces. He organized the interiors with a "telescoping of function," as he explained in a 1937 *Architecture Record* article, and therefore kept form and color simple, as opposed to "the special treatments usually given to rooms designed for a given purpose." To the sleek spareness of the place he added discrete sculptural elements, notably carved blocks of wood by artist Edgar Miller, which lent vitality and "humanistic logic," Rebori said.

Clearly Rebori's heart lay with the modern, even though his usual, big-money commissions were of a more traditional type. Modernism remained an architectural ideal that was seldom realized in 1930s Chicago. "From the point of view of what may be termed organic, as contrasted with mere functional mechanisms, it can be said that modern architecture is not yet a reality," Rebori wrote. "It is only a potentiality in process of being discerned, sought, and practically and occasionally attained."

CROW ISLAND SCHOOL

Although pragmatism defined much American architecture of the 1930s, a streak of idealism had persisted at least since the Progressive Era. It certainly underlay the Crow Island School—an important example of what might be termed "Euro-American modernism." The project was a collaboration between the Finnish-born Eliel Saarinen (1873–1950), his son Eero (1910–1961), and the Chicago firm of Perkins and Will. Lyrical in some ways and utterly practical in others, Crow Island School was widely published and influenced school design for at least a generation.

The project, completed in 1940, was in the North Shore suburb of Winnetka, which had an extremely advanced school system at the time. Its Winnetka Plan loosened strict separations between disciplines and between grades, and its visionary superintendent, Carleton Washburne, was determined that the school's facility embody its educational theories. To that end he hired the Saarinens, who had moved to Michigan after the Tribune Tower competition and were teaching at Cranbrook

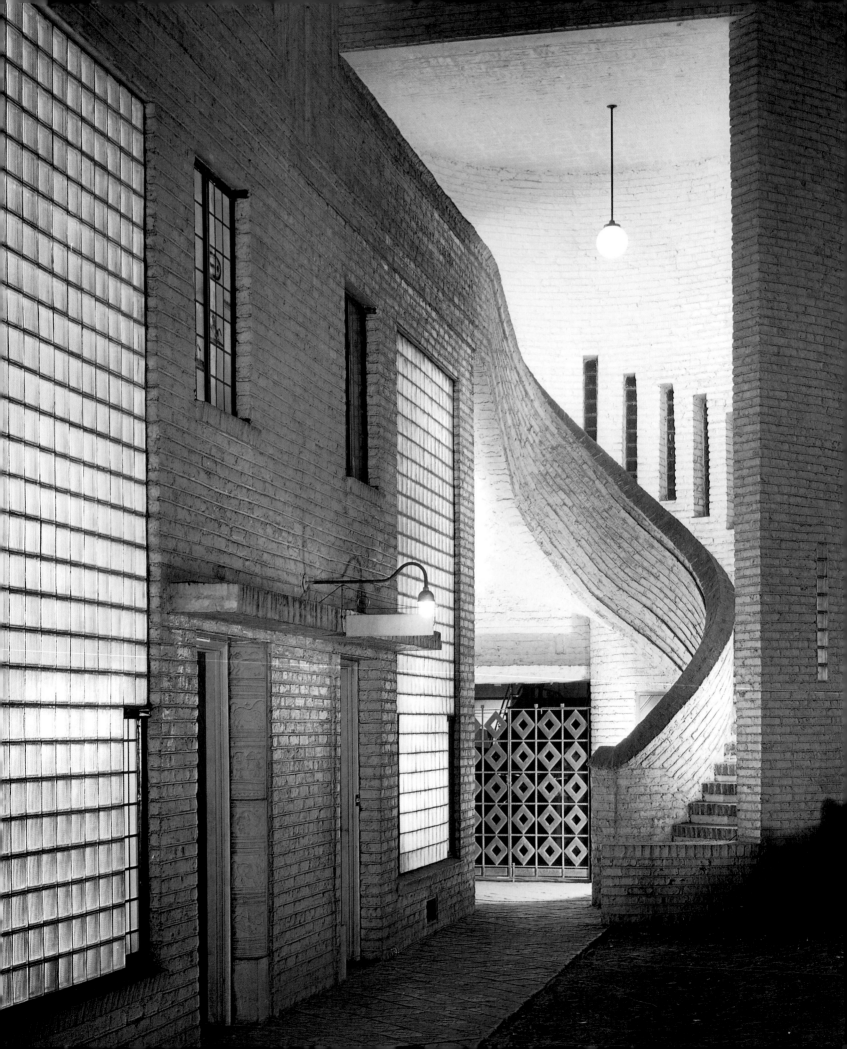

FRANK FISHER APARTMENTS

Rebori used abstract carvings and sculptural brickwork (opposite) to imbue his buildings with "humanistic logic," which he said softened the mechanistic spirit of modernism.

CROW ISLAND SCHOOL

1112 WILLOW ROAD, WINNETKA, ILL.
1940
ELIEL SAARINEN AND EERO SAARINEN WITH PERKINS AND WILL

The school (below) was to be a "beautiful, practical, homey, architectural embodiment of an educational philosophy," as the client put it. Its simplified geometric shape was International in style, but its organic materials and relation to its site hark back to the Prairie School.

Academy of Art. The Saarinens had also designed a new Cranbrook campus, mixing the formal, straight-line modernism of Europe with a warmth and a connection to the site akin to the traditions of Midwestern architecture.

Like Prairie School designs of decades past, Crow Island was built low to the ground and emphasized local materials like brick and wood. The school, which remains in operation, opens out on its wooded site in many places; other features reflect the ideas of organic architecture more subtly. Intentionally, the design was not to "seem complete and finished beyond any addition or adjustment to later demands," a school administrator involved in the project wrote in *Architectural Forum*. A sense of craftwork was desirable, but it did not have to be overly sophisticated for an elementary school. The simple brickwork and the molded plywood furniture (designed by the architects) were meant to "form a harmonious background with honest child effort and creation—not one which will make children's work seem crude." The Crow Island School was to meet not just the aesthetic needs of the site but the psychological needs of the children inside.

MIES IN CHICAGO

Mies had already emerged as one of Europe's premier architects in the 1930s, but his greatest triumphs were to come in America and mostly in Chicago, where he moved in 1938 to head the School of Architecture at Armour (now Illinois) Institute of Technology.

He had left Germany with regret. Even as Nazi influence rose, Mies had tried to carve a role for himself. Despite political pressures from conservatives who deemed avant-garde art subversive, he had supervised the Bauhaus, Europe's polestar of modern design, for three years, until Hitler closed the school for good in 1933. Although evidence suggests that Mies attempted a personal truce with the government, ultimately the Nazis tagged modern architecture "degenerate," and he was unable to work in his own country.

At the same time, he was fascinated by the United States. Compared to Germany at the time it was aesthetically free and obviously in the thrall of new and powerful technology. He was excited by the abundance of steel and its use in large buildings. It is no exaggeration to say that Mies came to discover more in the possibilities of the metal frame than any architect since William Le Baron Jenney. Mies's work in Chicago opened the door to the proliferation of steel and glass towers and the transformation of skylines around the world.

In some ways, Chicago was a natural place for Mies to call home. He had studied Chicago School architecture, as all European modernists had, and admired how well it suited its day and age. "We must learn to work with technology, using the materials of our time," Mies once said. "All of Chicago was created in the spirit of the technological age." His own work had other affinities to Chicago's architectural heritage—not only the Wrightian concept of space and interest in materials, but a Sullivanesque emphasis on unadorned structure and powerful forms. "Mies van der Rohe's skyscraper apartments revive the tradition of the Chicago School of the 1880s," wrote Sigfried Giedion in 1963.

Mies's relocation to the city brought into clear focus the connections between European modernism and Chicago architecture, and the brilliance of the work he did there lent Chicago the mystical aura of an architectural hallowed ground. But his approach also indisputably diverged from the Chicago School before him. In contrast to Sullivan's assertion that "Form ever follows function," Mies declared: "We refuse to recognize problems of form, only problems of building. Form is not the aim of our work, but only the result." Even superficial differences between the two architects are telling. Sullivan idealized the pastoral, Thoreauesque world; Mies embraced the ethos of industry. Sullivan loved handwork, in the spirit of Ruskin; Mies loved the effect of machines, as taught by the Bauhaus. And in his doctrinaire approach to his buildings, Mies makes even the famously unyielding Sullivan seem forgiving and flexible.

And despite his admiration for and stylistic links to the city, it was by no means preordained that Mies would settle there. He had received his first overture to emigrate from Joseph Hudnut, dean of the architecture faculty at Harvard, in 1936. Mies had hoped to accept a position at the university, but withdrew his name when he discovered Harvard was vacillating on his appointment. Indeed, bringing such a stark modernist to the ivied precincts of New England would have been an interesting experiment—perhaps too interesting for Harvard, which balked.

Illinois Institute of Technology (I.I.T.) had no such misgivings. Its school of architecture was largely unformed and needed a leader. They found in Mies an architect of strong ideas and a willingness to transmit them to students. And in Chicago Mies found a city that offered clear advantages to his own work. He was attracted above all by its long tradition of openness to innovation, certainly more so than in Eastern cities, which were still tied to the beaux arts. "Mies loved the power and clarity of Chicago buildings," said architect Myron Goldsmith, who worked for Mies in the 1940s and went on to a distinguished career at Skidmore, Owings and Merrill. "Chicago gave Mies courage." On a more practical level, the steel mills near the city provided a convenient and relatively inexpensive source of the material that would distinguish his postwar buildings.

Mies's courage was matched by that of the forward-looking clients he found in Chicago. First in this group was Herbert Greenwald, a developer who was just twenty-nine years old when they began their collaboration in 1946. The architectural history of Chicago, and of other American cities, might have been far different without Greenwald, who had left rabbinical studies to enter real estate (and who would die tragically in a plane crash in

1958). With a notion to build large apartment towers, Greenwald sought to form a relationship with an architect of international renown. Mies was on his list, as were Wright and Le Corbusier, and Greenwald was surprised to learn that Mies was already in Chicago. Upon meeting, the developer and architect found that Greenwald's philosophical training put him on equal footing with Mies's abstract "t'inking," as Mies described the most important part of his work. It was Greenwald who enabled the esoteric Mies to build the first of his great glass apartment buildings and to become America's—and the world's—preeminent high-rise architect.

Glass towers were considered risky business in the late 1940s. No one knew whether people would rent apartments with transparent walls dozens of stories above the street. In fact, they did. Many city dwellers were instantly attracted to the sense of light and space and left their darker, heavily draped, traditional interiors behind. They also appreciated the unconventional grace in Mies's buildings. He was a master of detail and proportion, and even his earliest apartment buildings showed how a structure made entirely of steel and glass could please the eye in surprising ways. For example, the side-by-side towers that Mies designed and Greenwald developed in 1952 at 860–880 North Lake Shore Drive became famous—among the public for their glassy walls, and among architects for the structural I-beams that run up the outside of the buildings from the bottom to the top. These unadorned steel courses function indispensably as braces against wind and mullions for glass panels, and Mies ingeniously made them decorative as well. They give the exterior a subtle touch of three-dimensionality that would have been missing with a sheer curtain wall.

While Greenwald is remembered as a businessman who supported innovative architecture, Mies was an artist whose work corresponded with business objectives. Indeed, Mies was motivated in fundamental ways by economics. Flexible floor plans, for example, were an almost universal attribute of steel construction, a lesson first understood by the old Chicago School. So Mies designed the skeleton frame with a core for utilities down the center of the building, leaving the remainder of each floor open. Apartments could be divided into various sizes as the need arose. "To Mies, that was the sign of a good building, to maintain flexibility," said Joe Fujikawa, who worked on 860–880. "He always said that the ways we use buildings constantly change. The reason they tear buildings down is that they have outlived their usefulness."

Mies's interest in flexibility evolved into a concept known as "universal space." The idea sprang from the basic attributes of the architect's material—the great strength of structural steel allows construction of spaces that are entirely flexible, with no need for interior bearing walls or supports that would impede the inner space. While Mies's European career focused on the geometry of interconnecting rooms, in America it was the single, large, unencumbered interior that fascinated him—as did the potential to expand universal space to the exterior and into infinity by the use of transparent glass walls. Mies's finest examples of universal space can produce an almost supernatural calm, yet his intention was to be entirely practical as well.

Witness Crown Hall, which was built to house I.I.T.'s architecture and design schools. As Mies's biographer Franz Schulze explained, Crown Hall was the modern equivalent of the medieval *Bauhutte* (masons' guildhall), a place large enough that the master builder could work within view of apprentices and tradesmen at all times. For a school the idea is admirable. In one universal space, students in different classes and at various levels can separate themselves for lectures, drafting, model building, and other activities. Yet they can experience interaction, cross-germination, and creativity born of being in the same place.

860–880 NORTH LAKE SHORE DRIVE
INTERIORS BY POWELL/KLEINSCHMIDT
1985–89

Miesian design inspired interiors at 860–880 long after the buildings rose. Homes with open plans define "rooms" by screens and art, or merely by architectural geometry. Following pages: When the towers went up, it was unclear whether people would opt to live with walls of glass at vertiginous heights, but floor-to-ceiling views quickly became de rigueur for Chicago's best real estate. A sense of universal space makes the relatively small apartments feel uncrowded.

THE MEANING OF MIES AND THE RISE OF MODERNISM

CROWN HALL AT ILLINOIS
INSTITUTE OF TECHNOLOGY

3360 SOUTH STATE STREET

1956

LUDWIG MIES VAN DER ROHE

Crown Hall (below) was Mies's
most important experiment
in universal space and one of
Chicago's most unexpectedly
beautiful buildings. The steel
trusses surmounting the roof free
the hall of interior supports.
Here Mies created a *Bauhutte*
(opposite, above), where students,
artisans, and masters could
work in groups large or small.

ILLINOIS INSTITUTE OF
TECHNOLOGY CHAPEL

3200 SOUTH STATE STREET

1956

LUDWIG MIES VAN DER ROHE

The chapel (opposite, below)
demonstrates how fine brick and
a floor-to-ceiling curtain wall can
inspire contemplation.

People at I.I.T. disagree whether the *Bauhutte* idea really works, but the building itself is flexible enough for any use. Crown Hall's interior is entirely free of supporting members, allowing for easy division of space. Beyond its great unencumbered size, the hall's barely visible but precise sense of proportion—in the gridwork of the ceiling and the rhythm of its glass wall panels—make it well suited to temporary division. Such subtle, masterful details cue small groups or even individuals to feel the intimacy of a much smaller place. The universal space is shared, but "rooms" are implied.

To experience Crown Hall is to understand implied space and transparent divisions as the crux of Mies's art. It is also to realize that the building that appears to be the most minimal is actually the most complex, the embodiment of a simple concept that is difficult, perhaps impossible, for most to master. Miesian architecture required not only an understanding of materials and function, but also Mies's almost spiritual command of the way people perceive space.

The Trial of Farnsworth House

While Mies was the most esoteric of artists, architecture is a practical art, so unsurprisingly he had his share of clashes with the real world. Such a conflict related to one of his masterpieces, the 1951 Farnsworth House, an exquisite glass and steel home he designed for an acquaintance, Dr. Edith Farnsworth. What began as a wonderful collaboration between architect and client ended with Mies's dismissal from the job before the interior was complete. Farnsworth also sued Mies, unsuccessfully, for a variety of sins, including cost overruns and even alleged incompetence.

No one knows precisely what happened to make the Farnsworth commission a case for the court. There are convincing suggestions of a romantic relationship between Mies and Dr. Farnsworth, a prominent Chicago physician. When the affair went sour, the story goes, the client fired her architect. Fortunately the structural design had been executed before the break, whatever its cause. In spite of the unpleasantness, Farnsworth House can be counted among America's architectural

Mies combined glass, steel, and travertine with a sense of classical proportion to create a building as suited to its site as the trees and gentle rise in the land (preceding pages). It has been described as a glazed box floating on a steel frame—and, reduced to its essence, it really does seem to float (opposite). Mies had contemplated a new line of furniture for Farnsworth House, but pieces he previously designed suit its spirit (above).

landmarks. But the history of this famous building, on the Fox River in tiny Plano, Illinois, also testifies to the fragility of the architectural process, at least a process as refined as that practiced by Mies.

People who worked on Farnsworth House have said that Dr. Farnsworth, a highly intelligent and cultured woman, was well aware of what she was getting in a Mies van der Rohe house. That might be an overstatement, given that the house is widely considered the apotheosis of Mies's concept of universal space and therefore unprecedented. But Myron Goldsmith, an apprentice to Mies at the time of construction, insisted that Dr. Farnsworth was enthusiastic about the house from the beginning; she even made picnics for everyone working on the site.

The client seemed to agree with the architects and others who were present when the steel frame went up—it was simple but stunning in its rectangular, almost pristinely classical proportions. As the glass walls enclosed the structure, all witnessed the magic of universal space being created. Well before Farnsworth House was finished, people working under Mies recognized that it might be the most intense expression of modern architecture ever built. They had reason to assume that the client was happy.

In the end, she was not. The reasons were never clear, but the outcome was all too real. Mies was unable to finish the project and others did the interior design. Myron Goldsmith said that Mies had discussed ideas for the

FARNSWORTH HOUSE

Utilitarian touches do not detract
from the house's monumentality or
spoil its elegance inside and out.

furniture, including an intriguing one for chairs uphol-
stered with untanned leather to offer soft roughness;
he was also mulling plastic furniture. Goldsmith pointed
out that Mies's office was not then set up to design furniture, so perhaps he would have been satisfied with the
Barcelona chairs and other old designs that a later owner
installed. But the pieces Dr. Farnsworth chose for herself—modern, blond wood furniture from Italy—were by
no means what the architect would have selected.

The overriding issue between Mies and his client was not
taste, however, but fees. Toward the end of the project,
Goldsmith recalled, Farnsworth mentioned in passing
that she did not know how much Mies would be charging
for his services. Goldsmith was taken aback but gave no
reply. When Farnsworth later battled one of the world's
most famous architects in a five-week trial in a tiny rural
courtroom, it was the overruns and unexpected bills that
commanded the judge's attention.

The case revolved around how much Mies had said the
place would cost, when he said it, and whether or not
the price was guaranteed. Mies finally won the suit,
based on the customary rules governing the relationship
between architect and client, which hold that architects
can provide only estimates. But a small detail, which
architect Paul Schweikher mentioned years later in an
interview, is telling. Schweikher had served as expert
witness in the case on behalf of Mies. Just before the
trial, Mies told him that he found a "notation with
Edith." It was a piece of paper that stated, apparently
before construction began, that projected costs for
the house were only an estimate.

Schweikher was careful not to vouch for the truth of
Mies's story. Nor was this "notation" submitted as critical evidence in the case. But the tale has a deeply symbolic aspect, as Mies supposedly found the slip of paper
when paging through a book of German philosophy.
Schweikher remembered it as being one by Friedrich
Nietzsche, to whom Mies was devoted. Nietzsche celebrated the self-mastering superman *(Übermensch)* and
believed creativity and passion could free individuals
from the bonds of everyday life. The irony was that Mies
may have been reading Nietzsche when he lost track of
a simple document that might have helped resolve an all-
too-earthbound misunderstanding with a willful client.

CHAPTER 6

MODERN AND POSTMODERN CHICAGO

In the 1960s and 1970s, as firms like Skidmore, Owings and Merrill pushed the technical limits of skyscrapers beyond anything Mies had devised, it became increasingly difficult to detect the human hand behind the design. In previous generations significant buildings were firmly associated with individual architects, who made known the sources of their creative inspiration: Louis Sullivan claimed kinship with Walt Whitman; Mies invoked Saint Thomas Aquinas. But now the architect of the moment was a company, not a person, and its buildings, including Sears Tower and John Hancock, were recognized more for their engineering than their art.

Skidmore, Owings and Merrill (S.O.M.) drew its inspiration from the businesslike tenor of its times, and its pragmatic direction was set by individuals who were as passionate in their own way as their more romantic predecessors. First among them was Louis Skidmore (1897–1962), who began his career during the depression. It was a bad time for architects, and Skidmore was lucky to be made chief designer of the 1933 Century of Progress, Chicago's second great world's fair. Conceived more as a technological fantasy than a mere trade show, the fair was developed with strict architectural standards, which Skidmore was responsible for enforcing. He approved designs that achieved the futuristic theme—Keck's House of Tomorrow among them—and turned

down others that fell short. The rakish young architect was not cowed by the rich and powerful; among his rejects was a forty-five-foot pyramid of vinegar bottles, the proposed pavilion of H. J. Heinz Company. John Heinz himself stormed, "Who is this wax mustache bozo in the raccoon coat and earmuffs who turned down my display?" But Skidmore held his ground, which earned him more admiration than enmity. He went on to build a firm with major offices in Chicago, New York, and San Francisco that would change the look of corporate America.

Skidmore became his era's equivalent of Daniel Burnham. Both were central figures in world's fairs; both excelled more at salesmanship and organization than design. And just as many Daniel H. Burnham & Company buildings were more profitable than aesthetically inspired, S.O.M. produced quite a few buildings that were noted more for their mammoth size than their ability to stir souls. Yet some Burnham buildings became Chicago icons, and it would be equally hard to think of modern Chicago architecture without S.O.M.'s most important skyscrapers.

INLAND'S STAINLESS IMAGE
The story of S.O.M.'s influence on Chicago architecture begins with the Inland Steel Building, which was com-

INLAND STEEL BUILDING

S.O.M.'s Davis Allen designed stainless steel furniture for Inland Steel's offices; some of it, like his steel mesh chairs, became classics. The building's clear-span interior gives designers flexibility and freedom to divide offices using glass partitions. Art and sculpture from the Block family collection also served to define space in these pleasant, light-filled interiors.

pleted in 1958. It was only the second major new office building in downtown Chicago since the depression and seemed to soar with enormous pent-up energy. At nineteen stories the Inland Steel Building was hardly vertiginous, but its technology and styling—its function and form—pushed modern architecture's bold defiance of gravity several steps forward. It quickly became a milestone in the development of the twentieth-century skyscraper.

Among Inland Steel's innovations is that the building contains clear-span space on each story; narrow steel columns around the perimeter provide support, allowing utterly free and open interiors. In effect, the Inland Steel Building is a vertical manifestation of universal space, advancing the concept a step farther than Mies did by shifting the mechanical core of elevators and stairwells from the center to the side; the result turned out to be as practical for the clients as it was interesting to the architects involved. And while S.O.M.'s treatment of building materials was not driven by philosophical concerns, as Mies's seemed to be, the stainless steel cladding made a striking exterior and also a kind of billboard for an important product sold by the company doing business inside.

Stainless steel is used throughout the interior of Inland Steel as well. It was in fact the interiors that drew the most attention when the building was completed, and the story of their design testifies again to the importance of rapport between architect and client. Inland Steel was then run by Leigh Block, who with his wife, Mary, first imagined a modern corporate headquarters. There

were not many at the time, though New York's Lever House, built by S.O.M. in 1952, was bringing Lever Brothers considerable recognition beyond its stature in the soap industry. By 1956 the Blocks had settled on the structural design for the Inland building, but the interior was not yet planned when they left for a vacation that would take them to Istanbul. As S.O.M. was then working on the Istanbul Hilton, Louis Skidmore asked his man there to look in on his clients when they arrived. That was architect Davis Allen (1916–1999), who took the Blocks on a whirlwind tour of the city—lunch with the British ambassador and yachting on the Bosphorus. He also invited them for a look at his work on the interior of the Hilton, a design later described by S.O.M. partner Nathaniel Owings as "a salubrious blend of strong Turkish architectural motifs and American plumbing and heating." In fact, Allen had done what would become increasingly important in modern architecture. He gave otherwise plain modernist buildings distinct and memorable touches. The Blocks wanted Allen to do the same for Inland Steel in Chicago.

When he arrived in Chicago, Allen had several luxuries to work with in the Inland Steel tower. One was the space, entirely free of interior columns. The other was the Blocks' interest in purchasing large-scale modern art, which came to include works by Alexander Calder, Willem de Kooning, Harry Bertoia, and Seymour Lipton. Selections such as those provided considerable inspiration for Allen, who designed a refined but thoroughly modern environment for the company. "They didn't want any of that pseudo-Chippendale baloney," Allen said of the Blocks. Instead they chose furniture designed by

JOHN HANCOCK CENTER

875 NORTH MICHIGAN AVENUE

1968

SKIDMORE, OWINGS AND MERRILL

John Hancock's diagonal braces represented an innovative engineering solution. The building (opposite) tapers to provide large floor plates for the offices on lower floors and smaller ones for the apartments above. While meeting many such practical needs, the design was also a great artistic success. The exposed braces were even desirable design features for the interiors, as seen in the residential lobby on the forty-fourth floor (above left). Above right: A living room in the building, circa 1969.

modernists like Mies van der Rohe and Georg Jensen; they also encouraged Allen to design furnishings and office suites that were as original as the building itself.

Allen created elegant office furnishings from utilitarian materials, and many of the pieces became classics. For executive offices he designed lounge chairs of industrial-grade steel mesh. The boardroom table, known as "the surfboard," was accompanied by leather-upholstered chairs on slender, slightly splayed steel legs. Allen also designed the so-called tin desk for midlevel Inland offices, and its sleek, economical design quickly was adopted by Steelcase, the company that manufactured it, as a trademark product. Inland's was one of the first interiors to be integrated so completely with modernist architecture on such a large scale. "What was true outside became true inside," remarked Allen. Handsome inside and out, Inland Steel convincingly blended design, technology, and corporate image making. Other companies, including Chase Manhattan Bank in New York, would follow Inland Steel's lead by hiring S.O.M. to design sleek urban monuments for them too.

JOHN HANCOCK, SEARS TOWER, AND THE "EFFECTS OF SCALE"

S.O.M.'s success in the two decades that followed was unprecedented. The firm became the leading candidate to design countless corporate headquarters, apartment buildings, college campuses, and other large-scale works. In many ways, S.O.M. was in the right place at the right time. Founded in 1936, it was on the ascent in the 1950s, and its surge coincided with one of the largest economic expansions in history. By the 1960s the firm's vision and capacity corresponded perfectly with the needs of many large American companies—including Sears, Roebuck and John Hancock Insurance—which likewise were growing.

Primary credit for the designs of both Sears Tower and John Hancock Center was shared by architect Bruce Graham and engineer Fazlur Khan. But in S.O.M.'s corporate spirit of teamwork, other architects and engineers assumed important roles as well. Among them was architect-engineer Myron Goldsmith (1918–1996), whose early career included stints with Mies and Pier Luigi Nervi, an Italian innovator of curvilinear modernist forms. In 1952 Goldsmith completed a master's thesis at I.I.T., "The Effects of Scale," which examined the idea that structures of different size have different ideal forms— from Gothic cathedrals in Europe to nineteenth-century railroad sheds to early Chicago skyscrapers. Goldsmith went on to theorize about ideal forms for buildings not yet built and proposed a system of diagonal trusses as the optimal and most economical design for a steel-framed skyscraper of unprecedented height.

One result of his engineering insights was John Hancock Center, completed in 1968, which became one of the world's most recognizable modern skyscrapers. Based on Goldsmith's theories and S.O.M.'s exhaustive calculations, the crisscrossed trusses of the ninety-seven-story skyscraper not only proved practical—they reduced the amount of steel needed to support such a building, saving millions of dollars—they also contributed to a

SEARS TOWER

233 SOUTH WACKER DRIVE

1974

SKIDMORE, OWINGS AND MERRILL

America's tallest building demonstrates that mammoth modernism can be elegant. Sears Tower's engineering feat was its steel-tube construction, but it also drew from Art Deco skyscrapers and setbacks that maximize natural light. While its modern profile is inspiring from a distance, street-level modifications beginning in the early 1980s provided a more welcoming approach. S.O.M. designed the vaulted steel entrance on Wacker Drive.

unique form, a tapering tower rising effortlessly toward the clouds.

Unusual engineering solutions likewise contributed to the ultimate effect at the 110-story Sears Tower, completed in 1974 and the world's tallest building until 1997, when the Petrona Towers in Kuala Lumpur took the lead. The brashly original concept for Sears began with Fazlur Khan's engineering of the building as a cluster of nine vertical sections, rectangular steel tubes that were mutually supporting and largely free of interior columns. Bruce Graham's architectural scheme raised the tubes to various heights, creating setbacks in the building's profile and celebrating, not concealing, the underlying principle of the tower's structure. (The story is that Graham found inspiration for the design in the cigarettes

protruding from a new pack of Lucky Strikes.) In both Sears Tower and John Hancock, form marries function; architecture and engineering are inextricable. Among the economic features designed into both buildings are large work spaces in the lower stories to meet the needs of one class of occupant, and increasingly narrow, light-filled, and expensive floors as the buildings rise.

McCORMICK PLACE

One of the reasons for Skidmore, Owings and Merrill's success was its skillful rapport with good clients. Not all successful buildings, however, have been blessed by inspired clients and positive working relationships. An example was McCormick Place, a project that overcame catastrophe, politics, and indecision on a scale that would have scrubbed many projects. Design of present-

McCORMICK PLACE

22ND STREET AND LAKE MICHIGAN

1971

C. F. MURPHY AND ASSOCIATES

Several designs for the convention
center were scrapped before the
simplest, most Miesian of schemes
was approved. Gene Summers's
design is a masterwork of proportion on Chicago's lakefront.
The seventy-foot-wide overhangs
all around the center enhance
the sense of indoor-outdoor space.

McCORMICK PLACE ADDITION

1989

SKIDMORE, OWINGS AND MERRILL

S.O.M.'s addition to the esteemed
convention center (above and
following pages) used cable trusses
as rooftop supports, maximizing the
interior spans.

day McCormick Place, on Lake Michigan, began in
1969, almost immediately after the previous McCormick
Place exposition hall burned to the ground. Mayor
Richard J. Daley asked the firm of C. F. Murphy Associates to plan a new one at once. Daley's choice of firms
was predictable. C. F. Murphy was considered "palace
architect" to his administration, and most of the city's
important public work was sent its way.

The following day a partner from the Murphy office
called a young architect by the name of Gene Summers
(b. 1928), inviting him to join the firm and undertake
the design of McCormick Place. It was a tempting pro-
posal for Summers, who had recently begun his own
practice after working for Mies van der Rohe. The building's lakefront site was stupendous. It was an opportunity to create interior space on an unprecedented scale.
But Summers, determined to build his own business,
initially was uninterested.

Still, he listened to the Murphy offer over lunch at the
Arts Club, and at the end said he would consider it only
under conditions he himself regarded as outrageous.
The firm would have to make him a ten percent partner,
and to name him director of design for the entire practice, not just the McCormick Place project. Summers
returned to his office assuming the matter was finished,
but the next day the firm's venerable chief, Charles
Murphy, called to finalize a deal. So began an architectural marriage that was, at least initially, mismatched
and troubled.

C. F. Murphy Associates' history stretched back to 1911,
when Charles F. Murphy, a nonarchitect from Chicago's
South Side, was hired as a typist at Daniel H. Burnham
& Company. Burnham died a year later, and Murphy
joined its successor firm, Graham, Anderson, Probst and
White, becoming personal assistant to Ernest R. Graham.
Graham died in 1936, and Murphy fell out with his

heirs. But having studied at night to get an architecture degree, he went off with two partners to start a new firm, Shaw, Naess and Murphy (later Naess and Murphy). The firm grew slowly until 1955, when it designed the Prudential Building, the first major building in or adjacent to the Loop since the depression and, for more than a decade, the city's tallest. A few years later the firm's fortunes soared with its design for Chicago's Central District Water Filtration Plant. This project, in a parklike setting alongside Lake Michigan, was no architectural masterpiece, but Murphy's execution of the unobtrusive facility overcame much political resistance from lakefront defenders, for which Mayor Daley was eternally grateful. A long string of public commissions followed— a few of architectural merit. The largest of them was O'Hare Airport, completed in 1963.

Summers, for his part, was an anomaly at the Murphy firm—he was more artist than political insider. His first job in architecture was working on the interior core of Mies's Farnsworth House. He later became lead designer and supervisor on several buildings late in Mies's career, including Die Neue Nationalgallerie (New National Gallery) in Berlin, completed in 1968. When Summers set out to practice on his own, his idea was to have a small office much like that of Mies, a famously deliberate thinker who never hurried to solve creative problems. Perhaps hoping to cultivate a similar environment for the McCormick Place commission, Summers asked Mies to collaborate. "Not if it was the Parthenon on the Acropolis," replied Mies, who had once designed a convention hall, never built, for Chicago. He was near the end of his career. He also knew Chicago politics. Summers was on his own.

The project seemed star-crossed from the start, Summers later recalled. Problems began when the general manager of the city's convention authority insisted that the

MODERN AND POSTMODERN CHICAGO

HAID RESIDENCE

MICHIGAN AVENUE, EVANSTON, ILL.

1968

DAVID HAID

Haid was Mies's attentive student and employee in the 1950s. His work calls to mind something Mies once said: "Building has obviously less to do with the invention of new forms than with the organization in a construction of the clearly defined relationship between things." Haid's own one-story home, International in style, sits comfortably in a neighborhood of grander Queen Annes.

HAID RESIDENCE

A subsequent owner of Haid's house renovated it in 2001. The interior design by Powell/ Kleinschmidt demonstrated the building's timelessness and flexibility. Good Miesian design adapted easily to an infusion of color and a judicious mix of the modern and traditional.

new building be a multistory structure. The rationale eluded those involved in the project, but Summers obeyed—resulting in an initial scheme for the building that was panned by everyone who saw it. Summers was embarrassed but gamely went back to the drawing board. The second scheme was more representative of Summers's modernist work: a large universal space beneath a bridgelike structure with suspension cables overhead. Drawings show a handsome design, which won considerable praise from architects as well the convention and tourism industry. But one feature drew the ire of Henry Crown, a powerful Chicago philanthropist: Summers had downsized and placed underground the theater that in the original McCormick Place had been named for Arie Crown, Henry's father. The plan was scuttled.

Discouraged and by now under considerable time constraints, Summers made a third, less original attempt—

a giant pavilion with proportions similar to the Berlin museum's. It was a Miesian design grown to mammoth size, and it worked practically, artistically, and politically. Structurally, it was made possible by an innovative truss system worked out by Summers's associate on the project, Helmut Jahn, an I.I.T. alumnus; the system provided ample interior space for large conventions. Its expansive glass walls and seventy-foot overhangs allowed McCormick Place to take advantage of its lakefront site and views, among its greatest charms; an indoor-outdoor feeling was enhanced by an open sight line from the entrance through the building and out over the lake. The design even muted public criticism from dissenters who lobbied for a lakefront without buildings. McCormick Place remains a serene piece of architecture that tends to ennoble, not destroy, its stretch of lakefront. Ultimately, Miesian architecture needs no further justification than McCormick Place.

LAKE POINT TOWER

GRAND AVENUE AT LAKE SHORE DRIVE
1968
SCHIPPOREIT-HENRICH ASSOCIATES

Still one of Chicago's most desirable high-rise residences, Lake Point Tower typifies architectural design conceived from the inside out. The structure's central supporting column and utilities core free the surrounding interior space to be divided at will. The curvaceous three-leaf floor plate assures the best possible views and a distinctive exterior. In plan, Lake Point Tower achieved a modernist ideal—clear, simple structure and open, flexible space.

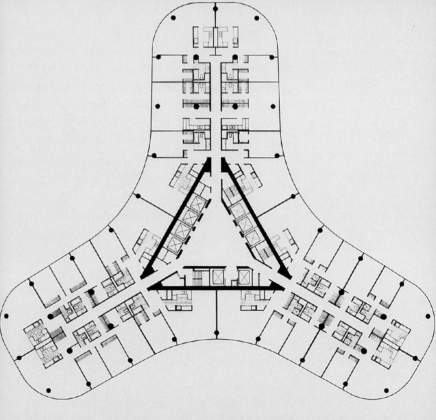

COMPOSITE FLOOR PLAN

THE HERETICS: BERTRAND GOLDBERG AND HARRY WEESE

In the 1950s and 1960s the glass and steel rectangles
of the International style dominated new architecture,
and most architects of large-scale buildings scarcely
dared consider an alternative. A few, however, saw the
world differently. One of them was Bertrand Goldberg
(1913–1997), a Chicagoan who had studied at the
Bauhaus for a year when Mies headed it. Goldberg
returned to America in 1933, just before the Nazis shut-
tered the school. He was deeply influenced by what he
learned in Europe, especially the overarching lesson that
new materials should lead to new architectural form—
the Miesian postulate. Goldberg differed, however, in
that he believed the great diversity of modern building
technologies rendered any kind of orthodoxy moot. In
a career that extended fifty years, mostly in Chicago,
Goldberg consistently renounced the German master's
somber intellectualism and followed his own path.

Early in his career, Goldberg worked in the office of Keck
and Keck, which must have fed his taste for innovation.
He also grew interested in prefabrication, an idea that
had guided the Kecks since the House of Tomorrow at
the 1933 world's fair. After establishing his own practice,
one of Goldberg's first commissions was for a 1938
prototype for a chain of ice cream shops called North

Pole. The result was a mast-hung structure, with a central post supporting a roof by tension wires and glass
panels suspended from the roof line. Without the usual
columns at the periphery, the structure seemed almost
to float. The shop was designed to be disassembled
and moved with ease, allowing the ice cream business
to follow the warm weather and prompting Goldberg or
someone close to him to call the prototype "a building
on wheels."

The North Pole's instant charm demonstrated Goldberg's
dedication to the Miesian notion that pure function led
to architectural beauty. Yet no avowed modernist could
have developed more differently from Mies. For the next
two decades, Goldberg followed no doctrine, using
pressed metal, plywood, masonry, and other materials
in addition to the modernist's classic glass and steel. He
built houses. He did interiors. He even designed kitchen
and bathroom systems that saved space and could supposedly be moved and installed with ease. He developed
an original, uncategorizable style, exemplified by his
most famous masterpiece, Marina City.

Planning for Marina City began in 1959 and was based
on a program to bring people back to the inner city they
had been fleeing for years. Financed largely by the union
of building janitors and elevator operators—whose liveli-

hood depended upon the central city's vitality—Goldberg's plan was initially driven by economic and political factors. Success meant overcoming not just "white flight" from Chicago but also zoning laws that then prohibited mixed-use projects, with apartments, retail, recreation, and office space in the same building. Goldberg later said that such laws were part of a "Marxist" conception of cities that segregated commercial, residential, office, cultural, and recreational districts. Goldberg was able to convince city officials to modify zoning impediments, but convincing people to return to the city was largely up to him.

The architect's challenge was to restore a sense of neighborhood—and to find a new approach for doing so. The overriding tendency of the day was to build pristine, Miesian towers—theoretically perfect buildings—that were isolated from rather than integrated with other buildings, often by forbidding plazas or uninviting parkland. The doctrinaire Mies had acknowledged that people would have to "learn" to live in his buildings—an idea Goldberg found distasteful. "I am not trying to modify society through architecture," he once said. "I am trying to reflect society through architecture."

Goldberg's concern for human beings appeared to be a part of his nature; his finding a way to serve their needs, however, came only with trial and error. Marina City's first scheme, for example, barely resembled the landmark it would become: It showed a pair of rectilinear towers rising over a complex of buildings close to the ground. When Goldberg discerned that two squarish high-rises would have been crowded on the three-and-a-half acre site and, most important, would have blocked each other's views, he rethought the plan. His solution, which actually reduced the total number of apartments, was two round towers that have been variously described as corncobs and grain silos. A central core provides services, as well as structural stability, and allows the apartments surrounding it—like kernels around a cob—to have unimpeded views.

Goldberg may or may not have had agriculture in mind when he was designing, but he later enjoyed the comparison, saying that the loss of grain elevators in downtown Chicago at the turn of the century marked the end of the river as a working thoroughfare and the beginning of "the confusion of the American city." That confusion was what he sought to rectify with Marina City, at that point

NORTH POLE ICE CREAM PARLOR
RIVER FOREST, ILL.

1938

BERTRAND GOLDBERG

Goldberg, who studied at the Bauhaus, made an early break from the sober dictates of German modernism. Back in America, he executed his commission for a prototype ice cream shop with a central column and cable supports—an adaptation of ideas exhibited a few years before at the Century of Progress.

MARINA CITY

300 NORTH STATE STREET

1961

BERTRAND GOLDBERG

Marina City still defines the neighborhood, although in 1973 it
acquired a distinguished neighbor,
Mies's IBM Building (seen to the
right). Goldberg was ahead of his
time in defying buildings' rectilinearity and in using reinforced
concrete when most urban towers
were framed in steel.

his largest project. In addition to the two sixty-story apartment towers, Goldberg incorporated a theater, a gym, the marina, stores, a swimming pool, a skating rink, a bowling alley, and two commercial buildings into the Marina City complex—all in an effort to reintegrate the city's many functions and create a lively community.

Silos or no, Marina City's form went against the grain of Mies's modernist rectangle; it also rebelled against the classic steel frame. Instead, Goldberg used concrete, producing the world's tallest reinforced concrete building at the time. Concrete may have lacked steel's elegance, but it was cheaper and more suitable for a project designed not just for wealthy cliff dwellers but also for teachers, office workers, and urban professionals. Only later did Goldberg realize that he could apply the plasticity of concrete to his work in general. Goldberg's subsequent buildings, including his last major project in Chicago, the 1986 River City mixed-use development, executed what he called a "geocentric" plan. The term described a system in which curvilinear structures provided residents with places to live, work, and converge naturally in communal spaces. "I was revolting against a century of static space, against the straight line, against the idea of a man made in the image of a machine," he explained.

Another Chicagoan who revolted against the dictates of the square box was Harry Weese (1915–1998). Born in Evanston, Illinois, he attended Yale, graduated from M.I.T., then went to Cranbrook Academy of Art in Michigan, where Eliel Saarinen ran the graduate architecture program. Cranbrook was imbued with the Scandinavian love of crafts and taught an architecture that used a wide selection of materials, including brick, plywood, and metal—in almost direct opposition to Miesian theoretical perfection. Weese cleaved to no doctrine. Over a long career, his residences, his commercial high-rises, and his many other projects—including the Washington, D.C., Metro subway system—earned him a reputation as a heretic but also a humanist.

Influences on Weese were as varied as his results. He traveled extensively in Europe as a young man and later said an architect should see everything ever built before drawing a line. He had a lifelong interest in sailing and naval engineering, and he built boats as a hobby. "For Harry, boats were the ultimate testing ground for the strength of materials and the deployment of dynamic forces and natural elements," wrote his wife, the designer Kitty Baldwin Weese. He sailed often on Lake Michigan and found the well-being the activity bestowed inextricable from the structure of the craft.

When Weese opened his own office in 1947, after a stint at S.O.M., he applied modernist ideas pragmatically and selectively. Initially he built small, distinctive residences. His reputation soared with his designs of urban high-rises, such as the 1968 Time-Life Building in Chicago, with bronze-tinted glass that blazed brashly at sunrise and sunset. Other of his skyscrapers used an unorthodox geometry of triangles instead of rectangles, creating amenable spaces within, as did Weese's Metropolitan Correctional Center, completed in 1975. "If it is possible to design a high-security federal prison in a compassionate way, Weese has done it," wrote critic Allan Temko in a 1987 book on Weese's work. The box-defying triangular form maximizes perimeter space in relation to square footage, providing each cell an exterior window. The three-sided floor plan also allows for central open-cell areas that Temko likened to common rooms in a college dormitory.

EDWARD DART

Like Goldberg and Weese, Edward Dart (1922–1975) was an independent-thinking architect of the 1950s and 1960s who diverged from the predictable modernism of his time. Dart earned his reputation on smaller-scale projects, primarily residences and neighborhood churches, that he designed from the inside out, resulting in buildings with striking personality. Later he applied his interest in flowing interior space to large commercial structures, including Water Tower Place, a vertical, urban shopping mall.

Dart was a New Orleanian who graduated from Yale in 1949. At college he studied under a number of distinguished modern architects who were teaching there in rotation, Louis Kahn and Eero Saarinen among them. He also studied with Paul Schweikher, who later brought Dart to Chicago, hiring him to work in his rural Schaumburg, Illinois, studio. Schweikher's work, which combined the minimalism of the International style with a Midwestern feel for modest materials like wood and brick, appealed greatly to Dart—and so did Chicago itself. He believed progressive architecture was possible in Chicago as it was nowhere else. "He did not want to build Cape Cod houses which seemed to be all the fash-

METROPOLITAN CORRECTIONAL CENTER

71 WEST VAN BUREN STREET

1975

HARRY WEESE

Weese's federal detention center is known for its piercing image on the South Loop skyline. He based it on the premise that prisons require humanistic design. The jail's triangular configuration was driven primarily by interior considerations: to maximize perimeter space for exterior windows and minimize the distance between the cells and the common areas (opposite). Its twenty-seven stories allow for the easy separation of men from women and of first-time offenders from hardened criminals.

FIRST SAINT PAUL'S EVANGELICAL LUTHERAN CHURCH

1301 NORTH LASALLE STREET

1970

EDWARD DART

The curvilinear church harmonizes with the rectilinear buildings all around it, conveying distinction and quiet stateliness. Except for the crosses, the exterior gives few hints that it houses a church. Inside, Dart's mastery of space is manifest in his conception of form and use of building materials. He addressed acoustics with a textured brick design in the sanctuary. The result, one pastor said, was an "ancient type of worship."

ion in the East," wrote Dart's sister, Susan McCutcheon, in her biography of him.

After two years with Schweikher Dart established his own practice, quickly finding clients interested in his contemporary style. Dart loved devices that were uncommon at the time, such as exposed beams and interior walls of common brick, and he used them to achieve pleasing effects of space and light. By 1955 his work was sufficiently well regarded to be included in an architectural tour, organized by Lake Forest College, along with houses by Wright, the Kecks, and other unconventional architects.

Dart's original approach to interior space came across most vividly in what is usually a staid form, the church. In the 1960s churches presented an interesting challenge for modern architects, as religion's role in society was in flux and many denominations were reexamining everything connected to their form and function. A num-

ber of church officials began opening themselves to experiments in church design, and Edward Dart was among their foremost candidates.

Of Dart's many churches in the Chicago area, First Saint Paul's Evangelical Lutheran is among the best known. Completed in 1970, it is sited in the middle of a densely populated urban renewal district. Passersby don't always recognize the seemingly simple brick, steepleless building as a church, but it entirely satisfied the commission's complex aesthetic and ecclesiastical needs. The client, pastor of Chicago's oldest Lutheran congregation, requested that it blend with the modern residential neighborhood, yet appeal to the church's traditional parishioners. Dart's solution, a round structure amid a sea of squarish apartment buildings, sprang from no obvious antecedents. Rather, the architect first thought about the commission in terms of the interior space, then about the walls that enclose it. As a result, First Saint Paul's looks indisputably modern, but the pastor

WATER TOWER PLACE

MICHIGAN AVENUE AND CHESTNUT
STREET

1976

**LOEBL, SCHLOSSMAN, BENNETT
AND DART**

Unloved when it was built, Water
Tower Place has aged well. Its
proportions and scale stand up
even to such distinguished
neighbors as John Hancock Center.
Today it seems more contemporary
than many more-recent additions
to the Magnificent Mile. It also
excels at its primary function, as
a shopping center.

who worked with Dart on the project judged the largely
unadorned brick interior as a place for "a much more
ancient type of worship."

The ellipse at the end of the nave is indeed cavelike. It
implies rather than delineates a chancel or sanctuary,
suggesting a gradual division between altar and congregation, not a strict one. The interior is plain but has
distinctive features: a highly textured red brick wall that
is decorative but also absorbs echoes, and clerestory
windows that direct streams of light to the altar. The
granite lectern and baptismal font are bold forms upon
which the eye easily rests. Dart used these pieces as
he said he used antiques in residential designs—to provide moments of visual respite in dynamic spaces that
stimulate the eye.

Residences, churches, and other buildings of a down-
to-earth, human scale kept Dart busy through most of
his career. Then in 1965 he joined the large commercial
firm of Loebl, Schlossman and Bennett. With them he
embarked on the commission that would be the most
impressive and most frustrating of his life, Water Tower

Place. A huge mixed-use project, anchored by an eight-
level indoor shopping center, Water Tower Place again
demonstrated Dart's skill designing interior space. The
mall comprises a sequence of interconnected spaces,
moving from the street-level entry up a two-story set of
escalators and into a soaring, balconied atrium. Its exterior, however, was attacked by many critics upon its
completion in 1976; they assailed it as hopelessly plain
and "a shapeless montage." But as good buildings do,
Water Tower Place has aged well. It is hardly a sculptural
masterpiece, but its simplicity and proportions have
retained a fresh look that contrasts with the already
dated postmodern buildings that later joined it on North
Michigan Avenue. Inside, the commercial space of Water
Tower is the least pretentious of the retail centers in
the area. It is also the most popular mall and among the
most profitable; at one time it accounted for more than
half of all retail sales on Michigan Avenue, Chicago's
premier shopping district.

The shame of Water Tower Place is that the building
could have been better integrated with the architectural
fabric of Chicago but for the developers' choice of mate-

203

rials. Dart's preference was for granite, but the shopping center magnates who hired him insisted on a shiny white marble, which inspired one critic to call the design "men's room modern." People who knew Dart at the time said the decision was painful for him, but the architect was powerless to oppose clients paying $160 million for the building. "He was caught in the big-business trap," said Ed Straka, an associate of Dart's from his small-firm days. "His latest work was devoid of human touch"— a harsh but understandable criticism. Dart's sister believed Water Tower Place underscored for him his error in moving to a large firm, and contended that it contributed to his sudden death, of a brain embolism, at age fifty-three.

MISCHIEVOUS POSTMODERNISM

Although Chicago's modernist movement spanned many decades and varied styles—from the Art Deco of Holabird and Root, to Rebori's sculptural use of brick, to Goldberg's inventive applications of concrete—Mies's crystalline towers had the most widespread influence by far. By the 1960s they had inadvertently given rise to a modern architecture characterized by glass boxes of increasing anonymity, which in the following decade prompted a rebellion among architects and their clients. So began the era of postmodernism—a rejection of minimalism and its utter disregard for historical references. The style typically grafted historical or pseudohistorical architectural ornament and forms to otherwise modern structures. A signature example is Philip Johnson's 1984 AT&T (now Sony) Building, a New York City landmark with a Chippendale-derived pediment. Architect-

ure's renewed interest in history was a clear indication that the ideas that drove modernism had run their course.

Chicago's break with stark modernism was gradual, though, and it originated with a generation of young architects who had studied at the history-oriented Ivy League—Yale, Harvard, Cornell—and M.I.T., rather than I.I.T. These architects—Laurence Booth (b. 1936), Thomas Beeby (b. 1941), Stuart Cohen (b. 1942), and Stanley Tigerman (b. 1930), among others—were careful to express admiration and even reverence for Mies. But they found that, in the hands of the master's imitators, the modern tradition had grown cold and unresponsive to social needs.

Their advancement of postmodernism initially occurred on paper, when the economic recession of the mid-1970s dried up commissions and young architects had plenty of time to ponder theory. The movement gained momentum in 1975, when Cohen and Tigerman organized a group of like-minded architects to stage exhibits and to direct attention to their non-Miesian work. Underscoring their break from convention, they called themselves the "Chicago Seven," taking their name from the radicals who had been prosecuted (on grounds of inciting to riot) for protesting the Vietnam War during the 1968 Democratic National Convention in Chicago.

One of the group's exhibits was the 1976 "Chicago Architects" counterpoint to the Museum of Contemporary Art's Mies-centric overview of the city's architectural history. "Chicago Architects" not only promoted the underappreciated works of Chicago's richly eclectic history but showcased recent work, including Tigerman's design for a vacation home called "Frog Hollow." The house, in nearby Michigan, was a classic barn shape covered in roofing shingles from top to bottom. It was widely published at the time, drawing attention for a whimsical attitude that defied modernism's seriousness.

Houses of Light

Another Chicago Seven exhibit that would prove influential was the Townhouse Competition in 1978, inspired by an incipient return to the city by young professionals. That significant demographic movement was accompanied by new interest in single-family houses on narrow residential lots—typically 25-by-125 feet—in old neighborhoods beyond the Loop. The exhibit, meant to help envision the new Chicago town house, included designs ranging from the traditional to the futuristic, with many combinations therein.

Architect Laurence Booth recalled that the exhibit was conceived "against this sort of crusade that the Miesians were on . . . their kind of earnestness." The exhibit was indeed playful—some designs were unbuildable—and the wild diversity of the designs was more obvious at the time than their similarities. However, common elements appeared, including the open interiors and abundant natural light that were important elements from Chicago's architectural past, and many entries presaged ideas that would be developed in following years.

Booth himself went on to build many town houses on expensive property on Chicago's North Side. Probably his best known was the 1981 House of Light. His objective was to "get a sense of freedom of not being confined in a very confined situation," he later said, echoing Frank Lloyd Wright. Details of Booth's houses harked directly back to works by Chicago's architectural luminaries, although the results looked nothing like a Root or a Wright design. Booth's mission was to bring light into his houses from every possible aperture, in the front and back and on top.

In the House of Light, on Orleans Street in the Lincoln Park neighborhood, the first challenge was to get light into the house, then to decide how to use it. The solution, as in the best old Chicago buildings, was a flowing, open layout. Booth's living room opens to the dining room, which opens to the kitchen; light streams in from both ends. A central light well also brings light through a large skylight down to all three floors of the house.

Within this simple, well-conceived scheme, the romance of the design—its luxury and livability—results primarily from finely crafted details that emphasize space and light. Doorways between rooms widen at about hip level, resembling a squared keyhole and admitting extra light. Another extravagant embellishment is the twinned floating staircase that ascends both sides of the expansive central space, which underscores the importance of Booth's signature light well as it dramatically rises to the light. The staircase also draws the eye through space, much as its predecessors in Root's Rookery and Sullivan

LIBRARY FOR THE BLIND AND PHYSICALLY HANDICAPPED

1976 WEST ROOSEVELT ROAD

1978

STANLEY TIGERMAN

Tigerman designed this facility, which serves people with physical and visual handicaps, with vividness and simplicity. The building is short on historical references, but its playfulness is postmodern in spirit. Its bold colors and unusual geometry defy classic Miesian sobriety.

MODERN AND POSTMODERN CHICAGO

and Wright's Charnley House did long before. Booth's treatment of light-drenched interiors would also prove influential to residential design in the following decades, when Chicago's housing development boomed.

"Late Entries" and New Directions

The Chicago Seven went on to organize another thought-provoking exhibit that advanced postmodernism in Chicago. "Late Entries to the Chicago Tribune Competition," held in 1980, hinged on the premise that the 1922 Tribune Tower design competition was a great turning point in architecture—not on account of the office building that resulted, but for Eliel Saarinen's second-place entry. The wry point was that, if Saarinen's unbuilt tower could change the course of architecture, perhaps other never-to-be-built Tribune Tower designs could, too.

The submitting architects took "Late Entries" as an invitation not only to develop new ideas but also to comment on old ones. Helmut Jahn, a former student of Mies, drew a preposterous design, with a sleek all-glass caricature of the Tribune Tower mounted on top of the actual Hood and Howells design. Thomas Beeby drew a building wrapped in an American flag, Christo-style, in a rebuke to the newspaper whose distinguished history had been overshadowed in recent decades by a rabidly jingoistic editorial policy.

"Late Entries" was an exercise in rhetoric more than architecture. But it contributed to architects' growing awareness that political, social, and humorous elements could drive a building's design; it also spurred their

eagerness to create buildings that expressed meaning, not just structure. The message resonated, particularly among architects who had long bristled against the constraints of classic modernism. In the years that followed many focused their designs on history, context, and whimsically ornamental touches—such as the parking structure Tigerman designed with a facade resembling the grille of a Rolls-Royce.

Over time, however, the word "postmodern" became a catchall label for urban structures embellished with simplified and often cartoonish pediments, arches, columns, and other elements from architectural history; it evolved into a derogation implying superficial, random decoration. The most extravagant displays tended to afflict the fast-growing Sun Belt, including a glassy San Diego hotel with notes of Hadrian's Villa and the kitschy pyramids and Venetian-style canals that typified Las Vegas development in the 1990s. Although Chicago was spared the style's worst excesses, as early as 1984 Booth disavowed postmodernism as "the arbitrary manipulation of form. . . . Thus we are confronted with countless architectural oddities. These buildings, some well done, others not, can be seen around Chicago, but we cannot be sure what they mean." By the 1990s the label was abhorred by architects and their clients alike.

But to its credit postmodernism, during its brief reign, showed that architecture could move beyond the dead-end simplification of modernist rectangles. It brought color, which modern architecture eschewed, back to commercial building. And by contrast to the blank glass

NBC TOWER

Smith's design blends with the fabric of the city in the sky and has the strength to stand against the aristocratic Tribune Tower (seen at far left, opposite). It blends equally well with the street-scape; at ground level it is a major element of Cityfront Centre, the mammoth and largely successful riverfront redevelopment project.

boxes that had come to dominate recent architecture, postmodernism could be eye-catching and witty. Its most thoughtful examples breathed much-needed life into architecture. And in contrast to stark, isolated Miesian towers, postmodernism was often responsive to its surroundings, though it frequently achieved that contextualism by unsubtly mimicking older structures nearby.

POSTMODERN CONTEXTUALISM AND THE NBC TOWER

NBC Tower, completed in 1989, was in some measure a postmodern exercise yet strove to moderate the style's excesses with a deep understanding of historical and contextual themes. NBC was no pastiche of spare parts from ancient Rome, say, or medieval Bavaria. Rather, its backward glance related to an existing thread in Chicago's urban fabric—the streamlined Art Deco sky-scrapers of the 1920s.

NBC's designer, Adrian Smith (b. 1944) of S.O.M., imbued the forty-story tower with a quality rarely associated with commercial buildings at the time—subtlety. It avoided the empty decoration that had caused typical postmodern buildings of the period to be compared to "old ladies with too much jewelry." It fit in with its broad-shouldered neighbors—specifically the 1925 Tribune Tower, which could be regarded as the grandfather of Chicago's Jazz Age skyscape. "People glimpse NBC tucked back between the Gothic newspaper headquarters and the Miesian Equitable Building," *Inland Architect* wrote shortly after it opened, "and wonder how they could have missed seeing it 'all these years.'"

MODERN AND POSTMODERN CHICAGO

Blending with its surroundings was the source of NBC's
charm but also a stunning departure from other high-rise
designs by S.O.M., avatars of classic modernism. Since
the 1950s no firm had so successfully adapted the unornamented rationalism of Mies van der Rohe to the
needs of corporate America, as it had done with Sears
Tower and John Hancock Center.

The impetus behind Smith's decidedly different approach was an architectural mishap opposite the new
tower's site in Cityfront Centre, a massive redevelopment
project on the north bank of the Chicago River. Directly
across the river sat the Illinois Center, a mixed-use
complex of Miesian high-rises built in the 1970s and
1980s, which had matured into a maze of faceless buildings segregated from the city. In response to Illinois
Center's cold, unloved towers, Cityfront Centre's planners prescribed contextualism, which Smith interpreted

as designing in "the ethos and character of what was
already there," as he later put it.

Smith's design echoed but did not imitate elements of
the streamlined skyscrapers nearby and was especially
praised for its resemblance to NBC's New York headquarters in the Art Deco Rockefeller Center. "I did NBC
with the conviction and philosophy of contextualism,"
he said. "I believed that the traditional city needed to
be reinforced instead of being eroded with more buildings in the modern style." While NBC Tower did not
presage a new era in American architecture, it was one
of the first buildings in years to be welcomed as a handsome and intelligent addition to Chicago's skyline.

FLASH GORDON AND "STARSHIP CHICAGO"

In its restraint, however, the NBC Tower was atypical of

the structures rising in Chicago at the time. Throughout the 1980s the city's own brand of postmodernism was dominated by the hard-to-categorize architect Helmut Jahn (b. 1940). His idiosyncratic buildings often alluded to the architectural past but defied the contextualism the NBC Tower embraced. Jahn was trained as a modernist and he demonstrated an early flair for structure in glass and steel and a keen interest in interior space. But instead of Miesian boxes, his trademark became audacious, unprecedented office buildings, otherworldly inside and out, which earned him the nickname "Flash Gordon."

Despite his German origins and a career that spans the globe, Jahn's roots sink deeply into Chicago's architectural tradition. He emigrated to Chicago at age twenty-five, lured by the legacy of Mies van der Rohe. He studied at I.I.T. with Myron Goldsmith and Fazlur Khan. In 1967 he joined Gene Summers at C. F. Murphy as a design associate on McCormick Place, where he is credited with having devised the steel truss system that supports the immense pavilion. When Summers left C. F. Murphy in 1973, Jahn replaced him as director of design. He may have won the promotion by default, as

the firm was then in crisis and other candidates had recently left. But from that point on, his rise and the firm's resurgence were meteoric. So powerful was Jahn's role as both designer and salesman that he was made president of C. F. Murphy in 1982. The following year he bought out the Murphy family and assumed full control.

Jahn's talent lay in his ability to respond to the postmodern trend without fully submitting to it or conceding his own daring originality. Although he abided by the modernist lesson that architecture is a direct expression of its materials, Jahn recognized that the essence of construction in the post-Miesian period was flexibility. He found ways to work arches, columns, and even domes into his designs, sometimes abstractly, but always in a way that satisfied clients impatient with monotonous skyscrapers.

Jahn's triumph was to steer C. F. Murphy away from strict glass-box modernism to accommodate such changing tastes. One of Jahn's first important designs to make that transition was the Xerox Centre, built in the Loop in 1980. Xerox was an understated office tower, but it featured touches of flash and responded to its site in

CHICAGO ARCHITECTURE AND DESIGN

JAMES R. THOMPSON CENTER

100 WEST RANDOLPH STREET

1984

MURPHY/JAHN

The Thompson Center remains one of the city's most controversial buildings, although Chicagoans appreciate its indoor-outdoor plaza and oversize Dubuffet sculpture (opposite, right). The exterior suggests a modified, perhaps weightless, dome with decorative columns detached from the structure's perimeter. Inside, the seventeen-story atrium provides soaring architectural drama, suggesting a street lined with skyscrapers.

The United Airlines Terminal is unique but has Chicago antecedents ranging from John Wellborn Root to Mies van der Rohe; its lofty steel superstructure evokes nineteenth-century European railroad sheds. The terminal conveys the sense—now mostly lost elsewhere—that travel is romantic and exciting. Jahn's often successful combination of structuralism and whimsy was termed "romantic modernism."

ways that were uncommon at the time. Its otherwise rectangular form is rounded at the corner, a gesture that subtly recalls Louis Sullivan's Carson Pirie Scott building two blocks away.

The sleek white high-rise is also set back from the street a few feet more than usual, in effect both expanding the open space around First National Bank (now Bank One) Plaza across Monroe Street and deferring to Xerox's next-door neighbor, the old Marquette Building on Dearborn Street by Holabird and Roche. Xerox was original but not outlandish.

More large commissions followed, and as Jahn's buildings became more sculptural and imposing, he established a national reputation. He attracted a large share of the vast amounts of capital spent in the real estate boom of the 1980s, appealing especially to developers interested in trademark buildings. In 1982 Jahn completed his glass-wall addition to Holabird and Root's 1930 Chicago Board of Trade. The twenty-three-story addition echoes the proportions of the Art Deco original and is likewise crowned by a prominent decoration: Where the 1930 building has a statue of Ceres, Jahn's addition sports an octagonal sculptural element that has been likened to a Mercedes-Benz hood ornament. His equally bold design for the 1987 Northwestern Atrium Center (now Citicorp Center), a mixed-use tower, features a bright blue, rippling glass facade that may have been inspired by Art Deco setbacks but most vividly suggests a forty-story waterfall.

Every bit as brash as his buildings, Jahn cultivated his own image as an architectural superstar: His photogenic wardrobe of capes and hats became well known, his personal style—down to the kind of pen he used (Mont Blanc) and the color of ink (sepia)—was widely flaunted. Jahn not only branded himself, but with distinctive design he branded his corporate clients' buildings; he even branded Naperville, a suburb west of Chicago where cornfields predominated before his arrival. There he designed a large office block, called Two Energy Plaza when completed in 1986, in the shape of an N, for Naperville.

It is fair to ask, however, if Jahn pushed the limits too far in his most conspicuous Loop design, the state government's James R. Thompson Center, dedicated in 1985. Sometimes called "Starship Chicago," the build-

ing remains an eyesore to many Chicagoans, notwithstanding its spectacular, lofty interior and the praise of many European critics. The problem is that Jahn's steel and glass building speaks a fractured architectural language. Its broad outline is reminiscent of something reassuringly classical—an ellipse, perhaps, or a dome. That might be an interesting and even noble idea for a government building, except that Thompson Center leans disconcertingly, perhaps to suggest a defiance of gravity (a notion that might also explain the decorative columns in front of but unconnected to the building).

Sometimes advanced ideas need only time to be understood and accepted, but Thompson Center has not withstood that test. Among its nagging miscalculations are the exterior glass panels of light blue and salmon, a color scheme more appropriate for a discount department store than a government center. And whatever one's opinion was of the daring design, the building suffered from poor construction. Although the mechanical problems were later corrected, Thompson Center became famous for its unbearable heat: Those working there used to bring umbrellas to shield them from the radiant heat of the sun.

Despite the scathing reaction to Thompson Center, Jahn landed on his feet with a commission for the United Airlines Terminal at O'Hare Airport. This design also drew flak when it was built in 1987, mostly because it differed markedly from the airport's existing calm, Miesian terminals. But the United terminal soon won acclaim for being both dramatic and simple. Like most Jahn buildings it is structural and modern, but its form harks clearly to the past, to glass-roofed railroad terminals and a time when travel was exciting and romantic.

Mies himself might well have approved of the United terminal's overall simplicity, though its network of steel beams and patterned glass is decorative in a way that Mies's work never was. Its tall, arching metal supports recall century-old glass-and-iron interiors like the Rookery, or even the railroad sheds that inspired it. Jahn's mastery of structure demonstrates technology's potential to create functional space. But the building also testifies to Jahn's ability to incorporate original and vividly expressive form, which became the signature of this confirmed 1980s postmodernist.

THE LIBRARY COMPETITION

In 1988 a city-appointed jury of eleven people awarded the design of Chicago's new main public library to architect Thomas Beeby, and Chicago collectively sighed with relief. The city's Library Board, which to its growing embarrassment had been without a central library for twelve years, triumphantly announced the decision. The architectural community, which generally dislikes competitions, could only express satisfaction that this one was over. And the public, which had gotten restless over the competition's protracted public drama, was pleased finally to be getting a building, especially one that did not present a fierce aesthetic challenge.

The choice of Beeby's historically eclectic entry was by far the safest among the five finalists in a contest that invited comparisons to the Chicago Tribune competition sixty-odd years before. As with the Tribune competition, the most daring designs did not win. Beeby's design is a sometimes jarring combination of beaux arts, Richardsonian Romanesque, and other styles from Chicago's past, but a jury member proclaimed it "a gentle building. It's beautiful. This looks like a library. This is a building that you can trust." "Trust" was clearly the quality that won over the jury, which had hoped to avoid the rabid architectural controversy that had greeted other recent projects, notably Jahn's Thompson Center.

The story of Beeby's Harold Washington Library Center began in 1976, when the original library, designed by Shepley, Rutan and Coolidge and dedicated in 1897, was deemed too small. Its books were moved to a ware-

CHICAGO PUBLIC LIBRARY COMPETITION

1988 (UNBUILT)	
TOP LEFT:	**MURPHY/JAHN**
TOP RIGHT:	**LOHAN ASSOCIATES**
BELOW LEFT:	**ARTHUR ERICKSON**
BELOW RIGHT:	**SKIDMORE, OWINGS AND MERRILL**

Jahn's radical entry had little chance of winning in the wake of his controversial Thompson Center. Lohan's submission, widely regarded as the most "Chicago" of the entries, featured steel, glass, and a light-filled atrium. Erickson's massive concrete building won public approval, but the architectural establishment dismissed it as something out of *Star Wars.* S.O.M.'s entry, at once conservative and postmodern, failed to inspire.

The jury thought Beeby's design
looked like a library and reflected
the city itself, with notes of the
Chicago School, the Columbian
Exposition, and even Mies van der
Rohe folded into one building.

CHICAGO PUBLIC LIBRARY

The street-level view (above) doesn't hint at one of the gems inside, the library's ninth-floor Winter Garden (opposite). The vast glass-ceilinged structure is a splendid reference to Chicago's architectural past. But, hidden from view, the Winter Garden misses at one of the primary functions of the Chicago School light court: to welcome people in from the city's hard, often cold streets.

house on the Chicago River, which was to be a temporary home while a new library was designed and constructed. Library patrons would soon have cause to wonder what "temporary" meant. After an initial delay, planners unveiled a plan to renovate the former Goldblatt's department store on State Street for use as the library. It seemed like a practical yet creative solution; the century-old building, a fine example of the Chicago School by Holabird and Roche, was vacant and threatened with demolition. Over the next several years detailed studies of the adaptive reuse plan were made, but before they were finished a strangely ferocious campaign against the Goldblatt's plan by *the Chicago Sun-Times* upended it.

Cautious politicians were unsure of their next steps. Finally in 1986 a vacant lot was chosen for an all-new library building, and a "design/build" competition was announced. Under the rules, architects would form teams with engineers and contractors, jointly presenting their detailed designs and proposals guaranteeing the $130 million price. Many architects were horrified by that approach; for one thing, developing designs on that scale requires an enormous investment, and only the wealthiest firms would be able to enter. The process would also prevent the client, in this case the city, from interacting with the architect and playing any substantial creative role in the design. One of the strongest objections to the competition came from the local chap-

ter of the American Institute of Architects, which pointed out that working at arm's length from the client never results in the best possible building.

Of the five entries submitted to the jury, that of Dirk Lohan, a prominent Chicago architect (and Mies van der Rohe's grandson), was perhaps the most "Chicago" of the designs—a light-filled glass and steel structure with a large atrium and grand staircase. Helmut Jahn's was predictably radical; he assembled geometric shapes with his customary whimsy. Skidmore, Owings and Merrill submitted a vaguely postmodern version of a Chicago School office block. The Canadian Arthur Erickson submitted a huge concrete structure with rounded shapes

so massive and emphatic that some dismissed it as a set from *Star Wars*.

Beeby's was the most conservative design, harking post-modernistically to Sullivan's Auditorium, just two blocks away, with thick masonry walls and large Romanesque arches. Beeby also paid homage to the 1893 World's Columbian Exposition, which Sullivan deplored, by blending in pediments and swags that recalled the fair's extravagant classical style. Continuing in a historicist vein, Beeby reprised the city's Miesian past by designing the back of the nine-story building as a sheer curtain wall of green glass. Beeby's mix of architectural styles and fragments was decorative but also delivered a post-

modern message: that history itself is fragmentary and
that Chicago architecture, contrary to myth, never
evolved in a single, straight line.

The library has aged well in the years since its 1991
opening. Its materials and scale harmonize with the rest
of the old Chicago neighborhood, and even the mammoth "owls"—metal sculptures set into the corners of
the roof line—have lost their strangeness. But the library
remains disappointing, as its exterior charms fail to
penetrate the surface. The entrance promises grandeur,
but has no atrium and no natural light. The escalators
lack the drama even their department store counterparts
can muster. Perhaps a certain dullness was inevitable,
given a library's complex functional requirements. The
library's one exceptional interior space is the glass-
roofed winter garden on the top floor. Bathed in light
and richly detailed, it suggests a Rookery-like light court
and the vastness of universal space. Sadly, it is separated from the library's human flow and is usually empty.
Perhaps Beeby is sending a message here as well: that
Chicago's architectural splendors are sometimes hidden,
neglected by architects, and lost to the public at large.

RATIONAL POSTMODERNISM

Theoretical architectural debate often pits one side
against the other—Chicago School versus the beaux
arts, for example, or the modern versus the postmodern.
Real architecture is almost never an either/or proposi-

tion, however, and Chicago architecture's strength in
the last decades of the twentieth century was its ability
to embrace all sides of such matters, combining elements of the modern and the postmodern, the rational
and the romantic.

For instance, the 1991 Oceanarium addition to the
Shedd Aquarium, by Lohan Associates (now called
Lohan Caprile Goettsch), blended gracefully with the
original 1929 beaux arts building by Graham, Anderson,
Probst and White. Yet the new building adds more
than just classically proportioned size to the old one.
The interior features a pool for performing dolphins and
whales, a great glass wall behind it, and a vista that at
times seems to connect the pool inside with the distant
panorama of Lake Michigan outside—the quintessential
universal space.

Another example of Chicago architecture from this
period blends industrial notes into a whimsical interior
design. The Painted Apartment, in the Mies van der
Rohe building at 2400 North Lakeview, overlooks
Lincoln Park. The apartment, designed in 1981 by
Krueck and Olsen, features glass walls and perforated
metal that add to a sense of weightlessness and transparency. Architect Ronald Krueck (b. 1946), who earned
his architecture degree from I.I.T. and then studied
painting at the Art Institute of Chicago, said Mies's
handling of invisible space inspired this interior.

The result looks anything but
Miesian, but architect Ron Krueck
applied the master's lessons
by combining basic materials with
grace and care. Although constructed of industrial-grade metals
and glass, the apartment is a
refined dwelling. Divisions of space
are either transparent or merely
suggested.

The Painted Apartment began as a fantasy of the client, who told Krueck she could not afford the modern paintings she liked so she wanted to "live inside one." Krueck created the design from a "palette" of high-tech elements like stainless steel and plate glass. Such materials might otherwise outfit a factory but here they serve to add brightness and color throughout. Light penetrates and plays variously on surfaces, often changing with the time of day, and giving the apartment a large measure of its richness and comfort. Its success owes partly to an understanding of spareness and glassiness handed down by modernists of the previous generation, and also to the fascinating range of materials used, uncommon to a residential interior.

The most important Chicago architecture of the late twentieth century demonstrated that architects could still discover innovative forms while responding directly to modern values. The New York firm of Kohn Pedersen Fox did just that at 333 West Wacker Drive, which sits neatly but boldly on a narrow site at a bend in the Chicago River. The green glass high-rise drew much praise when built in 1983. It was then considered surprising and original, although it harks back to modernist forebears with a light and glassy curtain wall. It also has an organic connection to its site: One facade gently curves along with the river, and the other squares off against the grid on the Loop side. Those features, among others, represent an exercise in geometry and proportion that should satisfy any architect with a modernist bias, but add to it a welcome contextualism.

THE PROMISE OF PRESERVATION

Much as postmodern architects of the 1970s rediscovered beauty and interest in the architectural past, so too did cities slowly begin to appreciate historic buildings for their charm, character, and diversity. In the name of "progress" Chicago had unsentimentally razed important structures throughout the modernist era. Richardson's 1887 Marshall Field's Wholesale Store was demolished back in 1930, and Jenney's 1885 Home Insurance Building met the same fate the following year. Sullivan's 1889 Auditorium would have been razed without a second thought after World War II, except that the proposed demolition would have cost more than the value of the land. But even in the modernist heyday of the 1960s, many of Chicago's old buildings were more appealing than the new ones rising around them.

The teardown trend continued into the 1970s, as developers sought larger buildings, and even architects sometimes failed to protect important buildings from the wrecking ball. Self-serving architects were among those who testified in the mid-1970s that Louis Sullivan's 1884 Troescher Building was not worth saving—and then vied to design the high-rise that would replace it. The occasional building managed to escape the bulldozers by chance or luck: The old public library on Michigan Avenue, for example, was slated for demolition in 1972, until the mayor's wife declared her love for the building, and it was reborn as the Chicago Cultural Center. But that didn't keep Michigan Square, Holabird and Root's much-loved Art Deco shopping center, from being leveled the very next year. A chorus of distress sounded when Michigan Square went down, but not until the 1980s did such protests coalesce into a true preservation movement.

One of the original leaders of that movement in Chicago is a working architect—and anything but a quaint antiquarian. John Vinci (b. 1937), who graduated from I.I.T. in 1960, was trained as a Miesian and acquired a reputation for frankly modern new designs, such as the 1991 Manilow House, on which he collaborated with the English architect Max Gordon. Yet Vinci was also enchanted by the past, and while being trained in the essence of glass and steel at I.I.T., he used his spare time to salvage ornamental detail from the Louis Sullivan houses that were coming down with disturbing regularity. As Vinci later explained, he was doing more than hunting antiques; he was learning volumes about how ornament could enhance appreciation for structure, not conceal it.

Vinci's interest in salvage continued after college. His first paying job was to remove plaster and terra-cotta details and copy stencil designs from Sullivan's Schiller Theater (by then called the Garrick Theater) on Randolph Street. Schiller's was one of the first demolitions local preservationists vocally opposed, and Vinci was among a small band of faithful who picketed the sidewalk outside in an attempt to save it. The Schiller was doomed, however, and after the demolition permit was issued, Vinci and others were given a little time and a little money to salvage what they could.

The preservation movement was still too weak in 1971 to save Adler and Sullivan's Stock Exchange on LaSalle

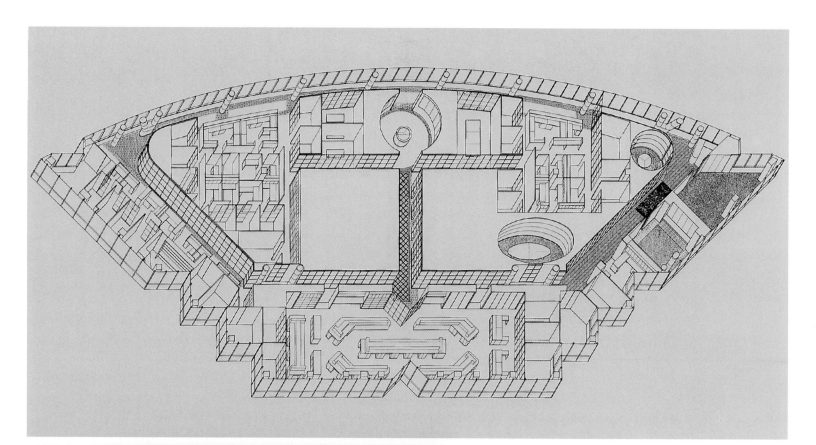

333 WEST WACKER DRIVE

1983

KOHN PEDERSEN FOX

The postmodern office building was often more curvilinear than the modernist one, sometimes for the most practical of reasons—such as an odd-shaped lot. The 333 office tower fits snugly into a bend of the Chicago River. Its subtle architectural imagery brought it wide praise as one of the city's best buildings of the 1980s. Its curtain wall is almost sheer and provides dramatic reflections. But mullions and spandrels in slightly different colors suggest floors, offices, and real life inside. Though small, the lobby provides drama inspired by the exterior's curves and transparency.

MANILOW HOUSE

CHICAGO

1991

MAX GORDON WITH JOHN VINCI

English architect Max Gordon
designed this house as a home
and gallery for a major collector
of art. The exterior is reminiscent of houses Mies designed
in Germany before World War II.
Also like Mies's work, the over-

all simplicity, set off by finely
crafted finishes, makes a fitting
backdrop for large-scale art.
An Anselm Kiefer canvas, period
furniture, and early modernist
steel-frame windows combine
harmoniously in the living room.

Street, one of Sullivan's finest office building designs in Chicago. But this time the protests of architects and historians helped in extracting additional time and money from the developer for a more extensive collection of fragments before the building's demise. Salvage on this large a scale was relatively new, and the preservationists involved weren't sure how to approach it. Vinci suggested a creative solution: The most powerful memorial to the building would not be scattered specimens of ornament, but rather the re-creation of an entire section of the building. With no idea where they would rebuild it, they chose the Stock Exchange's interior centerpiece, the old Trading Room, and began dismantling it piece by piece. "I thought it was important to see

how this room's infinite number of architectural details could come together in a complete space," Vinci said.

The Trading Room's splendor was certainly faded, with a dropped ceiling hiding art glass, paint over Sullivan's elaborate and largely forgotten stencils, and dozens of other coarse alterations. Vinci improvised a project in "architectural archaeology," carefully noting the room's configuration and plotting the placement of each detail recovered. Using old photos, Vinci and his colleagues developed a precise conception of the once glorious space.

By April 1972 Vinci's official salvage job was completed. However, one of his fellow salvagers, a photographer

CHICAGO STOCK EXCHANGE TRADING ROOM

NOW IN THE ART INSTITUTE OF CHICAGO

1894 BY **ADLER AND SULLIVAN**

RECONSTRUCTED 1977 BY **VINCI-KENNY ARCHITECTS**

Though filled with ornament, the Trading Room retains a calm sense of organization, a tribute to Sullivan's genius. His stenciled patterns are mind-bogglingly intricate; their reconstruction required sixty-five shades of green, red, blue, and gold.

named Richard Nickel, had arranged an informal truce with the wreckers, who allowed him in with crowbar and camera. While Nickel was alone in the doomed building, trying to pull some last pieces from it, a large section suddenly collapsed, killing him instantly. If there was a shred of consolation in this story it was that news coverage of the tragedy highlighted the passion that many felt for old buildings.

A year later, a happier event furthered the preservationists' cause. The Art Institute of Chicago was developing an east wing, which was in the final planning stages. Many curators and trustees doubted that the predictably modern design—with broad planes of masonry and

glass—would meet the high standard set by the museum's classical main building on Michigan Avenue. Someone proposed that the Trading Room would lend a historical touch to the museum's unlovely modernist addition. The idea was met with enthusiasm, a quickly launched fund-raising effort, and substantial institutional support.

Vinci had scarcely dreamed of so happy an outcome before the Stock Exchange was razed, but in many ways the hard work had just begun. Reconstruction of this sort was a new process, untried on such a scale, and every step demanded painstaking thought and improvisation. Problems included the discovery that the original

Trading Room was out of square; fortunately the museum's construction contractors got the news in time to build corresponding interior walls. And workers adept in the crafts prized in Sullivan's day were hard to come by in the 1970s. To re-create lost ornament that appeared in documents, Vinci tracked down craftspeople as far as California, where he found one eccentric artisan who knew how to do scagliola, or marbleized plaster, on the surface of columns.

The result of all this effort is an astonishment, especially to people who know Sullivan interiors only from black-and-white photos. The Trading Room has light and color, a stimulating freshness that must have been exciting to a trader on the old stock exchange. At the same time, its high ceilings and harmonies of design inspire calm. As is so often the case with Sullivan, elaborate form follows complex function—in this case, a stately but stirring space for financial trading.

With increasing frequency in the 1970s, enlightened building owners and history buffs were finding architectural treasures that had been hidden by decades of neglect; architects were discovering whole chapters of architectural history that were simply not being addressed in the modernist-oriented schools. Architectural restoration was gaining momentum, but its execution was still improvisational. When Vinci was asked to restore Louis Sullivan's magisterial Carson Pirie Scott storefront, for example, it was nearly by chance that he found experts to help. A typical example was the chemist of modern paints who incidentally had an interest in old Chicago architecture. Together he and Vinci mixed colors that matched Sullivan's original, which was a convincing simulation of oxidized bronze. Elsewhere on

MODERN AND POSTMODERN CHICAGO

The Rookery's restoration recovered elements from the original John Wellborn Root design that had been hidden during a 1907 renovation by Frank Lloyd Wright. One of Root's cast-iron columns was discovered within a Wrightian casing of incised marble and left exposed. In the background are elevator doors from a later renovation during the Art Deco era.

the facade, tiles needed replacing; Vinci somehow located the retired president of Northwestern Terra Cotta, which had done the original work in 1903. Together they combed through old documents and found a way to fabricate replacements.

By the late 1980s the increasing interest in old buildings had spawned a full-fledged industry dedicated to architectural preservation, with a growing expertise that made extensive projects feasible. McClier, a large local architectural firm that had developed a preservation department, undertook a number of important restorations in Chicago during this period. In 1988 the firm tackled a project of unprecedented scale, the restoration of John Wellborn Root's once magnificent Rookery. Then a century old, the Rookery had fallen on hard times, aesthetically and economically. The glass ceiling of its light court was tarred over in the 1940s, its ornate facade required attention, and the building was hanging on as low-grade office space. In 1983 the Continental Bank bought the Rookery, planning a $20 million rehabilitation. But five years later the company fell into a financial crisis, halted the project, and put the building on the block.

The buyer, Thomas Baldwin, a wealthy futures trader, believed the Rookery's original qualities of flowing space and natural light could be recaptured and the building refashioned into what is known as class A office space. He was charting largely new territory, in terms of both the architectural restoration and the new type of real estate that would result. When the project began in 1988, the only thing certain about the project was that it would be the largest and most expensive restoration of a rental office building to date.

Leading the project was Gunny Harboe, head of McClier's preservation group and then a recent graduate of restor-

ation programs at Columbia and M.I.T. Harboe organized and managed the wide range of specialists essential to such a project. He personally redrew sections of lost ornament, using old photographs to project full sections from the bits that survived. He found a mosaicist who used computers to reproduce pavements. He even led a group to Carrara, Italy, to retrieve marble from the quarry that had supplied the original. Harboe described the project as working on an "epic novel," not only for the grandeur of Root's original design but because of the building's long history. Along with what remained of Root's 1888 interior, a 1907 renovation by Frank Lloyd Wright was carefully preserved, as were later touches of Art Deco, while the desecrations of more recent decades had to be overcome.

The restored Rookery revived some of Chicago's most subtle lessons of architecture. It revealed once again the timeless fascination of Root's entrance, light court, and winding, cylindrical oriel staircase. It illustrated with renewed clarity the interpenetration of spaces, the fiery luminescence of direct sunlight on gold leaf, and the sensations stirred by a gravity-defying metal-frame structure. It proved how inspired works in masonry, metal, glass, and marble can touch the soul. It also demonstrated the commitment—financial and philosophical—such extensive restoration demands. When completed in 1992 the final price tag for the Rookery's restoration came to $25 million.

But the Rookery was more than an aesthetic triumph; quickly attracting first-class tenants, it was a financial one, too. Perhaps most important, it provided impetus for the preservation movement and gave courage to subsequent restorations. Its success showed that historic preservation is not merely sentimental but can thrive in the hard-knocks urban real estate market.

CHAPTER 7

CHICAGO'S SECOND MODERN PERIOD

Chicago at the dawn of the twenty-first century prospers and grows, as it has almost continuously since its founding in the early nineteenth century. Developers try to keep up with ever-rising land prices by constructing larger buildings at a faster pace, just as they did in the 1800s. And many new buildings, like many of their predecessors, fail to reach architectural heights. Reviewing recent construction on the edges of the Loop in 2003, the *Chicago Tribune* described a rash of high-rises as "architectural weeds" and declared Chicago's reputation for architecture as an echo from the past.

Yet news of Chicago's architectural demise has been grossly exaggerated. Partly it is the weeds—and there are always weeds—overshadowing the fewer buildings of real quality. More important, the passage of time is essential to our understanding of what is beautiful and right, especially when new ideas assertively push beyond the boundaries of the familiar. Even now-iconic Chicago School structures—including the Rookery, the Auditorium, and Reliance—were greeted with ambivalence before gaining recognition for their architectural nobility.

In fact, evidence of vitality and even genius abounds in Chicago's contemporary architecture. Some examples—including Frank Gehry's Millennium Park band shell, with its curling ribbons of stainless steel—have incited

flurries of popular excitement. The city's enduring attraction as a place to build is apparent in the numerous acclaimed architects from elsewhere—Kevin Roche, Ricardo Bofill, Cesar Pelli, among them—who have made significant contributions to Chicago's skyline in recent years. Lucien Lagrange emigrated from France in 1968 and built an active practice in Chicago, producing high-rises like 510 West Erie, the steel-framed condominium completed in 2002. Rafael Viñoly, born in Uruguay and based in New York, unveiled the University of Chicago's Graduate School of Business in 2004, while Italy's Renzo Piano has designed a new wing of the Art Institute of Chicago, expected to open in 2007 on Monroe Street, directly opposite Millennium Park.

Perhaps never since the years following the Great Fire of 1871 has Chicago's landscape undergone change so active and so infused by talent from beyond the city limits. While some complain that awarding Chicago commissions to outside architects deprives local practitioners, others welcome the energy and vision architects are bringing to the city from elsewhere. And many of Chicago's own architectural firms—including Skidmore, Owings and Merrill, Lohan Caprile Goettsch, and Murphy/Jahn—are themselves enjoying enormous international careers.

510 WEST ERIE STREET

The tower of loftlike condominiums rises above an airy lobby (above).

SONY CENTER

POTSDAMMER PLATZ, BERLIN, GERMANY

2000

MURPHY/JAHN

Chicago's architectural influence extends to twenty-first-century Europe. Jahn describes his well-loved Sony Center in Berlin (above right) as a "successor" to his Thompson Center in Chicago, though the design evolved away from its predecessor's postmodernism. Both used advanced technology to create a breathtaking urban space.

BARRINGTON AREA LIBRARY ADDITION

BARRINGTON, ILL.

1995

ROSS BARNEY + JANKOWSKI

This addition to a suburban library simultaneously blends with its wooded site and distinguishes itself. The uplifting, memorable work (opposite) reflects the spirit of a library.

With such productive architectural cross-pollination, lessons learned in one city reverberate around the world. Helmut Jahn even describes his glass and steel Sony Center, which was highly praised after opening in Berlin in 2000, as an evolutionary development that sprang from his 1985 James R. Thompson Center in Chicago. Although new influences are streaming into the city, Chicago's own rich history continues to inform designs that are transforming cityscapes, stimulating new ideas, and developing new conventions in contemporary architecture across the globe.

A SENSE OF PLACE

Chicago's architectural tradition of responsiveness to the environment continues to produce buildings that harmoniously reflect the area's flat land and unforgiving climate. Chicagoan Carol Ross Barney (b. 1949) clearly draws on the philosophy, perhaps best expressed by Frank Lloyd Wright, that structures should grow "out of the ground and into the light." Each of Ross Barney's projects is so attuned to its specific physical and cultural environment that her work defies categorization.

The architect was thrust into the limelight when her firm, Ross Barney + Jankowski, was chosen to design the U.S. Federal Campus in Oklahoma City, to replace the Alfred P. Murrah Federal Building that was destroyed in a 1995 bombing. Her widely praised design for the replacement, completed in 2003, acknowledges the site's distant and recent past: Its floor plan gently arcs, a reference to tribal council rings and Oklahoma's Native American history, and the surrounding green space and bollards subtly convey a much-needed sense of security.

A very different project, Ross Barney's 1995 addition to the Barrington, Illinois, Public Library, relates just as closely to its own setting, a wooded site in a semirural village northwest of the city. Nature and a sense of quiet guided the design of the building, whose unobtrusive exterior opens to an unexpectedly dramatic interior. Closely spaced wood columns supporting branchlike joists rise toward clerestory windows, simultaneously evoking a light-dappled forest and a cathedral's nave. It hardly resembles a Prairie School structure but nonetheless exemplifies Wright's credo that a building "grow up out of conditions as a plant grows up out of soil" and be "dignified as a tree in the midst of nature but a child of the spirit of man."

THE CHALLENGE OF HISTORY

The relationship between contemporary architecture and its recent past is complex everyplace architecture matters, but especially in Chicago, where architects are haunted by what critic Lynn Becker called "the great

The new Arts Club is a direct homage to Mies van der Rohe, who designed the original. The red brick exterior recalls the master's early German period. The interior, particularly the glass-enclosed stairway (opposite), re-creates the flow and intimacy of its predecessor, which was demolished.

undead of modern architecture," Ludwig Mies van der Rohe.

In the postwar years Mies elevated architecture to a transcendent art; he discovered the essence of modern construction and reduced it to the most seductive simplicity. But he left a difficult legacy: No one could emulate his skill or do justice to his deeply philosophical, classically precise International style, and his genius became the great burden of the following generation. In one way or another—whether by acceptance, rejection, or some rapprochement in between—architects continue to grapple with Mies's exquisite understatement, and to this day little is built in Chicago without some relationship to his work.

Questions surrounding the contemporary relationship to Mies specifically and to the architectural past in general influenced the sharp debate that revolved around one high-profile project on the near North Side. The Arts Club on Ontario Street, designed by Vinci-Hamp Architects and completed in 1997, pays deep homage both to Mies (with whom architect John Vinci studied at I.I.T.) and to the old Arts Club that stood two blocks west, whose interior the master designed in 1947. That building, which the Arts Club did not own, was com-

pleted in 1951 and demolished in 1995, along with two neighboring turn-of-the-century gems, to make way for a shopping-and-cinema complex the *Wall Street Journal* described as architecturally "horrid."

To the club's good fortune it was able to build a new structure of its own, funded by the sale of an important sculpture by Constantin Brancusi. Arts Club directors invited some forty architects to vie for the commission, and a jury of three pared the finalists to two Chicagoans: Vinci, the modernist architect and ardent preservationist; and Ron Krueck, designer of the Painted Apartment in Mies's high-rise at 2400 North Lakeview, among other, mostly residential, work.

Vinci's winning design inspired debate more prickly than customary even in architectural circles. Friends and foes alike described Vinci's freestanding two-story structure as "restrained"—so restrained that its brick walls with large glass panels might easily escape notice amid the bustling streetscape. The interior is equally subtle, attempting no more than the unembellished movement through space that Mies achieved so strikingly in the original Arts Club. Vinci even installed the old club's most famous element, a two-flight travertine stairway, with a result nearly as weightless and ethereal as the

original. Mies himself might have described Vinci's thoughtful design with his highest compliment: simple.

Yet a nagging issue dogged the new Arts Club even after it was built: Was Vinci's design—as Miesian as any could be thirty years after Mies's death—appropriate for the 1990s? The question was especially pointed because the Arts Club's mission since its founding in the 1920s was to promote avant-garde art.

Krueck's design was certainly more contemporary. Like Vinci, Krueck was an I.I.T. graduate and influenced by the Miesian interest in glass and transparency. Unlike Vinci, he used a range of materials that did not exist during Mies's lifetime. His elevations and interiors for the new Arts Club featured transparent and translucent space dividers and an eye-catching design.

Krueck bitterly argued, even after Vinci's building was completed, that the jury's selection had been a mistake. He insisted that his own design, like the original Arts Club, represented "an important statement of contemporary architecture" Suggesting that John Vinci's build-

ing did not, he referred to Vinci as a "restoration architect." While Krueck's disappointment was unfortunate, his campaign focused attention on questions of the past and the future in the architecture of the present.

Vinci's design obviously looked backward—in part because of the commission's unique circumstances, which were inextricably tied to the demolition of the old Arts Club. That well-publicized architectural vandalism clearly informed Vinci's winning design. Many were sorry that his Arts Club failed to make an architectural statement blazing with zeitgeist. But others saw the new building as an appropriate reminder of the loss that had made its construction necessary.

CONFRONTING MODERNISM

No confrontation between architectural past and present has been as raucous in recent years—or as apparently successful—as the one that erupted at Illinois Institute of Technology, where Mies taught and whose most important buildings he designed in the 1940s and 1950s. Purists long regarded the campus as a paragon of modernist clarity, and I.I.T. duly prohibited subsequent

CHICAGO'S SECOND MODERN PERIOD

architects from diverging even slightly from the International style. Yet the campus, on the edge of public housing on the South Side, had gradually become bleak and unwelcoming, a sign that some aspects of modernism were not aging gracefully.

By the mid-1990s the administration finally admitted that too much Mies was serving neither the school nor its students and commissioned two buildings in new styles. The first was the McCormick Tribune Student Center, whose architect was chosen in a competition. The finalists included Helmut Jahn, Peter Eisemann of New York, Iraqi-born Zaha Hadid of London, and Rem Koolhaas of Amsterdam—all architects of great stature, each one promising genuine change.

The selection of Koolhaas (b. 1944) was arguably the most radical. The Dutch architect was a famous iconoclast; he built his early reputation with convention-shattering books such as *Delirious New York,* which argued against city planning and celebrated congestion as a condition architecture should encourage. An essay he wrote upon winning the I.I.T. competition, entitled "Miestakes," promised an overthrow of the precepts of old modernism. He affirmed a published college poll that voted I.I.T. "America's least-beautiful campus," describing in his essay an unlovely complex in an unlovely part of Chicago, "a void within a void."

The jury had not intended the selection of Koolhaas as a repudiation of Mies. Its members included Phyllis Lambert, a former student of Mies, who was uninclined to disrespect the master. (Lambert, the daughter of Seagram's chief executive, had recommended that Mies design the 1958 Seagram Building in New York.) Yet Lambert and her fellow jurors understood Koolhaas's impatience to challenge the calm, cool order of Mies's International style. Koolhaas claimed that he "loved" Mies but didn't "respect" him; he was defiantly determined to bring the famous campus up to date architecturally.

Koolhaas's approach to the student center commission was typically contrarian. The school's original program was for a multistory building that would raise its main levels above the elevated railway that clattered along the site. Instead Koolhaas designed a low, flat building directly beneath the tracks—and rather than insulating the building, he soundproofed the trains themselves. He wrapped the tracks in a long, steel-clad tube, the bottom of which rests on the building's concave roof. The tube appears to be crushing the building, which is just one of many visual effects that create ambiguity and tension and mark the building as distinctly un-Miesian.

Unlike most architects Koolhaas prefers chaos to order. To combat the rectilinearity of the old campus, he had

McCORMICK TRIBUNE CAMPUS CENTER AT I.I.T.

3300 SOUTH STATE STREET

2003

REM KOOLHAAS

Koolhaas's student center defied Mies's black-and-white modernism and jolted I.I.T., most of whose campus Mies designed in the 1950s. Among the iconoclastic touches: The master's portrait on glass (opposite, right) chromatically divides his head in two. A mild sense of instability, including the impression that the transit line overhead is crushing the structure's roof (above), infuses the center with energy.

his assistants plot the pedestrian traffic patterns. The lines that emerged from that exercise created an irregular web of diagonals, which the architect used in his building's floor plan, exploding conventional divisions of space. Corridors without walls pass through open spaces. Eating places, a post office, student lounges, and computer stations occupy spaces that overlap—not calmly and coherently as in classic modernism, but confusingly, with an effect much like the urban congestion Koolhaas claims to admire. He augmented the chaos with vivid color—orange, green, black, and red—that wildly contrasts with Mies's monochrome palette.

The new student center incited controversy and even antipathy, but a good flare-up was exactly what Koolhaas

thought the school needed. Older architects generally disapproved of his building, but many were particularly irritated by one aspect: Koolhaas had tucked one of Mies's buildings, the 1953 Student Commons, almost invisibly between the new building's two wings. Koolhaas "intentionally clashes with Mies," said John Vinci during a flurry of debate as the new building was going up. Koolhaas "does damage with a building [the new student center] that is really quite ordinary," said Stanley Tigerman.

But the school was happy with the result. Architecture dean Donna Robertson said that today's students cope well with—and even enjoy—chaos. And the controversy helped rejuvenate I.I.T., lifting it out of a dreary twilight

and declining enrollment. However Koolhaas's building
is ultimately appraised, it undeniably tests the power of
the Miesian campus to stand up to a design that intentionally challenges it. It will be interesting to see how
the original black and gray campus relates to a burst of
color and a bit of chaos in its midst. Some expect Mies
and Koolhaas to highlight each other's genius—reinforc-
ing the lesson that modern architecture's essence lies in
the manipulation of space, whether subtle and somber
or playful and disorderly.

JAHN GOES BACK TO SCHOOL
Another encouraging development at I.I.T. was a commission that went to Helmut Jahn about the same time
that Koolhaas designed the student center. State Street

Village, a student-housing complex, was the first major
project in Chicago Jahn had secured since the 1980s,
when his widely disliked James R. Thompson Center
compromised his reputation.

The passage of time and major projects, including work
at airports from Bonn to Bangkok, had matured the onetime wunderkind, and his new restraint and seriousness
are evident in the I.I.T. dormitories, completed in 2003.
The buildings are spare, economical, and well suited
to their function, and they relate pleasingly to their site.
They demonstrate how, in the years since Thompson
Center, Jahn increasingly focused on building technology
rather than the idiosyncrasies of design—not ignoring
aesthetic questions, but faithfully adhering to the adage

STATE STREET VILLAGE DORMITORIES AT I.I.T.

3300 SOUTH STATE STREET

2003

MURPHY/JAHN

Jahn designed and built the dorms on a tight budget, using minimal structure to address student needs that included quiet courtyards, a pleasant commons, light-filled rooms, and cable-ready infrastructure. Following pages: The shape of the dorm buildings alludes to the train that unavoidably clatters through I.I.T.'s campus.

"form ever follows function." He has collaborated closely since 1995 with the structural engineer Werner Sobek, another native of Germany interested in pushing the limits of the way buildings function. Their joint approach seeks to wed technology to art, rather than imposing one on the other. The result, Sobek said, is buildings that "are becoming clearer, simpler, more logical."

For Jahn addressing the issue of the elevated rail line that loudly rumbles past I.I.T. was central to the design. Some solutions were conventional, such as placing concrete stairwells and service cores closest to the tracks, shielding the living quarters. One of Jahn's counterintuitive solutions was to punctuate the dorm buildings with a series of courtyards, separating them from the train

with large panels of high-tech layered glass that preserve a sense of light and openness while effectively muffling the noise. Jahn also wittily alluded to the omnipresent railway in the dorms' design. The buildings are clad in stainless steel, and the outer walls curve gently to meet the roof, evoking the streamlined trains of the 1930s, as well as those clattering by.

Flash Gordon and the Power of Natural Light

An exceptional example of Jahn's technological progression is his 2001 HALO Building (now occupied by Shure Electronics) in suburban Niles, Illinois. Sharply contrasting with Jahn's 1985 Thompson Center and the initial problems it had with radiant heat and glare, the ultramodern, ecologically sensitive HALO Building

241

STATE STREET VILLAGE DORMITORIES AT I.I.T.

Although the campus is not situated on a rolling glade, State Street Village provides the luxury of indoor-outdoor space. The six dorm buildings, clad in corrugated stainless steel, are separated by courtyards. The courtyards are partially enclosed by metal mesh, which allows breezes in, and high-tech glass, which keeps out much of the transit line's noise. Groves of birch trees, which will improve with age, provide a sense of calm.

HALO BUILDING

5800 WEST TOUHY AVENUE, NILES, ILL.

2001

MURPHY/JAHN

Above, opposite, and following
pages: HALO's simple, if
unconventional, lines reflect the
architect's determination that light
is the essence of building design
and glass the keynote of modern
architecture. HALO is as transparent a building as current
technology allowed. Its skin is
a kind of screen that modulates
natural light and solar heat.

harnesses the sun's power, maximizing natural light
and conserving energy. Solar power also charges HALO's
aesthetic agenda, Jahn said. "Light is the essence of
the design. The building is luminous, not illuminated."

The seven-story box-shaped building is almost entirely
transparent, with a concrete structure clad in high-tech
insulated glass. Sensors gauge the natural light and
heat coming in from the outside, triggering automatic
responses from air displacement systems, artificial lighting, and aluminum shades that adjust to the sun's angle
and intensity. Early in Jahn's career his futuristic lean-
ings earned him the nickname "Flash Gordon," but the
moniker never before seemed so apt.

Finding high-tech solutions to environmental concerns
represents for Jahn the "second modern period." As
he explained in a 1999 interview, ever-improving materials, production techniques, and architectural knowledge
have given rise to architecture of "considerably greater
technological possibilities" that will increasingly achieve
the early modernists' objectives of constructive clarity
and transparent divisions of space. "We can rely," Jahn
said, "upon knowledge that . . . permits us to move
closer to the visions of earlier times with much greater
certainty."

THE STATE OF SKYSCRAPERS

Given the artistic triumphs of Chicago's historic skyscrapers, it's not surprising that the recent crop of commercial buildings would suffer by comparison—many of them deservedly. "Designing to a budget" was how one forgettable architect explained the aesthetic poverty of a high-rise of his own design. But other additions to the city's skyline do reach for the nobler qualities of commercial architecture, including two office buildings designed by James Goettsch of Lohan Caprile Goettsch, the Blue Cross/Blue Shield headquarters and UBS Tower.

Goettsch (b. 1941) was a designer with Murphy/Jahn until 1989, when he joined the firm then called Lohan Associates. Both firms descended from "the great undead" Mies van der Rohe; Helmut Jahn was Mies's most famous student and Dirk Lohan was Mies's grandson. In both cases Goettsch's single degree of separation from the master provided him an intimate understanding of the modernist legacy and the profession's struggle to contend with it.

Through the 1980s and into the 1990s Goettsch watched architecture search unrewardingly for new ideas. Postmodernism, he said, "was in many ways a reaction to the oversimplistic minimalism of the post-Miesian idea . . . . People couldn't figure out how to make buildings interesting." The two extremes left him, like many architects of his age, equally cold.

For Goettsch, the way back to a vital commercial architecture was guided—in the best Chicago tradition—by attention to a client's specific, pragmatic needs. Blue Cross/Blue Shield of Illinois needed two million square feet of office space that could expand by eight hundred thousand square feet over the next sixteen years. At the time, local vacancy rates were as high as ten percent, but the company could not find suitable existing space. Nor could it economically build a structure that would suit its eventual requirements and rent out the excess space until it was needed. With those and other design restrictions, Goettsch and his colleagues proposed a building, on the edge of Grant Park, that could expand with the company—not horizontally but vertically.

Goettsch designed the Blue Cross/Blue Shield building, completed in 1997, as a simple but stately thirty-story structure capable of accommodating another twenty-four stories on top. Within the glass-clad rectangle he included a number of other features that responded directly to the client's needs, including a full-height light court, which provides drama and natural light and includes open-shaft elevators, with room for more elevators in the future. Goettsch also designed atrium stairways as "interconnecting tissue" for employees stationed on different floors, having researched the company's traffic flow and finding that interdepartmental collaboration was typical. Now staff members routinely walk up or down a flight or two to conduct business and often confer on the landings. "It's amazing how many people actually use those stairs," Goettsch said.

The same idea of form following function drove the UBS Tower, which opened in 2001. Like Blue Cross, the fifty-story UBS building was conceived during a period of double-digit vacancy rates. Unlike Blue Cross, it was built not by the primary tenant but by a speculative building developer, John Buck, which only intensified the significance of the high vacancies and the pressure to create something uniquely attractive to prospective tenants. Buck had a history of responding to trends with distinctive architecture: In 1987 he developed Chicago's most extravagant postmodern building, 190 South LaSalle Street, a forty-story tower by Philip Johnson in the financial district. But a decade or so later, high-quality tenants were looking for not just the latest office style but also the latest office technology.

When the UBS project (then called One North Wacker) began in 1998, Buck set out to provide a prestigious address and a highly efficient space. Efficiency was not just a matter of reasonable operating costs but also involved state-of-the-art infrastructure for telecommunications and other utilities, such as electrical and cooling systems. Goettsch's design incorporated those important elements as well as an aesthetic approach that reflected the client's and tenants' high-tech priorities.

"There was a time when you wanted to obscure the building's technology," Goettsch observed. By contrast, the exposed systems at UBS Tower celebrate that technology, much as Renzo Piano's pioneering Pompidou Center, completed in 1976 in Paris, emphasized its mechanical apparatus with a facade of color-coded shafts and ductwork.

The most striking feature of the UBS Tower is its forty-foot glassed-in lobby, which is enclosed by a sheer glass

251

BLUE CROSS/BLUE SHIELD OF ILLINOIS BUILDING
300 EAST RANDOLPH STREET

1997

LOHAN ASSOCIATES

James Goettsch's Blue Cross/ Blue Shield design (left, above, and opposite) was shaped by the client's need to expand vertically in the future. Simple proportions and a restrained exterior design allowed for later additions. Inside, a large and dramatic atrium/elevator core provides abundant natural light, space for additional elevators when needed, stairways for short trips between departments, and landings where employees can meet casually or by design.

UBS TOWER
ONE NORTH WACKER DRIVE

2001

LOHAN CAPRILE GOETTSCH

Following pages: UBS Tower features the most transparent walls technologically possible, yielding a maximum sense of openness and light. Minimal and unadorned, the building has an advanced telecommunications infrastructure beneath its surface. Its handsome neighbor, the Civic Opera House (at extreme right), supplies the block's ornamental gestures.

curtain wall supported by a visible system of taut cables. The overall effect is a stunning, almost seamless connection between indoors and out. (This type of wall, with nonreflective, ultraclear glass, has a genuine Chicago provenance: It was first used on a large scale in 1994 in Munich's Kempinski Hotel, whose architect was Helmut Jahn. The Kempinksi's project manager later moved to Lohan Caprile Goettsch.) Altogether the building, completed in 2001, succeeded in attracting UBS and other tenants to occupy ninety-five percent of the space at a time of double-digit vacancies and set a new standard for top-notch office buildings.

Among other successful additions to Chicago's skyscape are the works of Ralph Johnson, leading design partner in the old Chicago firm Perkins and Will. Johnson (b. 1948) was educated, as were most of his peers, as a modernist. But he was particularly drawn to "dissidents" such as Bertrand Goldberg and "eccentrics" like Andrew Rebori, whose work attracted him as "less rigid in terms of its approach" than most modern architects, he said. Johnson was also greatly influenced by the long-dead Dutch modernist Willem Dudok, who was in turn much inspired by the Prairie School. Dudok's work was characterized by monumentality, craftsmanship in brick, and interesting, asymmetrical geometries related to the

European architecture of the 1920s inspired Ralph Johnson's design for Boeing. With 1920s modernism in mind, he expressed the office tower with a careful geometry that culminates in its conspicuous clock tower. The building is constructed over a rail yard on a prominent riverfront site; special truss work suspends its weight over the railway.

de Stijl movement—which also had been an early influence on Mies. For Johnson, Dudok's work demonstrated clearly the modernist ideas of order and clarity, blended with a decorativeness Mies eschewed.

Those role models, and Johnson's own quest for originality, are apparent even in his early work, undertaken during the postmodern era of the late 1980s, when developers were building towers along the river at an unprecedented pace. Johnson's contribution to the riverfront was his thirty-six-story Boeing Corporation headquarters, completed in 1990. With traditional granite facades and a monumental clock tower that is visible up and down the river, it was not immune to the postmodern trend. But an undisguised steel truss that supports a section of the building over a stretch of railroad tracks also celebrates the structural system in a high-tech variant of modernism.

Johnson's first residential tower, the thirty-nine-story Skybridge, added another strikingly decorative element to the skyline in 2003 and pushed skyscraper design a step forward. Constructed on the edge of Chicago's Greektown, it is the largest building in a flurry of development that has transformed what had long been a low-rise, distinctly ethnic neighborhood.

The Skybridge plan originated with developers looking to build something distinctively different, with loftlike layouts, high ceilings, abundant light, and a feature uncommon to American skyscrapers, sizable balconies. Johnson and his design colleagues imagined dividing the tower into stacked sections that would create "neighborhoods in the sky" and provide extraordinary light. To achieve those ends, they began carving an original form out of a regular, rectangular high-rise plan. "We started to cut slots down the center of the building," Johnson said, "also at the bottom and to the sides, to

SKYBRIDGE

ONE NORTH HALSTED STREET

2003

PERKINS AND WILL

The apartments in Ralph Johnson's skyscraper (opposite), with their terraces and glass walls, feel suspended in the sky. Giant columns set off the main residential entrance (below). Bright colors accent an otherwise white and gray building.

break it down into separate units while keeping the integrity of the original rectangle as a kind of ghost figure."

The largest slot, some twenty-five stories high, effectively splits the building into twin towers, which are connected by glass-enclosed walkways. All of the openings lend a transparency and lightness to the concrete structure. They also provide almost all Skybridge's apartments, nestled between Halsted Street and the Kennedy Expressway, with premium views of the Loop and Lake Michigan. The handsome, thoughtful result blends innovative function with sculptural form.

THE MUSEUM OF CONTEMPORARY ART: A CHALLENGE TO PUBLIC TASTE

Not every attempt at serious architecture in this period succeeded. The firm of Kohn Pedersen Fox, which in 1983 produced the graceful green-glass high-rise at 333

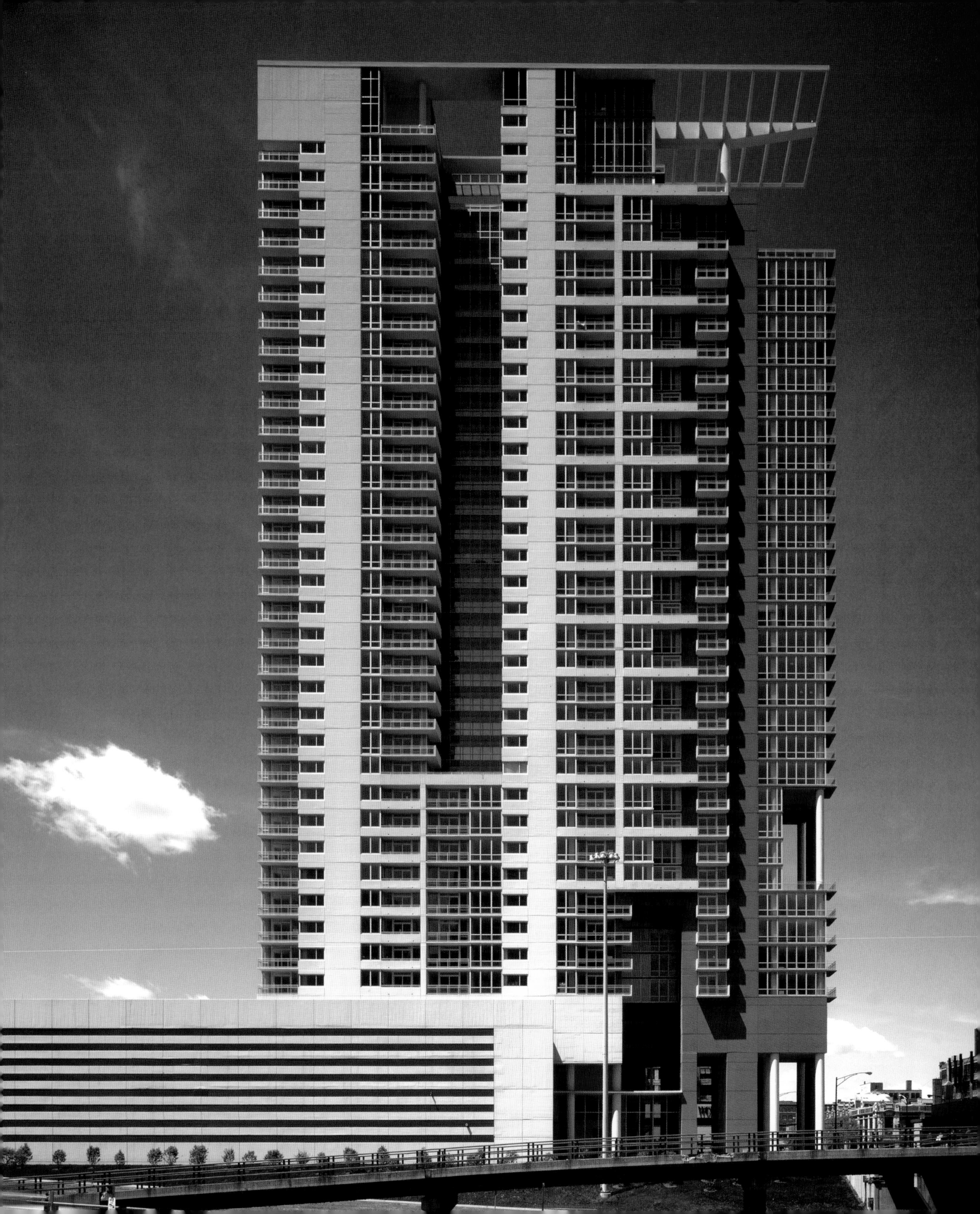

MUSEUM OF CONTEMPORARY ART

220 EAST CHICAGO AVENUE

1996

JOSEF PAUL KLEIHUES

The majestic exterior Kleihues designed for M.C.A. took utilitarian starkness beyond the public taste. The open, dramatic, and light-filled interiors more successfully pay homage to Chicago's architectural past.

West Wacker, followed that success in 1991 with 311 South Wacker. This stone-clad office tower, with proportions and detail that recall Tribune Tower, has modest postmodern charms that are unfortunately overshadowed by ludicrous details, such as false buttresses and an enormous, glaring lamp that calls far too much attention to the building at night.

Another mixed result came in 1996 with the completion of the Museum of Contemporary Art, which the city had anticipated as a milestone work of architecture. The museum, which had previously been ensconced in a converted bakery, was to occupy a choice site close to Michigan Avenue, with a clear view of the lake.

The competition for the prestigious project attracted entries from around the world. Museum officials selected Josef Paul Kleihues (1933–2004) of Frankfurt, in spite of customary objections that any number of

Chicago architects of equal stature should have been chosen. Museum officials countered that the M.C.A. was a museum of international scope and ought not be limited to local artists. They also believed that Kleihues—who had romanced the committee by disclosing his preference for the architecture of Rome and Chicago above all other cities—would create a building that both recalled the past and presaged the future.

Philosophically Kleihues's "poetic rationalism" sounded promising. His concept was to express the most advanced construction techniques ("rationalism") with meaningful ("poetic") references to the past. For example, Kleihues's 1986 Museum of Pre- and Early History in Frankfurt fused the nave of an old Gothic church to a rectangular modern structure, underscoring the strong contrasts and subtle similarities between the two. The M.C.A. administration expected him to produce a work of equal power in Chicago.

MUSEUM OF CONTEMPORARY ART

The entry's proportions are monumental but its materials impart a severity to the overall effect. Plain concrete panels attach to the building with large, undisguised screws. Skylights flood the interior with light.

Connecting architecturally historic themes with cutting-edge construction, Kleihues designed for M.C.A. a monumentally grand building with seemingly incompatible elements, including concrete block walls, steps that rise almost heroically to the entry, and a classically proportioned wall of glass. The design is deceptively simple; despite the austerity of the building's materials, the entry's dimensions and see-through facade give the place undeniable presence. Kleihues extended the idea of transparency to the interior, an open, balconied space that flows to a sculpture garden.

Notwithstanding the handsomeness within, the museum has become best known for its plain exterior, initially regarded as provocatively unfamiliar and now disliked as starkly inhospitable. Especially in the winter, the steep steps between concrete walls appear windswept and forlorn, contradicting Kleihues's claim that his buildings respond amiably to the people who use them. He seems to have misinterpreted something in his translation of Chicago history: Its architects found elegance, not plainness, in structure; tapped the beauty, not the harshness, of modest materials; and never intentionally challenged public taste.

THE FRUIT BOWL IN THE COLONNADE

Perhaps the most controversial project in Chicago since Thompson Center opened in 1985 was the renovation of Soldier Field, longtime home to the Chicago Bears football team. Debate raged not only over the new design but especially over the way the present collided with the past—a beloved and historic landmark, the neoclassical stadium by Holabird and Roche built on the lakefront in 1924.

The renovation by Wood and Zapata in association with Lohan Caprile Goettsch retained the original stadium's signature exterior colonnade, demolished the interior, and inserted an ultramodern steel and glass stadium within the shell. A portion of the raking grandstand is daringly cantilevered over the Doric colonnade along Lake Shore Drive, overwhelming the original more than complementing it.

The stadium has been excoriated by many and praised by others before and since its completion in 2003. One critic called it the "mistake on the lake," while another deemed it a "highly energized design." The federal government removed Soldier Field from its historic register, and even the iconoclastic architect Stanley Tigerman lambasted the design as a "fruit bowl jammed in the colonnade." Yet the asymmetrical new football stadium has obvious modern interest—described by one writer as a "scrimmage" between the old and new. Combining such disparate elements, Soldier Field is itself a manifestation of change in progress. And if experience is a guide, Chicago will in time claim the design as its own. As Tigerman wrote in the year following Soldier Field's opening, "We didn't ask for this massive structure on an otherwise sacrosanct lakefront, but it's here, it's ours (warts and all), and we will, I assure you, come to love it no less than we once loved our smelly stockyards."

AT HOME IN CHICAGO

At the turn of the twentieth century, affluence in many sectors of society and an empty-nest migration from suburbs to city produced robust demand for new housing in Chicago. Residential building booms erupted on all three sides of the Loop, creating great opportunities for architects intent on moving residential design in new directions.

Residential architecture often serves as a laboratory of contemporary design, as small-scale projects for individual families generally allow freer rein than large commercial ones do. The major constraint for most Chicago houses is their site, usually a long, narrow lot in an old neighborhood. Despite the physical limitations and settings that are usually more Victorian than modern, new construction is often experimental and reflects its owners' personal tastes and eccentricities.

A dazzling example is the Lincoln Park town house completed in 1993 on Lakeview Avenue by architect Perry Jahnke, then of Lohan Associates. Despite the vintage setting—a narrow lot amid stately neighbors—the last thing the client wanted was to blend in. Her father—who had collected modern art when the now classic works of Robert Rauschenberg and Claes Oldenberg were regarded as tasteless—had left her not only his collection but also a legacy of avant-garde iconoclasm. "It was important to me that people question this house," said the client, "even to the point of disliking it."

LINCOLN PARK RESIDENCE

2474 NORTH LAKEVIEW

1993

LOHAN ASSOCIATES

The client wanted this home to shock and challenge observers, much as the family's art collection once did. The architect sought to create an avant-garde design that would age as well as a Warhol or a Pollock. Clad in monochromatic granite and glass, the unconventional exterior form is less jarring than it might have been. The interior boasts space, light, and altitude.

Iconoclasm was important, but so was a degree of restraint in so quiet a neighborhood. The house achieves both. The exterior is a surprising cubist puzzle whose starkness is mitigated by the use of richly grained, dove gray granite and large panels of textured, ash-colored glass. The high-tech patterned glass provides views from the interior out to the street and park but prevents any view from the outside in. The glass also allows natural light to flood the interior, largely an exhibit space for paintings, freestanding sculpture, and vitrines. The house caused the desired uproar early on but, to its credit, soon blended into the fabric of its street, which is no less distinguished for this quietly radical addition.

A frequent challenge in residential architecture is the client who wants to push the limits of innovation while seeking the comforts of tradition—leaving the architect to reconcile such seeming contradictions. Laurence Booth successfully met the needs of one such client, who had sold a large Victorian house near Lincoln Park and planned to build a smaller modern house on the same street. The client "had psychologically exhausted her old house," Booth explained, but didn't want the new one to be too extreme, since the neighborhood had no experimental architecture.

Booth's solution, completed in 1995, was to assemble a variety of traditional elements in a thoroughly contemporary way. The exterior is classically proportioned limestone on a streetscape of brick and clapboard houses. The open interior and other elements are inspired by the Chicago atrium tradition but simplified to the basics.

Phillips melds a classic sensibility with the desire to experiment with new forms. For his own home, set upon what could be called "reclaimed" urban real estate, he borrowed basic elements from midcentury modernism. His Tower House also alludes to the fortress-like qualities of Richardson's Glessner House. Like Richardson, he eschewed an ornamental exterior, focusing instead on careful design from the inside out.

Japanese-style screen walls separate spaces; plain rails line the balcony above the first floor; and the stairway provides the comforts of loving craftsmanship while emphasizing the house's airiness and free movement. Booth kept asking himself the same question during the design process: "What can I do to make it lighter, to make it simpler? In the end, it was all reductive."

Some contemporary residential designs, like Booth's, can be deceptively traditional. Others can be deceptively modern, like the Tower House, completed by Frederick Phillips (b. 1946) in 2000. Phillips's earlier town houses have postmodern touches that blend them into their neighborhoods. But Tower House had little neighborhood to blend with; it was built on vacant land near the Cabrini-Green housing projects, which are being slowly dismantled. Phillips seized the opportunity to build for himself an unconventional town house he had long been imagining.

Raised on steel girders and clad in plate glass and corrugated metal, the four-story Tower House appears almost futuristic. The top and bottom stories are open, creating a carport and terrace. Yet the seemingly avant-garde design has touches of timeless classics: The exposed

steel skeleton is Miesian; the window glazing mimics the old "Chicago window" created by William Le Baron Jenney in the 1880s; and the underfloor heating and top-floor terrace recall Frank Lloyd Wright. The building seemed instantly at home on the postindustrial prairie; one can only wonder how its eventual neighbors will relate to the striking design.

Among the many houses built in recent years, a Lincoln Park home by Tadao Ando (b. 1941) ranks as one of the most expensive and probably the most sublime. On a triple lot in an old North Side neighborhood, Ando demonstrated the extraordinary skill he has deployed in numerous other buildings, mostly in his native Japan. Ando is a modernist, using simple geometry, basic materials, and natural light to create remarkable effects. While often awe-inspiring, his architecture also conveys something profoundly quiet and Zenlike in the play of space and light. Just as Mies's modernist simplicity has a mystical impact, Ando's spaces positively elevate the spirit.

Completed in 1997, Ando's Chicago house was his first major project in the United States; the clients hired him after seeing an eye-opening exhibit of his work at the

CHICAGO'S SECOND MODERN PERIOD

HOUSE IN CHICAGO

WRIGHTWOOD AVENUE

1997

TADAO ANDO

These and following pages: Ando created a sublime Lincoln Park residence in a patchwork urban setting. Buffered from the surrounding brick buildings by branches of trees and pools of water, the house exudes a cool serenity. Among the pleasing visual and tactile ambiguities are the concrete walls with their satiny finish. Ando's approach distills twentieth-century modernism through a timeless Japanese sensibility.

Museum of Modern Art in New York in 1991. Like most Ando buildings, this one is constructed of glass, steel, and reinforced concrete with a velvety surface. The house has three distinct sections—a guest wing, living area, and private quarters—all turned inward to face a shallow reflecting pool. The emphasis on light and water blurs distinctions between indoors and out, and the overall effect is that of a deeply contemplative cloister within the city.

STARS ON CHICAGO'S SKYLINE

The most spectacular structure to go up in early-twenty-first-century Chicago is the Jay Pritzker Pavilion, an open-air music hall that is the centerpiece of the city's new lakefront green space, Millennium Park. Designed by the Canadian-born Californian Frank Gehry (b. 1929) and completed in 2004, the band shell's ample stage is framed by Gehry's signature ribbons of wildly looping, shimmering stainless steel.

The design is reminiscent of the architect's other famed projects, including the Guggenheim Museum in Bilbao, Spain—and Gehry's distinctive stamp is seemingly unrelated to Chicago's developmental curve. But the project does in fact reiterate themes that recur throughout Chicago's architectural history, including clients who seek the new, a city that welcomes innovation, and a belief in function driving form, no matter how decorative.

The commission was initially to have gone to the hometown firm of Skidmore, Owings and Merrill, but that design was reportedly dismissed as predictable. S.O.M.'s Adrian Smith then induced Gehry—who had designed the Walt Disney Concert Hall in Los Angeles—to try his hand at the band shell. The architect agreed to meet with the client, Mayor Richard Daley, who had made a personal mission of building the enormous and costly Millennium Park. The mayor's enthusiasm to create an unprecedented new icon for Chicago quickly attracted Gehry to the project.

Gehry's design extends far beyond the concert stage and the undulating mane of metal that enlivens it. The band shell has seating for four thousand, with room for another seven thousand concertgoers on a two-acre lawn. Floating above the entire listening area is an airy, parabolic grid of steel pipes that defines the outdoor space, framing the stars in the lakefront sky. Beyond such aesthetic niceties, the grid serves the practical purpose of supporting lights and a state-of-the-art sound system, eliminating the need for view-blocking pylons.

The design is undeniably courageous, but what matters most is how well the band shell serves music, performers, and audiences. And the positive early response to the Pritzker Pavilion suggests that Gehry struck a chord, literally as well as figuratively. Musicians have raved about the onstage acoustics, while the scores of amplifiers distributed thirty feet overhead allow music to wash over the audience with a natural sound. Gehry's music

pavilion may appear at first glance to be almost arbitrarily decorative, but successful function was foremost to the design.

The globalization drawing international architectural stars like Gehry, Koolhaas, and Ando to Chicago's firmament is dramatically redefining the city's skyline. Buildings that will rise tomorrow in Chicago are being designed today in Los Angeles and New York, Amsterdam and Osaka—while Chicago's homegrown talent is producing signature buildings all over the world.

Such global crosscurrents are reenergizing architecture everywhere, but Chicago remains uniquely fertile ground. The city combines reverence for its rich architectural heritage with enthusiasm for innovative design and abundant opportunity to build. Its wealth of landmark buildings continues to set an example, teaching timeless, invaluable lessons. With a profound past and dynamic present, Chicago provides an unparalleled backdrop for architecture of the future.

MILLENNIUM PARK

MICHIGAN AVENUE BETWEEN
MONROE AND RANDOLPH STREETS

2004

VARIOUS ARCHITECTS

Chicago's newest oasis amid its famed skyscrapers is the 24.6-acre Millennium Park (right). Among its attractions are an ice rink, a theater for music and dance, fountains, landscaped gardens, and sculpture, including Anish Kapoor's massive ellipsis, whose highly polished surface reflects the skyline and anything passing by (in the foreground, opposite). The park's centerpiece is the Jay Pritzker Pavilion, the band shell designed by Frank Gehry (right and following pages), whose signature swirls of metal add another sculptural note.

GLOSSARY

ART DECO

The term came from the Exposition Internationale des Arts Décoratifs et Industriels Modernes, which was held in Paris in 1925. The exhibit lionized streamlined and geometric design in metals, glass, and other materials of the mass-produced world. Art Deco, or Art Moderne, also refers to buildings, mostly skyscrapers constructed in the 1930s, whose design was stripped down and emphatically modern.

ARTS AND CRAFTS MOVEMENT

English poet, artist, and designer William Morris began the movement in the mid-1880s with design that depended on handcrafts and eschewed the machine-made. Regarded as morally uplifting, Arts and Crafts emphasized the inherent beauty of materials and craftsmanship and led to a fashion for carved wood, painted tiles, wrought iron, and medieval images. American Arts and Crafts, advanced by Frank Lloyd Wright, among others, at the turn of the century, was more conspicuously modern but retained a fascination with materials such as wood, brick, and glass.

BEAUX ARTS

Beaux arts is a style of architecture named after the École des Beaux-Arts in Paris, where many American architects trained in the late 1800s. The École was considered up-to-date in that it taught the "primacy of the plan"—that interior space must be laid out before exteriors can be designed. But it was traditional and antimodern in that it called for strict use of classical forms.

CENTURY OF PROGRESS

Chicago's second great world's fair, the Century of Progress, took place in 1933 and 1934. Architecturally it was noted for streamlined modernism, and it foreshadowed the design of houses and buildings in the latter half of the twentieth century. The House of Tomorrow, designed by George Fred Keck, was showcased at this world's fair. It was largely prefabricated and featured walls of glass, air conditioning, metal-tube furniture, and a hangar for an airplane on the ground floor.

CHICAGO LOOP

Chicago's downtown has been called the "Loop" since the time streetcars formed a ring around the central business district. The Loop is bordered on three sides by water (the Chicago River on the north and west; Lake Michigan on the east), which made property therein dear and led to the need for taller buildings downtown.

CHICAGO PLAN

Daniel Burnham's city plan for Chicago was published in 1909. It depicted a parklike setting much influenced by the great cities of Europe. Burnham's plan was never entirely realized, but it encouraged Chicago architects toward openness and great size in the manner of the 1893 World's Columbian Exposition, which was directed by Burnham. It also pushed architects toward classicism and away from an indigenous style of Chicago's own.

CHICAGO SCHOOL OF ARCHITECTURE

The term refers to the commercial architects of the late 1800s who dedicated themselves to office and loft buildings of the simplest possible design. Exteriors did little to conceal the steel-frame cage that was their interior support system. These buildings have been admired for their truthfulness and "structuralism"—they are what they seem—and they represent a truly indigenous American architecture.

THE CLIFF-DWELLERS

This novel by Henry Blake Fuller was one of the nation's best-sellers of the 1890s. Set in Chicago, the action takes place in a skyscraper, a vivid symbol of power and ambition amid a bustling and sometimes frightful center of commerce and industry.

ILLINOIS INSTITUTE OF TECHNOLOGY

Ludwig Mies van der Rohe arrived in Chicago in 1937 to take over the architecture department at the Armour Institute of Technology. The school soon changed its name to Illinois Institute of Technology and moved to a new campus designed entirely by Mies. I.I.T. grew to be a world-famous mecca of modern architecture and design.

INTERNATIONALISM

The Bauhaus, a German school of design directed by Walter Gropius and later by Mies van der Rohe, began advancing important ideas in modern architecture in the 1920s. The Bauhaus advocated the use of machine-made materials such as metal and glass, powerful geometric forms, and utter rationality, as opposed to traditional styles that drew from local context or heritage. The term "Internationalism" was coined by the curators of an exhibition of European architecture in the 1930s at New York's Museum of Modern Art.

LIGHT WELL

Also known as a "light court," this is a central opening within office buildings that allows sunlight to pour in, illuminating interior offices. Chicago architects were among the first to develop the idea of the light well, as the crowded downtown required all manner of strategies to bring maximum light inside. Oftentimes the first few stories of a light well were covered with glass ceilings, creating elegant atrium spaces, most notably in John Wellborn Root's Rookery.

MODERNISM

This term refers to the effort by artists in the late nineteenth and early twentieth centuries to take art beyond the idea of representational beauty and express underlying content. As part of the movement, modern architects developed entirely new forms to suit the latest building technologies and current lifestyles. William Le Baron Jenney's steel-frame buildings are considered modern. Louis Sullivan's organic architecture was modern, as were the flowing and open spaces of Frank Lloyd Wright. The International style of Mies van der Rohe reduced architecture to its most fundamental terms, after which the modern movement in architecture floundered and postmodernism made its appearance.

ORGANIC ARCHITECTURE

Architecture is organic to the extent that it corresponds to the forms and forces of nature. A house that blends with the natural beauty of its site is considered organic. Organic architecture, which became an obsession for Louis Sullivan and second nature to Frank Lloyd Wright, came to mean architectural form that is deeply suited to its use.

POSTMODERNISM

The postmodern movement began as a rejection of the minimalism and uniformity inherent in modernism. Beginning in the late 1960s, this meant an inclusion of historic architectural forms in contemporary buildings—columns, arches, ornamentation—and a rejection of the "forced amnesia" that critics attributed to modern architecture. Ultimately, postmodernism led to caricature and excess, and the movement was eventually discredited.

PRAIRIE SCHOOL

The Prairie School refers to the attempt to develop an indigenous architecture of the Midwest led by Frank Lloyd Wright and a number of his contemporaries. Their Prairie-style residential designs were often low and long, reflecting the prairie horizon, used such modest local materials as oak and brick, and featured handcrafted fixtures throughout.

RICHARDSONIAN "ROMANESQUE"

As American architects searched for forms that were characteristically American in spirit, Henry Hobson Richardson alighted on the Romanesque. Although originating in medieval Europe, the Romanesque was powerful and somewhat raw, like America itself. It was appreciated also because its piers and arches expressed structure rather than concealed it with ornament.

SEVEN LAMPS OF ARCHITECTURE

This book by English art critic and aesthete John Ruskin, first published in 1849, attempted to reduce the canons of architecture to seven "lamps"—sacrifice, truth, power, beauty, life, memory, and obedience. It was widely influential among Chicago's early modern architects in the late 1880s.

SKYSCRAPER

In nineteenth-century Chicago, any building over ten or eleven stories high was regarded as a skyscraper, a building type made possible through the development of steel-frame construction. William Le Baron Jenney's ten-story Home Insurance Building in the Loop was one of the world's first such buildings. The 110-story Sears Tower, two blocks from the site of the now-demolished Home Insurance, was completed in 1974 and the world's tallest building until 1997.

TRIBUNE TOWER COMPETITION

In 1922 the *Chicago Tribune* held a design competition for a new office tower on Michigan Avenue. The newspaper selected a neo-Gothic skyscraper, which was built the following year, but the second-place entry by Eliel Saarinen of Finland drew the most critical praise for its sleek lines and powerful skyward thrust. Saarinen's never-built tower inspired a new generation of modern commercial buildings in Chicago and elsewhere. It also prompted Saarinen to move to the United States, where he was thrust into the limelight as an important modernist architect.

UNIVERSAL SPACE

Mies van der Rohe attempted to create large spaces unencumbered by bearing walls, an architectural challenge that allowed for the most flexible use by the occupants. Further, he clad buildings such as Crown Hall at the Illinois Institute of Technology in glass, suggesting by transparency that the interior space extends to infinity and is indeed "universal."

WORLD'S COLUMBIAN EXPOSITION

Chicago's 1893 world's fair was then the largest event of its kind, exhibiting the arts, sciences, technologies, and other trappings of civilized modernity. Architecturally, however, it was a reversion to the past, a beaux arts extravaganza of classical style. The fair gave Chicago a European patina but quashed the local taste for the simple but elegant buildings of the structuralist Chicago School.

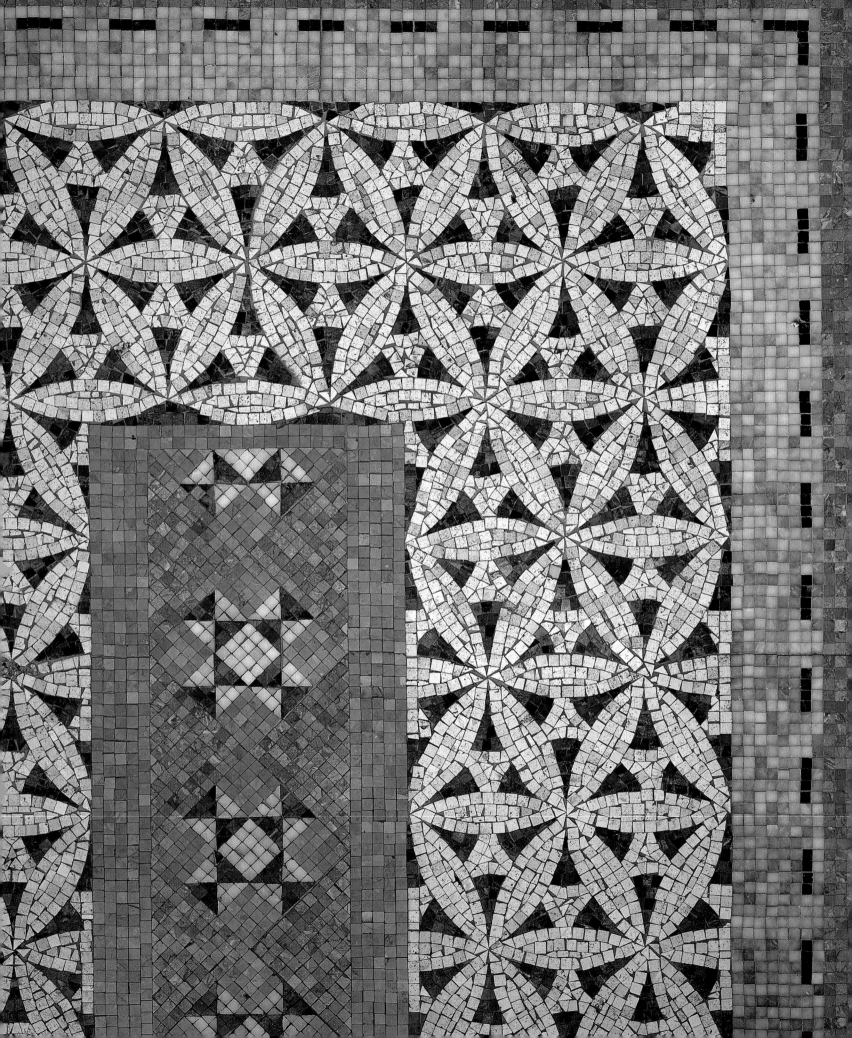

BIBLIOGRAPHY

RELIANCE BUILDING (DETAIL)
STATE STREET AT WASHINGTON
STREET
1895
DANIEL H. BURNHAM & COMPANY

Berger, Miles L. *They Built Chicago.* Chicago: Bonus Books, 1992.

Blaser, Werner. *Mies van der Rohe: Furniture and Interiors.* Woodbury, N.Y.: Barron's, 1982.

Boyer, Robert Piper. *Keck and Keck.* New York: Princeton Architectural Press, 1993.

Brooks, H. Allen. *The Prairie School: Frank Lloyd Wright and His Midwest Contemporaries.* Toronto: University of Toronto Press, 1972.

Bruegmann, Robert. *Holabird & Roche, Holabird & Root: An Illustrated Catalogue of Works.* 3 vols. New York and London: Garland Publishing, 1991.

Callahan, Carol J. "Glessner House, Chicago, Illinois," *The Magazine Antiques* 139 (May 1991): 970–81.

Chappell, Sally Anderson. *Architecture and Planning of Graham, Anderson, Probst and White, 1912–1936: Transforming Tradition.* Chicago: University of Chicago Press, 1992.

Cohen, Stuart E. *Chicago Architects.* Chicago: Swallow Press, 1976. Catalogue for an exhibition organized by Laurence Booth, Stuart E. Cohen, Stanley Tigerman, and Benjamin Weese.

Condit, Carl W. *Chicago 1910–1929: Building, Planning, and Urban Technology.* Chicago: University of Chicago Press, 1973.

____. *Chicago 1930–1970: Building, Planning, and Urban Technology.* Chicago: University of Chicago Press, 1974.

____. *The Chicago School of Architecture.* Chicago: University of Chicago Press, 1964.

____. *The Rise of the Skyscraper.* Chicago: University of Chicago Press, 1952.

Cowles, Linn Ann. *An Index and Guide to An Autobiography, the 1943 Edition, by Frank Lloyd Wright.* Hopkins, Minn.: Greenwich Design, 1976.

Dart, Susan. *Edward Dart: Architect.* Louisville, Ky.: Evanston Publishing, 1993.

Drexler, Arthur. *Ludwig Mies van der Rohe.* London: Mayflower Publishing Company; New York: George Braziller, Inc., 1960.

Eaton, Leonard K. *Two Chicago Architects and Their Clients: Frank Lloyd Wright and Howard Van Doren Shaw.* Cambridge, Mass.: M.I.T. Press, 1969.

Garrigan, Kristine Ottesen. *Ruskin On Architecture.* Madison: University of Wisconsin Press, 1973.

Giedion, Sigfried. *Space, Time and Architecture: The Growth of a New Tradition.* Cambridge, Mass.: Harvard University Press, 1941.

Gill, Brendan. *Many Masks: A Life of Frank Lloyd Wright.* New York: G. P. Putnam's Sons, 1987.

Glibota, Ante, and Frederic Edelmann. *Chicago: 150 Years of Architecture, 1833–1983.* Paris: Paris Art Center and L'Institut Français d'Architecture, 1983.

Goldsmith, Myron. *Myron Goldsmith: Buildings and Concepts.* New York: Rizzoli, 1987.

Grube, Oswald W., with Peter C. Pran and Franz Schulze. *100 Years of Architecture in Chicago: Continuity of Structure and Form.* Chicago: J. Phillip O'Hara, 1976.

Hitchcock, Henry-Russell. *The Architecture of H. H. Richardson and His Times.* New York: Museum of Modern Art, 1936; Cambridge, Mass.: M.I.T. Press, 1966.

Hoffmann, Donald. *The Architecture of John Wellborn Root.* Baltimore: Johns Hopkins University Press, 1973.

Hubka, Thomas C. "H. H. Richardson's Glessner House: A Garden in the Machine." *Winterthur Portfolio* 24 (Winter 1989): 209–29.

Joediche, Joachim. *Helmut Jahn: Design of a New Architecture.* New York: Nichols Publishing Company, 1987.

Johnson, Ralph. *Ralph Johnson of Perkins and Will.* New York: Rizzoli International, 1995.

Jordy, William H., and Ralph Coe, eds. *American Architecture and Other Writings by Montgomery Schuyler.* 2 vols. Cambridge, Mass.: Harvard University Press, Belknap Press, 1961.

Lynes, Russell. *The Tastemakers.* New York: Harper & Brothers, 1954.

Menocal, Narciso G. *Keck & Keck: Architects.* Madison: University of Wisconsin, 1980. Catalogue for an exhibition at the Elvehjem Museum of Art.

Monroe, Harriet. *John Wellborn Root.* Boston and New York: Houghton, Mifflin & Company, 1896.

Morrison, Hugh. *Louis Sullivan: Prophet of Modern Architecture.* New York: W. W. Norton, 1935.

Mumford, Lewis. *Roots of Contemporary American Architecture.* New York: Reinhold Publishing, 1952; Dover Publications, 1972.

O'Gorman, James F. *H. H. Richardson: Architectural Forms for an American Society.* Chicago: University of Chicago Press, 1987.

____. *H. H. Richardson and His Office.* Cambridge, Mass.: Department of Printing and Graphic Arts, Harvard College Library, 1974.

Pratt, Richard. *David Adler: The Architect and His Work.* New York: M. Evans and Company, J. B. Lippincott, 1970.

Ragon, Michel. *Goldberg On the City.* Paris: Paris Art Center, 1985.

Ruskin, John. *The Seven Lamps of Architecture.* Sunnyside, Orpington, Kent: George Allen, 1880; New York: Dover Publications, 1989.

Russell, Frank, ed. *Mies van der Rohe: European Works.* London: Academy Editions; New York: St. Martin's Press, 1986.

Salny, Stephen M. *The Country Houses of David Adler.* New York: W. W. Norton, 2001.

Schipporeit, George, project director. *Mies van der Rohe: Architect as Educator.* Chicago: Illinois Institute of Technology, 1986. Catalogue for an exhibition of the Mies van der Rohe Centennial Project.

Schulze, Franz. *Mies van der Rohe: A Critical Biography.* Chicago: University of Chicago Press, 1985.

Siry, Joseph M. *The Chicago Auditorium Building: Adler and Sullivan's Architecture and the City.* Chicago: University of Chicago Press, 2002.

Slavin, Maeve. *Davis Allen: Forty Years of Interior Design at Skidmore, Owings and Merrill.* New York: Rizzoli, 1990.

Smith, Adrian, and W. Cecil Steward. *SOM: Adrian Smith, FAIA, of Skidmore, Owings and Merrill.* Corte Madera, Calif.: Gingko Press, 2002.

Tafel, Edgar. *Years with Frank Lloyd Wright: Apprentice to Genius.* New York: Dover Publications, 1979.

Thorne, Martha, ed. *David Adler, Architect: The Elements of Style.* Chicago: Art Institute of Chicago in association with Yale University Press, 2002.

Twombly, Robert C. *Louis Sullivan: His Life and Work.* New York: Viking, Elisabeth Sifton Books, 1986.

____. *Louis Sullivan: The Public Papers.* Chicago: University of Chicago Press, 1988.

de Wit, Wim, ed. *Louis Sullivan: The Function of Ornament.* New York: W. W. Norton, 1986. Catalogue for an exhibition organized by the Chicago Historical Society and the St. Louis Art Museum.

Wright, Frank Lloyd. *An Autobiography.* New York: Duell, Sloan and Pearce, 1943; Horizon Press, 1977.

Zukowsky, John, ed. *Chicago Architecture, 1872–1922: Birth of a Metropolis.* Munich: Prestel-Verlag, 1987. Catalogue for an exhibition at the Art Institute of Chicago.

____. *Chicago Architecture and Design, 1923–1993: Reconfiguration of an American Metropolis.* Munich: Prestel-Verlag, 1993. Catalogue for an exhibition at the Art Institute of Chicago.

285

INDEX

RELIANCE BUILDING (DETAIL)
STATE STREET AT WASHINGTON
STREET
1895
DANIEL H. BURNHAM & COMPANY

PHOTOGRAPH CREDITS

Courtesy the Office of Tadao Ando: 268–71

Courtesy Art Institute of Chicago: 68, 95, 122; Hedrich Blessing photograph: 123; Ludwig Hilberseimer Collection: 140

Courtesy Booth/Hansen, Greg Murphey photographer: 30 (left), 57 (upper left)

Courtesy Chicago Architecture Foundation: 25

Courtesy Chicago Historical Society: 34 (below); Barnes-Crosby photograph: 24, 43; Hedrich Blessing Collection: 31, 64, 104, 110, 120–21, 129–31, 134, 138, 141–42, 145–47, 150–55, 158–59, 161–62, 164, 168–69, 174, 180, 181 (right), 184–85, 190–91, 194–97, 229; James D. McMahon photographer: 116; Raymond Towbridge photographer: 117

Courtesy Langdon Clay: 206

Courtesy Domino's Center for Architecture and Design: 105

Courtesy the Donnelley Library, Lake Forest College: 21, 114

Courtesy Arthur Erickson, Panda Associates: 216 (below left)

Courtesy Esto Photographics: 178–79, 181 (left)

Courtesy Evanston Historical Society: 108–9

Courtesy Gensler: 60 (top); Harry Weese Associates Archive, Jim Hedrich photographer: 200–201

Courtesy Hammond Beeby Rupert Ainge, Judith Bromley photographer: 217, 219; Kent Bloomer Collection: 218

Courtesy Hedrich Blessing: 57 (lower left), 60 (below), 75–77, 198; Chris Barrett photographer: 192–93, 236–37; Craig Dugan photographer: 82, 83 (top left), 248–49; Bill Engdahl photographer: 136; Steve Hall photographer: 13, 128, 232, 234 (left), 235, 260–62; Bob Harr photographer: 115, 118; Bill Hedrich photographer: 28; Ken Hedrich photographer: 20, 135, 148–49, 160; Marco Lorenzetti photographer: 143, 163; Scott McDonald photographer: 132, 252–53; Nick Merrick photographer: 26, 65–67, 69–71, 170–72, 176, 182 (right), 183, 207–9, 220–22, 256–59; Jon Miller photographer: 10, 30 (right), 80, 86–94, 98–103, 126–27, 165–67, 173, 182 (left), 254–55, 264–65; Jeff Millies photographer: 58–59, 83 (top right and two below), 282, 286; Bob Shimer photographer: 18, 34 (top), 35–39, 72–74, 125

Courtesy Historical Society of Oak Park/River Forest: 96–97

Courtesy Illinois Institute of Technology, Richard Barnes photographer: 238–40

Courtesy Balthazar Korab: 202

Courtesy Martyl Langsdorf, Hedrich Blessing photograph: 156–57

Courtesy Lohan Caprile Goettsch: 216 (top right)

Courtesy Mati Maldre: 106–7

Courtesy Marshall Field Archive: 22

Courtesy McClier: 112 (right); Hedrich Blessing, Nick Merrick photographer: 40, 45–51; Hedrich Blessing, Jeff Millies photographer: 231

Courtesy Millennium Park, Hedrich Blessing photographs; Craig Dugan photographer: 274–75; Scott McDonald photographer: 272–73

Courtesy Monadnock Block, Ron Gordon photographer: 52–54

Courtesy Greg Murphey: 224 (below), 225

Courtesy Murphy/Jahn: 6, 210–13, 216 (top left), 247, 250; Engelhardt/Sellin photograph: 234 (right); Timothy Hursley photographer: 214; Doug Snower photographer: 9, 241–46

Courtesy Richard Nickel Committee: 32; Richard Nickel photographer: 23, 57 (right), 81, 84–85, 278

Courtesy Shirley Paddock and Griffith Grant & Lackie Collection: 112 (left)

Courtesy Frederick Phillips: 266–67

Courtesy Skidmore, Owings and Merrill: 216 (below right); Ben Altman photographer: 186–89

Courtesy Tigerman-McCurry Architects: 204–5

Courtesy University of Chicago News Office: 29

Courtesy U. S. Equities, Inc.: 78–79

Courtesy Vinci-Hamp: 228; Phil Hamp photographer: 227; Bob Thall photographer: 62–63, 226

Courtesy Water Tower Place, Tony Soluri photographer: 203

Courtesy Wood + Zapata, Douglas Reid Fogelson photographer: 263